THE LANDSCAPE
BELOW GROUND II
Proceedings of a Second International Workshop
on Tree Root Development in Urban Soils

Edited by:
Dr. Dan Neely
Illinois Natural History Survey (retired)
Scott City, Missouri
and
Dr. Gary Watson
The Morton Arboretum, Lisle, Illinois

Held March 5 and 6, 1998
San Francisco, California

Published by
International Society of Arboriculture
P.O. Box 3129
Champaign, IL 61826-3129 USA

Copyediting and Composition: Peggy Currid
Printed by: United Graphics, Inc., Mattoon, IL 61938, 217-235-7161

International Society of Arboriculture
Web Site: http://www.isa-arbor.com
email: isa@isa-arbor.com

10 9 8 7 6 5 4
11-09/150/RF

ISBN 1-881956-23-7

PREFACE

The second Landscape Below Ground Conference was organized to bring the results of research to arborists. Research is an important component in the practice of arboriculture today. Arborists are seen in their communities as possessing special knowledge—knowledge of tree care. Membership and participation in the International Society of Arboriculture gives you access to that special knowledge in the form of research-based information. That knowledge, coupled with your years of experience, yields the privileged position that arborists hold in their communities.

While we appreciate that research is important to the arborist, we must also be aware that arborists are important to the research that is being done on tree care issues. Arborists support research by identifying topics that need research, by testing the validity and practicality of research results in the field, and by contributing to the funding of research.

The ISA forms a vital link between the community of researchers and the working arborists. Strengthening that link is the key to our future success. It is through research that we will gain more knowledge and improve our effectiveness as key players and management of urban ecosystems.

Edward Brennan
ISA Western Chapter President

TABLE OF CONTENTS

PART III — URBAN SOILS

PART IV — PLANTING

PART V — WATER UTILIZATION

INTRODUCTION

In 1993, the first international workshop on tree root development in urban soils, "The Landscape Below Ground," was held at The Morton Arboretum in Lisle, Illinois. In 1998, a second Landscape Below Ground workshop (also known as "Landscape Below Ground Resurfaces") was held in San Francisco, California. Although some time and distance separated the two workshops, both meetings had a common purpose: to provide a forum for the interchange of information relevant to the below-ground aspects of urban tree root growth and management.

Approximately half of the functional tree is below the ground, yet most research efforts have been directed toward the above-ground portion. Recognizing the need to understand all parts of the trees, these workshops have focused on developing and expanding the base of information on tree roots, the root environment, and the management of both.

In addition to researchers from across the United States, scientists from Denmark, England, Holland, and Sweden participated in the second Landscape Below Ground conference. Papers were presented on a wide variety of topics, including structural soils, planting pit design, stimulation of root regeneration, mycorrhizae, fill soils, soil compaction, construction-related root injury, root barriers, treeshelters, and water relations of trees.

Papers included in the these proceedings provide the reader with an up-to-date compendium of below-ground research related to urban trees. Combined with LBG I proceedings, an extensive compilation of below-ground research for the past decade can be found. With this information, a strong base for future research on urban tree root development has been established. We look forward to learning and reporting the results of many new research endeavors at Landscape Below Ground III in 2003.

Larry Costello
Gary Watson
Conference Co-Chairs

ACKNOWLEDGMENTS

The second Landscape Below Ground workshop could not have been possible without the support of the following organizations:

- Arbor Care, Inc.
- Arboricultural Research and Education Academy
- The Filoli Center
- International Society of Arboriculture
- International Society of Arboriculture, Western Chapter
- The Morton Arboretum
- San Francisco Recreation and Parks Department
- San Francisco Department of Public Works
- University of California Cooperative Extension

KEYNOTE ADDRESS

Tree-Friendly Lifestyles

Thomas O. Perry

Large trees require plenty of room! The branches of open-grown trees often spread to cover a circle with a diameter greater than their height. Their roots typically extend 40 feet beyond the branch tips (Figure 1). These roots grow horizontally and up to into the top inch of soil. The roots and their associated mycorrhizae occupy every millimeter of soil and preempt the available moisture and oxygen. One large tree can dominate an entire residential yard, while its roots trespass across several neighboring yards. (Urban foresters often ignore neighborhoods with small residential lots. Lots in the 1930s were commonly 110 feet wide by 180 feet deep; the grass covered space between the curb and sidewalk was 15 or more feet wide. Today's residential lots are commonly 60 by 90 feet—not large enough for a lusty tree. Various street widenings and utility installations have reduced the "tree lawn" to almost nothing. The situation is most extreme in San Francisco, where lots are only 30 feet wide by 100 feet deep. The space between the walls of residences barely accommodates a mason's trowel.)

Trees are fierce competitors and make growing of grass or other vegetation difficult. Grass will grow under trees only when humans destroy some of the tree roots and plant the grass. The grass is usually stunted by the competition with tree roots. However, as Gary Watson's studies (1) show, the grass takes vengeance on the tree roots.

Under natural circumstances, vegetation is sparse or nil under the crown of a large tree or a closed forest canopy. Trees heave sidewalks, invade and plug storm drains, threaten overhead utilities, and can fall on neighboring houses. Yet trees are beautiful living things. How can we modify our lifestyles so these awesome and graceful giants can persist in our yards, our neighborhoods, our cities, our countrysides, and our planet?

For one family living on a 2-acre lot surrounded on three sides by city parkland, the problems of living with large trees are simple. Under such circumstances, only the Perry family had to change its lifestyle. However, in today's residential neighborhoods, all people have to modify their lifestyles to protect a large tree or a population of large trees. On a neighborhood or city basis, adopting lifestyles that are friendly to trees becomes a complex political process with multiple actors. For simplicity, this paper is limited to circumstances for which only one family—mine—had to develop a "tree friendly lifestyle."

Thomas O. Perry, Owner, Natural Systems Associates. His address is #104 Carol Woods, 750 Weaver Dairy Road, Chapel Hill, NC 27514.

Figure 1. "The Magnificent Oak" outside of Savannah is one of the most symmetrical and viewable live oaks in the area. The crown spread of the tree is 147 feet. The distinct black roots extend more than 40 feet beyond the branch tips of the tree. As is typical of many open-grown trees, there is no distinct point for measuring dbh. The smallest diameter I could measure exceeded 9.5 feet. (The child in the crotch of the tree was about 3 feet tall.) Note that the branches extend out from the trunk and touch the ground. The leaves are confined to the outermost portions of the branches. Sampling reveals that the leaf area index is at its maximum, approximately 12 square feet per square foot of ground surface (counting both top and bottom surfaces of the leaf). Sampling also reveals that every square inch of the upper inches of soil is occupied by multiple root tips and their associated mychorrizae. Competition is intense, and neither grass nor woody perennials can persist without destruction of tree roots by humans.

The Perry Yard

Hazel spotted the newspaper ad: "Architect leaving town—Must sell lot next to Lake Johnson Reservoir." We looked wistfully at the developer's billboard-map. A quick phone call was made and the question "How much?" was asked. The answer: "$4,800." Our response was "If the lot is the one we think it is, you've just sold it." We were out at dawn the next morning. It *was* the lot we had hoped!

I telephoned the architect and had him hold the lot for ten days while I arranged for inspections and blessings by county soils specialists, hydrologists, the sanitation officer, and zoning officials. Then I called my father, an architect, and asked him to inspect the lot. The trees and the view across the creek thrilled Dad. He gave his blessing and lent me money to purchase the lot, urging that I build a house with a living room and balcony on the second floor.

My lifestyle changed in 1960, the minute I plunked $4,800 down for 2.1 acres of land next to the reservoir, 3 miles from my office at North Carolina State University. Most of our new homesite was and is occupied by a dense 130-year-old high forest. The entire yard had been logged several times in the past. A small part of the yard was used to grow cotton until the 1930s. Other areas had been fenced off and used for cattle pastures. A natural spring was located about 200 feet west of our property. The creek that runs through our yard runs into the local reservoir. A portion of the creek bottom and the steeper parts of the yard were never plowed. Fences prevented destruction of the root mat and the rich wildflower population in the yard and the surrounding parkland. An old farm road, fallen red cedar fence posts, and plow furrows attest to recent land-use history. Native Americans had been there first and had used the spring: I found a splendid quartz arrowhead within 35 feet of the back corner of the house. The lot adjoined the buffer for the city reservoir. There were no water or sewer utilities, and the Lake Johnson Nature Park did not yet exist.

Huge trees occupied the lot. Many were over 105 feet tall and 15 inches in diameter in 1960. I immediately had to develop a tree-friendly lifestyle. Every tree in the vicinity of the house site, the septic tank drain field, the well-house, and future garage site was mapped. The yard was blessed with a population of native shrubs (viburnum, azalea, storax, silverbell). The natural vegetation also included dogwoods, sourwoods, aronias, and other understory trees. The locations of these plants were also noted in planning the development of the lot. A contour map with 1-foot intervals was vital to locating the house and protecting trees.

An impressive 24-inch white oak that was more than 90 feet tall and featured a ramrod-straight trunk would likely be damaged. At first, it seemed as if there was no way to avoid cutting into the root zone of the tree and and still locate the house properly on the contours of the lot. I must have relocated the house foundation 15 times before deciding on an arrangement that placed the house corner a mere 20 feet from the tree. The location of the septic tank drain field and various water and electric lines were as important as locating the house foundation for saving the white oak.

To save other trees on the lot, every detail of the movement of machinery and equipment had to be carefully planned. Twice-daily inspections were required to ensure that the various contractors and subcontractors did not move out of their designated areas of activity. During construction, my contractor fussed at me about the restrictions, but I was paying cost-plus, so he could not really complain. Indeed, when the job was done he shook my hand and said that I had saved him money by keeping the worksite clean and attending to details that would have created a muddy mess and a population of dead trees.

Experience in my own yard and as a consultant has provided the basis for a condensed manual for protecting trees during the processes of development. The manual is included in the appendix to this document.

Continuing Tree-Friendly Lifestyles After Construction

Successful maintenance of the white oak required that we think about it every one of the days in the 38 years we have lived next to it. Here's what we did.

1. We did not rototill the tree's root system and plant grass. Instead, we watered the trees (not our lawn) with an inch water for every ten days that it did not rain. In the mild climate of North Carolina, watering was sometimes required during the winter months. We applied the water slowly, using aluminum pie plates to measure the amount (a quarter inch at a time). If robins came to play in the sprinkler area, we knew it was time to shut off the water: the robins were after the worms, which were coming up for air. We did not want to overwater and cut off the oxygen supply to the roots of the tree.

2. We fertilized the yard twice a year, adjusting the applications on the basis of soil analyses. Most native trees and shrubs are like azaleas and grow best with a pH of about 5.5. We used only one application of ground limestone during the first year we lived in the house. Fertilizer regimens for grass call for a pH of 7 or better. Many trees show iron chlorosis when there is too much lime (divalent cations compete with iron and copper ions and chlorosis results). Trees and most native vegetation grow best when supplied with ammonium nitrogen rather than nitrate nitrogen, so we usually applied ammonium sulfate. Uptake of the ammonium by the tree left the sulfate ion to acidify the soil. After a few years, sufficient phosphate accumulated in the soil so this element was no longer needed on an annual basis. (Note: the appropriate fertilizer application to favor healthy tree growth varies from one part of a city to another. Beware of fertilizer dealers who want to sell you a fertilizer that is supposed to be good for trees everywhere on the planet.)

3. We ground some of the leaves with a mulching mower and raked others to form rings of leaves about 4 inches deep at the base of each tree. A 6-inch ring next to the trunk was kept clear to prevent mice and moles from nesting next to the tree and girdling the trees. Excess mulch was hauled to piles in an informal area of the yard. We raked the yard two or three times each fall. The objective of raking the leaves was to prevent the trees from performing their ultimate dirty trick by smothering the volunteer violets, moss, spring-green-and-gold, blood-root, wild ginger. Solomon's seal, etc. We developed a garden of flowers and trees without planting anything.

4. Once a year, in mid-June, we mow the violets and wild flowers. Even wildflowers become rank, and we want the yard to look reasonably cared for. The mowing is timed to match the natural summer dieback of the flowers. The mower blade is set as high as possible (4 .5 inches) to avoid scalping plants back to the ground. Thousands of new seedling trees are mown back. Without the mowing, the yard would quickly become a jungle of tree seedlings. We use a sharp trowel to cut stubborn tree seedlings just below the root collar/ground line.

5. We planted a few daffodils and crocuses throughout the yard. We were careful not to tear up tree roots to plant flowers. We did plant some flowering trees and shrubs—never in the immediate vicinity of valued trees. Beware of gardening under trees! Death by hosta is as sure as death by bulldozer.

6. We use herbicides with great care. Roundup is not inactivated in organic soil where tree roots are concentrated. Repeated applications of Roundup and other

herbicides can stunt or kill trees. Poison ivy and other offending plants can be killed by carefully wiping the plant stems or foliage with appropriate mixtures. (I feel like the Wicked Witch of the North as I put on a rubber glove and then a cotton glove and dip my hand into my container of plant killer.)

7. Soil compaction is a major tree killer and is a problem around my pet tree. The compaction from our dog's activities or from the birds scrabbling below the feeder next to the tree is as lethal as any piece of heavy equipment. Indeed, the pounds per square inch exerted by a bird's foot are greater than that exerted by typical construction machinery or by human feet. To minimize compaction, we maintain a 5-inch layer of mulch in all areas around the bird feeder, which is only 8 feet from the base of the white oak. Also, all brick walks in the yard are applied to the topography—they were not installed by digging in and cutting tree roots. The tree roots run freely under the walks. A layer of sand, a sheet of geotextile, and another layer of sand underlie the walks. This allows water and oxygen to penetrate to the roots under the walks.

8. Finally, as utilities became obsolete or wore out, I avoided cutting tree roots by having a local machinist make a set of jointed pipes that I used with a huge ratchet wrench to drive a drill bit under the roots and into the house. I spent more than a month boring and tunneling under roots and into the house with new water and electric lines from the well-house. I failed to install my utilities in pipe chases, which was a bad mistake. Ideally, two pipe chases should penetrate the lot from the street: one for water, sewer, and gas and one for electricity and fiber optics. The trenches should be installed to avoid damage to tree roots. Tunnel if necessary!

9. When I was young, I used to climb and prune the white oak and other trees myself. Now I pay professional arborists to prune hazardous or dead limbs from the tree. Prune if necessary for safety—about once every 5 years.

For 38 years, we lived with the white oak next to the house, the beech tree in back, and various yellow poplars throughout the property. The trees and wildflowers prospered. The pet white oak is now 38 inches in diameter and 113 feet tall, and its branches dominate an area 62 feet across.

My study of how to live with large trees is unreplicated. However, the Perry clan must have done something right. Hurricane Fran knocked trees down all around us. None were damage in the formal parts of my yard, but I lost over 40 trees on the hillside across the creek. A neighbor had two cars and a well-house destroyed. The other neighbor had a tree fall through his roof next to the chimney and drive the furnace through the floor.

My pet oak tree is still there and thriving. Adoption of a "Tree-Friendly Lifestyle" worked!

Appendix:
Program to Protect Trees and Other Natural Resources During Planning, Engineering, Construction, and Maintenance Projects, Thomas O. Perry 1983 (Revised 1995, 1997)

Overview: Steps for Managing Natural Resources During Development

The following is a bare-bones outline of the steps required to manage natural resources during the development process. If supervisors of municipal developments, contractors, and individual homeowners follow the steps of this outline, in proper sequence, they will reduce development costs and increase the overall success, attractiveness, and profitability of their projects.

Some of the essentials of proper sequence and timing are described in the section that follows the outline. The outline format makes this guide short, readable, and useful.

Phase I: Mapping and Prescription

1. Determine the objectives of the client.
2. Prepare a map and an inventory of soil, vegetation, and other natural resources of the area.
3. Prepare a development plan, which should include
   a. what should be protected
      * vegetation
      * soils
      * wildlife
      * vistas
      * human resources
      * unique features;
   b. what must be altered to achieve the objectives of the client and still permit the contractors to proceed effectively;
   c. operations schedule; negotiation of design approval; arrangement of contracts for implementation of plans.

Phase II: Preconditioning and Cultivation

1. Build access roads and staging areas for construction workers. Whenever possible, these roads and staging areas should be part of the permanent design.
2. Remove trash and clean up the site. Precious soils and tree roots are often destroyed by careless use of front-end loaders. Work by hand rather than scrape precious soils and roots away. (Remember, the best soils and most roots are concentrated in the top 2 inches.)
3. Thin and remove unwanted vegetation.
4. Fertilize.
5. Install protective fences, drainage, and irrigation.

6. Establish a transplant and holding area to salvage native plants or trees.
7. Establish a place to hold topsoil and a place to hold construction spoil.

Phase III: Supervision and Education
1. Provide manuals and seminars for contractors and subcontractors.
2. Give instructions to bulldozer operators.
3. Give instructions to utility people about ditch witches and location of lines.
4. During the first days of construction, make sure that someone be specifically charged with insuring that protective fences are honored and that spoil from land clearing is not shoved under fences and on top of tree roots. Bulldozer operators must be closely supervised.
5. Check last-minute changes in plans must to ensure that precious resources are not destroyed in the enthusiastic actions that characterize the start of new construction projects.
6. Agree on construction limits, sites of material storage, parking areas for workers, and locations of construction trailer and port-a-johns.
7. Agree on material disposal procedure: excess cement, paint cans, plastic, etc. (these can be toxic).
8. Agree on program to manage water from the construction site. Water from washing cement and cleaning brickwork can be toxic to plants. Excess erosion and storm-water runoff can be as costly to the developer as to the surrounding community.

Phase IV: Intensive Care
1. Provide extra water and fertilizer; insect, and disease control. Prune injured trees. Use herbicides cautiously.
2. Establish favorable soil conditions in areas of disturbance.

Phase V: Routine Maintenance and After-Care
1. Remove temporary fences and irrigation systems.
2. Plan for growth and maintenance of plants.
3. Locate and manage unpredicted paths and erosion patterns.
4. Maintain permanent irrigation systems and facilities
5. Perform regular thinning, pruning, and removal of plants that grow beyond desirable size, shape, or form. When possible, use herbicides on sprouts and other undesirable plants, and reduce the area to be maintained as turf.

Sequence and Timing of Operations
Proper sequence and timing of operations are as important as managing the natural resources of a developing area.

The mapping and inventory of the site and its resources should be conducted before major investments are made in laying out roads, dividing lots, and siting buildings. The data should be made available to site planners, architects, and engineers before any investment in drawings is made. Then a plan can be prepared that meets the objectives of the client and at the same time takes maximum advantage of the natural resources of the site. Actions to protect soil, landscape plants, and existing resources that the client treasures should take place first—before construction begins.

Everyone (prospective owners, contractors, and subcontractors) will save money by repairing roads and building staging areas before they begin tearing down old buildings, clearing away old trash or rubble, or removing unwanted trees. Completing the temporary paving work first is essential for saving the trees and will make the entire construction process less costly. Electrical workers do not like to drag their drop cords in the mud. Sheet-rock workers, carpenters, and plumbers need a dry places to pile their supplies. Flooring contractors and interior decorators will avoid tracking mud and dirt in the new structure. Good roads and clean staging areas for workers and their equipment are essential to simple operations such as forest management and even more essential to complex operations such as urban real-estate developments.

A common tragedy of construction sequencing is that irrigation lines, flood lights, utilities, and other critical support features are installed after paving is complete and after damage to soil has been repaired and landscape plants installed. This results in damage to the expensive landscaping and more serious damage to the soil.

Irrigation lines, drainage pipes, and utility lines should be installed before installing driveways, walks, and parking areas. If this is impossible, then bury plastic pipe in appropriate places so that these expensive installations do not have to be torn up and redone.

All construction, utility installation, and paving should be complete before damaged soil is replaced and before landscaping is done. After the soil is replaced, soil compaction can be minimized by using planks or placing the plants first and then moving the soil around the plants. Landscape contractors find they actually save money by following these procedures.

Living things go through seasonal cycles. These cycles dictate that landscaping be properly timed. If the building and dedication ceremonies are scheduled for July and the owner or the client insists on a pleasant surrounding (an instant landscape), then clean up the mud and provide flowers and grass, but wait until the proper season to plant perennials.

Beware of instant landscapes. The client, developer, building inspectors, planning commission, politicians, and general citizenry should not expect an instant landscape—especially in the off-season. Plants grow very rapidly. Trees can even grow 5 feet or more in height and an inch in diameter per year if soil and moisture conditions are favorable. If budgets are limited, it is more effective and more economical to spend money on soil and water management than to spend money on big plants. Indeed, proper soil and watering are more critical when installing large plants than smaller ones.

Literature Cited

1.   Watson, G.W. 1988. *Organic mulch and grass competition influences tree root development.* J. Arboric. 14:200–203.

PART I

ROOT GROWTH

Seed Selection and Nursery Production Practices Impact Root Regeneration and Tree Establishment

Michael A. Arnold, Larry J. Shoemake, and Mitchell W. Goyne

Transplant studies utilizing regionally adapted and nonadapted half-sib families of sycamore were used to investigate the relationships among seed selection, post-transplant shoot growth, and root regeneration characteristics of container-grown trees. Chemical preventative and mechanical corrective techniques for avoiding or remediating the development of circling roots were imposed on container-grown shumard oak seedlings to investigate the effects of these practices on post-transplant performance. Arizona ash and desert willow seedlings were grown in containers filled with various combinations of media at three fertility rates to determine post-transplant responses to these nursery practices. Substantial landscape growth gains in height, trunk diameter, and survival could be achieved via selection of adapted sycamore seed sources. Regional genotypes outgrew those from geographically distant regions. Genetically improved genotypes appeared to retain their relative growth advantages only over a limited geographic range. Measures or rapidity of root regeneration were most consistently associated with successful transplant establishment of sycamore and shumard oak seedlings. Regenerated small diameter roots appeared to be important during the first few weeks of landscape establishment of shumard oak. Elevated fertility rates during container nursery production were not beneficial to post-transplant establishment of desert willow seedlings in the landscape. Kenaf-based media reduced survival of desert willow and Arizona ash in the field.

Commercial foresters have understood for many years the importance of genetic origin in the selection of seeds for nursery production and plantation establishment. The regional origin or provenance of the original genetic material of seeds selected for nursery production versus the location of planting has long been of concern. Differential growth responses to genotypic and environmental interactions, both within and among seedling populations from different provenances, have been the basis for successful forest tree improvement programs throughout the world (27, 28).

This concept has been less completely incorporated into urban forestry programs and has only recently begun to be recognized in the nursery and landscape industries

Michael A. Arnold, Larry J. Shoemake, and Mitchell W. Goyne are Associate Professor of Landscape Horticulture, former Graduate Teaching/Research Associate, and former Research Associate, respectively, in the Department of Horticultural Sciences, Texas A&M University, College Station, TX 77843-2133.

(2, 9). Horticultural enterprises have historically capitalized on clonal rootstocks for size control, modification of cold tolerance, and disease or insect pest resistance in fruit crops (25), but have paid little heed to provenance in the selection of seed-propagated ornamentals, aside from such aesthetic characteristics as flower or foliage color (2). Recognizing the importance of genetically adapted strains or seed sources is critical to achieving maximal performance of planted stock, particularly when minimal maintenance is desired and establishment inputs are limited.

Is the term "provenance" interchangeable with "seed source"? Not necessarily—a provenance refers to the geographic origin of the genetic material of a group of plants, while a seed source refers to the geographic location from which the seeds used to produce the group of plants was collected. If the seeds were collected from a native stand, then the seed source and the provenance are essentially the same. If the seeds were collected from a planted stand of trees, then the provenance depends upon where the genetic material for the planted seedlings originated. For example, if seeds were collected from a red maple tree (*Acer rubrum* L.) growing in a native stand near Atlanta, Georgia, one could call that collection of seeds a Georgia provenance and a Georgia seed source. However, suppose that the seeds were collected from a planted red maple tree in a suburb of Atlanta, Georgia, but the seed used to produce the tree from which the seeds were collected was originally obtained from red maple trees growing in a native stand in Michigan. In this case, the seed source would be Georgia, but the provenance would be Michigan. Atlanta, Georgia, was the geographic origin of collection, but the original parental genotype came from Michigan.

Why be concerned with the subtle differences between seed source and provenance? In keeping with our example, would one expect the same adaptive traits to environmental stresses, such as cold, heat, drought, or soil problems, from the Michigan and Georgia provenances even though both were Georgia seed sources? One might expect substantially different physiological and perhaps morphological traits associated with genotypes from the two contrasting environments. In fact, when these differences are sufficiently distinct from the species type, varieties or subspecies are designated to taxonomically acknowledge these differences. With red maple, an example would be the Drummond red maple (*Acer rubrum* var. *drummondii*), which is generally more tolerant to heat, high pH, and wet soil than the species type *Acer rubrum* var. *rubrum* (1, 22).

Limited studies with larger landscape size container-grown stock of northern red oak (*Quercus rubra*) and sycamore (*Platanus occidentalis*) and with bare-root *P. occidentalis* and American sweetgum (*Liquidambar styraciflua*) seedlings suggest that gains in nursery and post-transplant landscape growth are possible using regionally adapted genotypes (4, 17, 18, 20). Gains were realized both by use of half-sib seedlings from regionally adapted sources (provenance) and superior selections within regional populations (17, 18).

Landscape establishment of container-grown trees is ultimately dependent upon the ability of the transplanted tree to sufficiently regenerate roots outside of the planted rootball into the surrounding soil to support long-term growth and development of the tree (10, 23). Critical water deficits can be reached within hours to a few days following transplanting due to the limited water-holding capacity of most container media (12, 13). The majority of studies relating root regeneration to post-transplant field performance have been accomplished with smaller bare-root stock, and principally with coniferous species (19). Limited studies with container-grown hardwoods suggest possible relationships among short-term post-transplant root regeneration characteristics and successful transplant establishment of several species (3, 5, 6, 7, 8,10, 12, 19). Studies measuring shoot growth parameters of *P. occidentalis* indicated gains of 20%, 27%, and 77%, respectively, for height, diameter at breast height, and wood volume—suggesting that significant variation existed in the species and could be assessed in part as early as three years of age (14). Root regeneration characteristics have been studied for *P. occidentalis* only on small bare-root seedlings (16).

The objectives in the following studies utilizing half-sib families of *P. occidentalis* as a model system were to 1) investigate relationships among root regeneration and field performance as affected by family selection and seasonal factors, 2) compare responses of regional and nonregional, genetically improved and nonimproved genotypes, and 3) search for characters associated with (predictors of?) successful transplant prone genotypes. Selected results from studies with other species will be discussed to illustrate the importance of documenting production practices when studying or recommending various genotypes.

Description of Studies

Seed Selection

During 1994, seedlings of seven half-sib families of *P. occidentalis* were grown in 9.1-L containers filled with a 3 pine bark : 1 sand (vol:vol) medium in an outdoor nursery in College Station, Texas (17). Half-sib families included two selections (Brazos-C and Brazos-D) native to Brazos County, Texas; one (Putnam) from Putnam County, Tennessee; two half-sib families (WV-10 and WV-14) from the Westvaco Corp. (Kentucky/Tennessee operations); and two (TFS-09 and TFS-24) from the Texas Forest Service tree improvement program. Brazos-C, Brazos-D, TFS-09, and TFS-24 represented local selections, while Putnam, WV-10, and WV-14 represented geographically distant families. TFS-09, TFS-24, WV-10, and WV-14 represented genetically improved selections from tree improvement programs, while Brazos-C, Brazos-D, and Putnam represent genetically nonimproved selections from the same regions, respectively. Fifteen seedlings of each family were grown in each of six blocks in the nursery using industry best management practices (17, 26). Growth parameters were measured at the end of nursery production.

The five container-grown seedlings from each family and block were transplanted to field plots in November 1994, April 1995, and June 1995 on 1 m within-row and 3 m between-row spacings to determine landscape performance. The soils on the site were Boonville Series, Boonville fine sandy loam, fine, montmorillic, thermic, ruptic-vertic albaqualfs. Seedlings were drip irrigated as needed for the next two growing seasons.

Concurrent with the above study, 30 seedlings of TFS-09, Brazos-C, WV-14, and Putnam families were grown in 4.7-L containers in a completely randomized design using the same cultural methods as previously described (17, 26). Ten seedlings of each family were transplanted to root observation boxes in a greenhouse to determine short-term root regeneration characteristics concurrent with field transplantings in the above study. Root elongation rates on the four 22 × 27 cm Plexiglas observation panels of the 12.5-L root observation boxes were monitored for 21 to 28 days. Plants were then destructively harvested to determine various root growth parameters by diameter classes, including root number, length, surface area, and branching, as well as fresh and dry masses.

In the summer of 1997, a preliminary study was undertaken to determine if clonal selections from selected families would respond similarly to the seedling populations in terms of nursery performance and root regeneration characteristics. Forty semi-hardwood cuttings were taken from five surviving seedlings from the TFS-09 and Putnam half-sib families in the field plots. TFS-09 represented one of the best field performers, while Putnam was the poorest establishing family in the field. These cuttings were placed under intermittent mist in a greenhouse until most cuttings were well rooted. No auxin or auxin-like compounds were applied to the cuttings. Root number and length (three longest roots) and percentage of rooting were assessed, and the rooted cuttings were transplanted to 4.7-L containers and grown in the nursery for the remainder of the year. Correlations were determined for root parameters at the end of the rooting process and shoot growth characteristics at the end of the first growing season in the 4.7-L containers.

Residual Effects of Production Practices on Landscape Establishment

Mechanical and Chemical Control of Circling Roots. Shumard oak seedlings (*Quercus shumardii*) were grown in 2.3-L containers and transplanted to field plots and observation boxes in June and October 1993 (3). Twenty seedlings were grown in containers treated with $Cu(OH)_2$ to prevent development of circling, matted, and kinked roots at the rootball/container-wall interface. Sixty were grown in nontreated containers. At each transplant time, ten seedlings from nontreated containers received traditional root pruning consisting of four evenly spaced, 1-cm-deep vertical slashes down the exterior of the rootball and removal of the matted roots at the bottom of the rootball, while ten seedlings were butterfly pruned. Butterfly pruning consists of splitting the rootball in half from the bottom to one-third of the distance from the top and splaying these halves apart at planting. Ten seedlings from the nontreated containers were not root pruned. Half of the plants from each rootball treatment were transplanted to field plots, and the remaining plants were planted in root observation boxes, as previously described, at each transplant date. Root regeneration was monitored for 21 days in the root observation boxes. Growth parameters were monitored in the field for two growing seasons.

Influences of Nursery Fertility Regimes and Media Composition. Arizona ash (*Fraxinus velutina*) and desert willow (*Chilopsis linearis*) seedlings were planted in 15-L black plastic containers and grown in a nursery as previously described

(11). Thirty seedlings of each species were grown in media composed of three composted pine bark : 1 sand (vol:vol), 3 pine bark : 1 coconut coir dust, 3 kenaf stalk core : 1 peat moss, or 3 kenaf stalk core : 1 coconut coir dust. Ten seedlings of each species and media type were fertilized with a 18N-3.1P-8.3K preincorporated controlled-release fertilizer at 3.55, 7.12, or 10.68 kg/m³ at planting in the 15-L containers and were later top-dressed in the spring of 1996 at the same rate with the same fertilizer. The seedlings of each species were transplanted to adjacent field plots in June 1996 as described previously in the *P. occidentalis* study. Growth was monitored for two growing seasons.

Discussion of Results
Seed Selection
Regional half-sib families (Brazos-C, Brazos-D, TFS-09, and TFS-24) had greater height growth in the nursery and greater height and trunk diameter growth after two years in the landscape (Table 1). Foliage of regional selections exhibited less water stress symptoms than did geographically distant families (WV-10, WV-14, and Putnam). Survival also tended to be greater for regional selections (Table 1). Regardless of the seed selection, summer transplanted seedlings performed poorly compared to those transplanted the previous fall or spring (Table 2). Mid-day and predawn water potentials were more negative for summer transplanted seedlings during the initial establishment period (Table 2). Avoiding summer transplant would result in substantial improvements in post-transplant landscape performance and reduced costs associated with failed plants. First-year field survival was 100% for fall transplants and 98% for spring transplants but dropped precipitously to 54% for summer transplants. Long-term survival of summer transplants was even less favorable (17).

Most root regeneration characteristics were not consistent across seasons of transplant in separating the performance of half-sib families on the basis of their aboveground landscape performance. While most measures were ineffective in separat-

Table 1. Main effects of half-sib *Platanus occidentalis* families pooled across transplant season on required pruning, growth responses, and stress symptoms in the nursery or field following transplant from 9.1-L containers.

Half-sib family	Nursery height (cm)	Survival (%)	Height (cm)	Trunk diameter (mm)	Year 1 visual rating (1–5)[y]
			Field		
			Two-year		
TFS-09	155 ab[z]	84 a	200 a	28.3 a	3.3 a
TFS-24	148 bc	74 b	175 b	27.0 b	3.0 b
Brazos-C	158 a	86 a	203 a	29.3 a	3.3 a
Brazos-D	150 ab	72 b	157 bc	26.6 b	3.1 ab
WV-10	140 cd	69 b	143 c	25.2 c	2.8 c
WV-14	137 de	73 b	137 cd	24.4 c	2.7 c
Putnam	130 e	66 b	119 d	22.5 d	2.7 c

[y]Visual rating scale; from 1 (100% of foliage with drought stress symptoms) to 5 (none of foliage exhibiting drought stress symptoms).
[z]Means within a column followed by the same letter are not significantly different ($P \leq 0.05$) using expected least squares means procedure; values are means of 90 observations.

Table 2. Main effects of transplant season pooled across family on xylem water potentials (Ψ_{xylem}), post-transplant growth responses, and foliar stress symptoms in the field on *Platanus occidentalis* seedlings transplanted from 9.1-L containers.

Season of transplant	Mid-day $\Psi_{xylem}{}^w$ (MPa)	Pre-dawn $\Psi_{xylem}{}^w$ (MPa)	Year 2 Height[x] (cm)	Caliper[x] (mm)	Visual rating (1–5)[y]
Fall	–0.48 c[z]	–0.27 b	223 a	32.4 a	3.5 a
Spring	–0.88 b	–0.22 c	182 b	25.7 b	3.3 b
Summer	–1.05 a	–0.34 a	81 c	20.4 c	2.0 c

[w]Values are means of 175 observations.
[x]Values are means of 210 observations.
[y]Visual rating scale; from 1 (100% of foliage with stress symptoms) to 5 (none of foliage exhibiting stress symptoms).
[z]Means within a column followed by the same letter are not significantly different ($P \leq 0.05$) using expected least squares means procedures.

Table 3. Measures of rapidity of root regeneration following transplanting from 4.7-L containers that consistently separated the *Platanus occidentalis* half-sib families in the same rank orders as indicated by their initial above-ground field performance across transplant times.

Half-sib family	Days to first root	Root elongation (cm/day)
TFS-09	8 bc[z]	0.62 b
Brazos-C	8 c	0.65 a
WV-14	10 b	0.58 c
Putnam	11 a	0.57 c

[z]Means within a column followed by the same letter are not significantly different ($P \leq 0.05$) using expected least squares means procedures.

ing families in one or more seasons, two measures were consistent across transplant dates (Table 3). The number of days to the first root present at the root observation panel and the mean daily root elongation rate of roots monitored at the root observation panels consistently separated superior and inferior performing families across all three transplant dates. The consistency of these measures suggests that rapidity of root regeneration may be an effective predictor of initial landscape establishment of container-grown sycamores (17). More work will be necessary to verify this hypothesis.

Previous studies conducted in Tennessee comparing WV-14 and Putnam half-sib families as transplanted bare-root stock indicated substantial growth advantages for WV-14 over Putnam seedlings (4). In Shoemake's (17, 18) trials, half-sib families from tree improvement programs tended to perform better than nonimproved families within a regional group, but many of the growth advantages of WV-14 over that of Putnam seedlings were lost (Table 1). This may be due to increased environmental stress associated with moving the genotype outside its adapted range. While no hard-and-fast rules exist as to how far seed can be moved from its origin and retain performance, movements of 100 to 200 mi are likely approaching the limits (27). Generally it is safest to move provenances near the center of a species' natural range and most risky as the borders of the range are approached or in regions in which rapid changes in environmental conditions are encountered such as mountainous or boreal regions (21, 24).

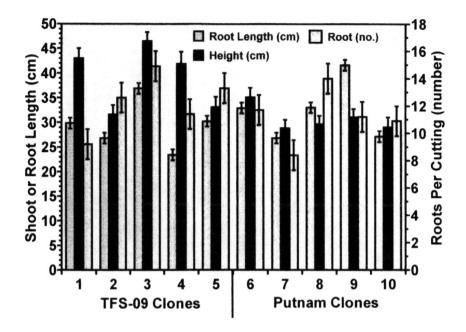

Figure 1. Mean (± s. e) shoot elongation at the end of the first growing season following transplanting to 4.7-L containers (solid columns) versus the number of regenerated roots (vertical hatching) and length of the three longest roots regenerated per cutting (horizontal hatching) at transplanting from the mist bench.

Preliminary work with rooted cuttings from five seedlings within the TFS-09 and Putnam half-sib families suggests that the adventitious root regeneration on cuttings (clones) may not be consistent with the root regeneration potentials indicated by the preceding work with seedling populations. While across families the number of roots per cutting ($R^2 = 0.15$) and length of the three longest roots per cutting ($R^2 = 0.14$) was weakly correlated ($P < 0.05$) with shoot height during the first year in container nursery production, no consistent differences were observed between the two families in terms of shoot extension and cutting root regeneration (Figure 1). Some TFS-09 clones did tend to have greater shoot extension during the first season in the nursery, but there did not appear to be a consistent relationship between cutting shoot extension and the number or length of roots regenerated in the mist bench (Figure 1). It may be that cutting-regenerated root systems react differently from seedling root systems. Oddiraju et al. (15) found that differences in root morphology among *Prunus* seedling populations disappeared when plants were propagated vegetatively from cuttings. Work is currently in progress to further investigate this phenomenon.

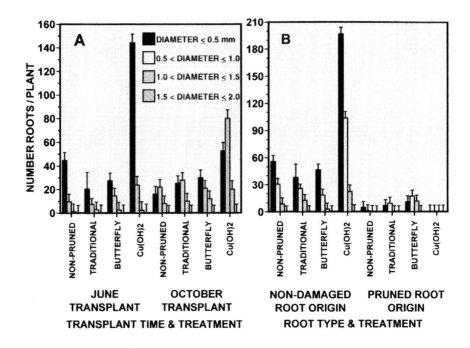

Figure 2. Mean number (± s.e.) of roots of various diameters that elongated beyond the transplanted 2.3-L rootball of *Quercus shumardii* seedlings grown in Cu(OH)₂-treated or nontreated containers or root pruned using traditional (vertical slashes) or butterfly pruning techniques at transplanting. Roots were separated into diameter classes based on month of transplant (A) or on origin from intact (nondamaged) roots or from roots that were severed or damaged (pruned) during the pruning and/or transplanting process (B).

Residual Effects of Production Practices on Landscape Establishment

Mechanical and Chemical Control of Circling Roots. Several key points can be illustrated from this study. Results strongly suggest the importance of small diameter roots, particularly those less than 1 mm in diameter, as a significant proportion of the new roots regenerated outside the rootball during the first few weeks post-transplant (Figure 2A). While there was a trend for slightly larger roots (those between 1 and 1.5 mm in diameter) to become a larger component of fall root regeneration than of summer root regeneration, the vast majority of roots regenerated outside the planted rootball were still 1 mm or less in diameter (Figure 2A). Plant size was confounded with the summer/fall contrast because fall-transplanted seedlings were somewhat larger (3).

The second point illustrated by this study is the importance of intact root tips as a source of roots regenerated outside the planted rootballs during the initial establishment period (Figure 2B). Across treatments for container-grown shumard oaks, numerically new roots overwhelmingly originated from smaller diameter roots rather than from larger diameter roots. While Dana and Blessing (8) found little effect of mechanical root pruning on plant water stress and no negative impacts on root re-

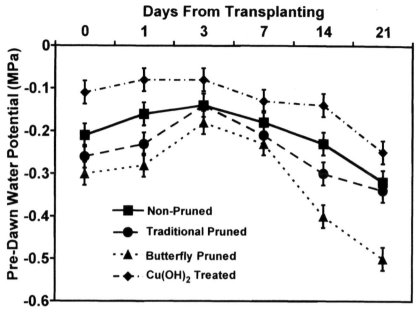

Figure 3. Mean predawn xylem water potentials (± s.e.) of the most recently mature leaves of *Quercus shumardii* seedlings following transplanting from 2.3 L-containers in October. Seedlings were transplanted from nontreated containers and root pruned by traditional (●——) or butterfly (▲ · · ·) methods to correct root circling, or not pruned (■——), or were transplanted from Cu(OH)$_2$-treated containers (◆— · —) designed to prevent root circling. Values are observations of five plants per treatment per observation date.

generation or post-transplant shoot growth of *Thuja occidentalis*, mechanical root pruning had a negative impact on shoot growth of *Q. shumardii*, particularly with butterfly root pruning (3). Mechanical root pruning resulted in greater water stress on *Q. shumardii* seedlings than on nonpruned plants (Figure 3). Seedlings grown in Cu(OH)$_2$-treated containers exhibited less-negative predawn water potentials than even nonroot-pruned plants from nontreated containers (Figure 3). Small diameter root regeneration during initial transplant establishment of Cu(OH)$_2$-treated *Q. shumardii* was two to three times that regenerated with any other treatment (Figure 2). Seedlings from the Cu(OH)$_2$-treated containers were the only plants to have a net increase in height during the first two years post-transplant (3). While the long-term importance of these small diameter roots may be debatable, they do appear to be associated with improved short-term landscape establishment in this study. Differential responses in this study may have been due to the coarser root system present on *Q. shumardii* versus that of *T. occidentalis*, suggesting the importance of utilizing multiple species with contrasting root and shoot morphology and phenology in transplant studies if the results are to be widely extrapolated.

Influences of Nursery Fertility Regimes and Media Composition. Several production practices other than seed selection, circling root development, root pruning,

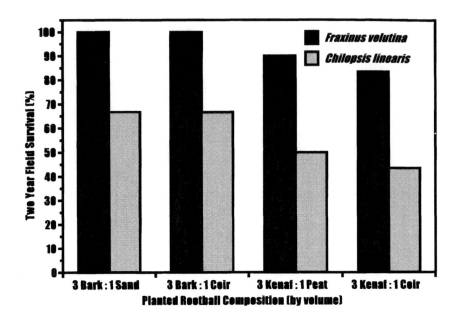

Figure 4. Two-year post-transplant field survival of 15-L container-grown *Fraxinus velutina* (solid columns) and *Chilopsis linearis* (horizontal hashing) seedlings grown in the nursery in 3 composted pine bark : 1 coarse builder's sand (vol:vol.), 3 composted pine bark : 1 coconut coir dust, 3 kenaf stalk core : 1 sphagnum peat moss, or 3 kenaf stalk core : 1 coconut coir dust. Percentage rate of survival is based on 30 seedlings per species and media combination, pooled across three fertility rates.

and root morphology modification can impact landscape performance. Many production techniques and inputs are selected solely on the basis of their impact on plant performance and cost:benefit analysis during the production cycle. Two examples of cultural practices with the potential to impact landscape establishment are illustrated in the results of experiments with *F. velutina* and *C. linearis* seedlings to investigate alternative container media and fertility rates during nursery production.

Kenaf stalk core is a byproduct of the processing of *Hibiscus cannabinus* stems for high-quality paper pulp, and coconut coir dust is a byproduct of coconut (*Cocos nucifera*) fruit coir fiber extraction (11). Composted pine bark fluctuates in price and availability with timber production. Sphagnum peat moss harvesting is politically and environmentally controversial. Kenaf stalk core and coconut coir dust were tested as potentially environmentally friendly container media substitutes for composted pine bark and sphagnum peat moss, respectively. While their suitability as a media component will not be discussed here, trials in which *F. velutina* and *C. linearis* were produced in these alternative media at different fertility rates then planted to the field yielded interesting results for urban foresters (11).

Fraxinus velutina had substantially greater survival than *C. linearis* under the conditions of the study, but both species responded adversely to the substitution of fresh kenaf stalk core for composted pine bark (Figure 4). Seedlings transplanted from

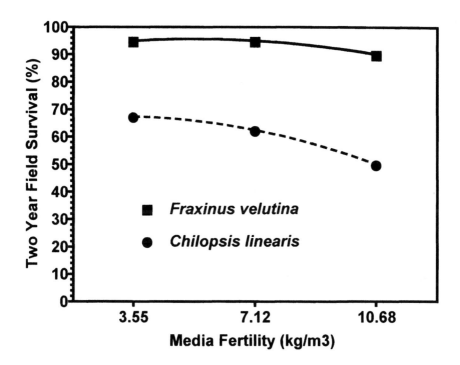

Figure 5. Two-year post-transplant field survival of 15-L container-grown *Fraxinus velutina* (solid columns) and *Chilopsis linearis* (horizontal hashing) seedlings grown in the nursery in media containing 3.55, 7.12, or 10.68 kg/m³ of 18N-3.1P-8.3K controlled-release fertilizer. Percentage rate of survival is based on 40 seedlings per species and fertility combination, pooled across 4 media types.

containers with a combination of kenaf stalk core and coconut coir dust had the poorest survival rates across fertility levels. This media combination had a very high water-holding capacity, reduced macropore space, and poor mechanical support properties (11). Seedlings transplanted from this media combination required more frequent attention to staking and tended to lean in the field.

Despite the "common wisdom" that well-fertilized nursery stock will establish more rapidly than similar stock grown under lower fertility regimes, the results with *C. linearis* and, to a lesser extent *F. velutina*, in these field trials suggest that more experimentation is warranted before issuing wholesale recommendations (Figure 5). These results actually suggest a trend to reduced survival with increased nursery fertility levels. Nursery production conditions need to be well documented for plant materials when researchers report results of transplant studies. Studies reporting results of transplant studies involving nursery stock may have little meaning if production conditions are unknown. It would likely be beneficial for landscape installers and urban foresters to also have a working knowledge of the production environment used to produce trees for their plantings. Locating reputable suppliers of high quality stock for use in a particular region is fundamental to establishment of successful plantings.

Take-Home Messages

Seed selection can be critical to successful establishment of some landscape trees. Proper seed selection can result in substantial improvements in nursery performance, post-transplant growth responses, and long-term survival rates. Marketing regionally adapted genotypes is a way to segment relatively undifferentiated products, such as seed-propagated trees, from those of less progressive competitors. Seed selection issues will likely increase in importance in the nursery and landscape industries for seed-propagated trees. Economic gains from capitalizing on this information could be substantial given the relatively low cost of investment for improved seed selection and collection that is possible with existing genotypes. The downside for nursery managers is that a single seed source or provenance will likely be inadequate in the future for a nursery that markets outside its immediate region, thus increasing inventory costs for stocking plants from multiple provenances or land races.

A plethora of potential confounding factors are present when evaluating source materials for commercial plantings and transplanting techniques or technology. Careful specification of nursery production conditions, handling practices, and installation techniques should be reported in any plant trialing or testing of transplant establishment aides. Specification of the appropriate production conditions may greatly aid landscape installers' odds of obtaining acceptable post-transplant tree survival.

Increased awareness of the need to control circling root development has occurred in recent years. Production practices should include efforts to minimize circling root development, particularly with container-grown stock. Media composition and fertility effects are deserving of further study to help elucidate the best nursery production practices for subsequent successful establishment of the plants in the landscape.

Acknowledgments

The authors thank Karen Major, Patty Reedy, and Steven Obst for their technical assistance with portions of this study. Financial support in the form of grants from the Faculty Minigrants Program of the Texas A&M University Office of Research and Graduate Studies, and donation of materials by Kinney Bonded Warehouses, Lerio Corporation, and the Griffin Corporation are gratefully acknowledged. Seeds for the sycamore studies were generously supplied by Dr. Randy Rousseau (Westvaco Corp.), Dr. William Lowe (Texas Forest Service), and Edgar Davis (Tennessee Technological University). The use of trade names in this publication does not imply endorsement by the Texas Agricultural Experiment Station, Texas A&M University, or the authors of the products named, nor criticism of similar ones not mentioned.

Literature Cited

1. Arnold, M.A. 1998. Landscape Plants for Texas and Environs. Stipes Publ. Co., Champaign, IL. (In Press).

2. Arnold, M.A. 1995. *Enthusiasm for "excellence."* Amer. Nurseryman 181(6): 12–13.

3. Arnold, M.A. 1996. *Mechanical correction and chemical avoidance of circling roots differentially affects post-transplant root regeneration and field establishment of container-grown shumard oak.* J. Amer. Soc. Hort. Sci. 121:258–263.

4. Arnold, M.A., and W.E. Davis. 1994. *Adaptability of forest tree improvement program seed sources of sycamore and sweetgum to ornamental field nursery production and transplant establishment following production.* J. Environ. Hort. 12:190–192.

5. Arnold, M.A., and D.K. Struve. 1989. *Green ash establishment following transplant.* J. Amer. Soc. Hort. Sci. 114:591–595.

6. Arnold, M.A., and D.K. Struve. 1989. *Growing green ash and red oak in CuCO₃-treated containers increases root regeneration and shoot growth following transplant.* J. Amer. Soc. Hort. Sci. 114:402–406.

7. Becker, C.A., G.D. Mroz, and L.G. Fuller. 1987. *The effects of plant moisture stress on red pine* (Pinus resinosa) *seedling growth and establishment.* Can. J. For. Res. 17:813–820.

8. Dana, M.N., and S.C. Blessing. 1994. Post-transplant root growth and water relations of *Thuja occidentalis* from field and containers, pp 98–112. In Watson, G.W., and Neely, D. (Eds.) The Landscape Below Ground: Proceedings of an International Workshop on Tree Root Development in Urban Soils. International Society of Arboriculture, Champaign, IL. 222 pp.

9. Flint, H.L. 1997 (2nd ed.). Landscape Plants for Eastern North America: Exclusive of Florida and the Immediate Gulf Coast. John Wiley and Sons, Inc., New York, NY. 842 pp.

10. Gilman, E.F. 1994. Establishing trees in the landscape, pp 69–77. In Watson, G.W., and Neely, D. (Eds.) The Landscape Below Ground: Proceedings of an International Workshop on Tree Root Development in Urban Soils. International Society of Arboriculture, Champaign, IL. 222 pp.

11. Goyne, M.W. 1998. Effects of Alternative Container Media Components on the Growth of Selected Under-Utilized Small Ornamental Trees. M.S. Thesis, Texas A&M University, College Station, TX. 95 pp.

12. Harris, J.R., and E.F. Gilman. 1993. *Production methods affect growth and post-transplant establishment of 'East Palatka' holly.* J. Amer. Soc. Hort. Sci. 118: 194–200.

13. Nelms, L.R., and L.A. Spomer. 1983. *Water retention in container soils transplanted into ground beds.* HortScience 18:863–866.

14. Nebgen, R.J., and W.J. Lowe. 1985. *The efficiency of early and indirect selection in three sycamore genetic tests.* Silvae Genet. 34:72–75.

15. Oddiraju, V.G., C.A. Beyl, P.A. Barker, and G.W. Stutte. 1994. *Container size alters root growth of western black cherry as measured via image analysis.* HortScience 29:910–913.

16. Rhea, S.B. 1977. The Effects of Lifting Time and Cold Storage on the Root Regeneration Potential and Survival of Sycamore, Sweetgum, Yellow Poplar, and Loblolly Pine Seedlings. M.S. Thesis, Clemson University, Clemson, SC. 108 pp.

17. Shoemake, L.J. 1996. Effects of Half-Sib Family Selection on the Root Regeneration Potential and Initial Landscape Establishment of Container-Grown Sycamore, *Platanus occidentalis* (L.). M.S. Thesis, Texas A&M University, College Station, TX. 91 pp.

18. Shoemake, L.J., and M.A. Arnold. 1997. *Half-sib family selection improves container nursery and post-transplant landscape performance of sycamore.* J. Environ. Hort. 15(3):126–130.

19. Struve, D.K. 1990. *Root regeneration in transplanted deciduous nursery stock.* HortScience 25:266–270.

20. Struve, D.K., and S.E. McKeand. 1994. *Importance of red oak mother tree to nursery productivity.* J. Environ. Hort. 12:23–26.

21. Wakeley, P.C. 1963. How far can seed be moved?, pp 38–43. **In** Proc. 7th South. Conf. For. Tree Improvement, Publ. No. 23, Gulfport, MS.

22. Wasowski, S., and A. Wasowski. 1997 (2nd ed.). Native Texas Plants: Landscaping Region by Region. Gulf Publ. Co., Houston, TX. 407 pp.

23. Watson, G.W., and E.B. Himelick. 1997. Principles and Practice of Planting Trees and Shrubs. International Society of Arboriculture, Champaign, IL. 200 pp.

24. Wells, O.O., and P.C. Wakeley. 1966. *Geographic variation in survival, growth, and fusiform-rust infection of planted loblolly pine.* For. Sci. Monograph 11.

25. Westwood, M.N. 1978. Temperate-Zone Pomology. W.H. Freeman and Co., San Francisco, CA. 428 pp.

26. Yeager, T., D. Fare, C. Gilliam, A. Niemiera, T. Bilderback, and K. Tilt. 1997. Best Management Practices for Producing Container-Grown Plants. Southern Nurserymen's Association, Marietta, GA. 69 pp.

27. Zobel, B., and J. Talbert. 1991. Applied Forest Tree Improvement. Waveland Press, Inc., Prospect Heights, IL. 505 pp.

28. Zobel, B.J., G. Van Wyk, and P. Stahl. 1987. Growing Exotic Forests. John Wiley and Sons, New York, NY. 508 pp.

Consequences of High Soil Temperatures

William R. Graves

Soil temperature is altered by urbanization and can increase enough to damage trees in urban landscapes. Although elevated soil temperatures affect the physiology and growth of both root and shoot systems of trees, species and selections within species are known to vary in their capacities to resist root-zone heat stress. A review of data collected on diverse, temperate taxa reveals that the development of below-ground urban heat islands probably will not cause direct heat injury of trees unless the temperature of soil remains above 32°C (90°F) for extended periods of time. Slight increases in root-zone temperature above 32°C (90°F) can result in reduced growth and water uptake of roots, reduced surface area and stomatal conductance of leaves, stunted stems, and alterations in nutrient content that cause severe chlorosis of young leaves. When considering the impact of elevated root-zone temperatures in urban ecosystems, it is necessary to recognize the effects of other root-zone stressors that may interact with temperature. We are just beginning to learn more about such interactions, but already there is evidence that the severity of the impact of drought on tree growth can depend on the temperature of the soil when the water deficit occurs.

The effects of urbanization on air temperature have been recognized for many years, and the so-called "urban heat island effect" has been documented in numerous metropolitan areas. As the name implies, urban centers tend to be warmer than surrounding suburban and rural areas. When characterized as average increases, most urban heat islands do not seem particularly severe; generally, gains in overall average temperatures do not exceed a few degrees. Examined differently, however, data on urban heat islands may provide more reason for concern. For example, differences between urban centers and outlying areas may be greater than 10°C (18°F) when only minimum nightly temperatures are considered. Additionally, as students of the urban forest, we recognize that the environment of individual, isolated city trees varies tremendously with the unique factors at each planting site. Is the urban heat island something about which proponents of city forests should be concerned?

A review of literature pertaining to the environments characteristic of urban trees shows that traits of tree microclimates can lead to dramatic increases in temperature that exacerbate the tendency for increased heat loads in cities. Among the microclimatic features that may foster heat stress of tree leaves is reflected radiation from parked automobiles and urban surfaces such as glass, metal, and concrete. Heat in

William R. Graves, Professor, Department of Horticulture, Iowa State University, Ames, IA 50011-1100.

aerial environments of trees in at least some areas likely contributes to reduced rates of photosynthesis and growth, to visible symptoms such as necrosis of leaf margins, and to the high mortality rates of city trees. But to focus our assessment of urban heat effects solely on the above-ground portion of the tree would be failing to consider the many temperature-sensitive processes that might be influenced if the urban heat island extends to the soil.

Those of us involved in this conference recognize that relatively little is known about tree roots and their environment, particularly roots of trees grown primarily for ornamental functions in urban soil or its substitute. Studying tree roots can be very challenging. Although assessing root development under ambient conditions in managed landscapes is difficult, it can and has been done, and data collected on root temperature in urban landscapes will be reviewed. Problems associated with imposing different root temperatures in a scientifically sound way on large trees are so great that we must rely on inferences from studies done in controlled environments with young plants. I will conclude this paper by summarizing data collected by my students and co-workers on root-zone temperature effects on tree seedlings or plants grown from stem cuttings.

Urban Soil Temperatures

The extent to which the urban heat island extends below ground has not been studied extensively. Johnson et al. (13) reported that average soil temperature at a depth of 10 cm (4 in.) within Urbana-Champaign, Illinois, was 4°C (7°F) higher than at sites in a nearby forest. An asphalt surface in a parking lot in New Brunswick, New Jersey, was associated with an increase in soil temperature 15 cm (6 in.) deep of 7°C (13°F) (12). Lethally high temperatures were observed in the planting pits of trees in downtown Indianapolis, Indiana, by Graves (2). Temperatures at certain sites increased with depth from 29°C (84°F) at 10 cm (4 in.) to 69°C (156°F) at 75 cm (30 in.). The researchers had been directed to these sites by city arborists because of the rapid death of trees planted there. The exceedingly high soil temperatures were attributed to the proximity of the planting sites to below-ground utility steam channels. Later, replacement trees were planted in large, raised containers placed over the planting pits. Figure 1 shows such a site in Indianapolis, as well as two other examples of sites designed such that they are prone to incidents of particularly high temperatures in tree root zones.

A study of soil temperatures in the cities of Lafayette and West Lafayette, Indiana (approximately 40.3°N latitude), revealed both generalities and variability (6). Fifteen sites at which trees were planted were selected for repeated measures of soil temperature during the summer of 1985. The sites were assigned to one of four classes. Sites in the urban street class were planting pits in the concrete pavement of sidewalks in downtown Lafayette. Downtown sites not adjacent to streets and characterized by surfaces of turf and organic mulch were placed in the urban nonstreet class. In West Lafayette, trees in the grassy parkways of a residential block were categorized as suburban street sites, and a site in a stand of native trees near the city limits was designated the native woodland site.

	Soil
Depth (cm)	temperature
10	29.3 °C
30	45.3 °C
75	69.3 °C

Figure 1. Three examples of sites in cities where tree roots are likely to be exposed to soil temperatures exceeding what would be optimal for root function. A. This is an above-grade planter in Salt Lake City, Utah; the walls of the planter are exposed to direct solar radiation. B. A series of raised planters within a slope of concrete in Bismarck, North Dakota. C. This is a site in Indianapolis, Indiana, where the soil temperature increased excessively with depth in the root zone due to steam channels below ground (see steam rising from a vent in the street). The data shown were collected at such a site in Indianapolis on September 4, 1984. Raised planters were installed to increase the distance between the heat source and the tree roots.

Average soil temperatures at depths of 5 to 50 cm (2 to 20 in.) during July were highest (26°C or 79°F) for the urban street class of sites and lowest (18°C or 64°F) for the native woodland site. Maximum temperatures in soils of urban street trees varied by site but were as high as 32°C (90°F). Soils of suburban street sites were warmer on average (24°C or 75°F) than soils of urban nonstreet sites (22°C or 72°F). Thus, the presence of pavement appeared to be an important factor associated with increased temperature. These average values show site class differences but do not illustrate other important findings. Among these was a uniformity of temperature with increasing depth at the urban street sites; a decrease of only 0.5°C (1°F) was found as depth increased from 5 to 50 cm (2 to 20 in.). In contrast, temperature decreased by nearly 2°C (4°F) at these depths in the native forest. Considerable variation observed among sites within a class was attributed to differences in the incidence of direct and reflected solar radiation on the surface. Finally, it is important to note that air temperatures were below normal during the period when these soil temperatures were obtained. During a different year (1987), mean and maximum temperatures from 2 to 20 cm (1 to 8 in.) deep at tree planting sites in downtown Lafayette were as high as 29°C and 33°C (84°F and 91°F), respectively (2).

The few data on soil temperature in managed landscapes clearly indicate that the urban heat island extends below ground. All studies of which I am aware have found higher temperatures at urbanized sites than at sites in natural areas surrounding a city. Lacking are data on soil temperatures in raised containers, rooftop landscapes, and other specialized locations. We may presume that soil temperature will be increased at many such urban sites, but questions regarding how increased heat loads affect tree function must be answered before we can conclude whether the urban soil heat island is a serious threat to tree health.

Root-Zone Temperature Effects on Trees

Direct evidence for effects of elevated root-zone temperature on the function of mature trees is lacking. Obtaining such evidence would be ideal, but temperature cannot be separated from other site-to-site differences in the urban environment. Nor would it be easy to design experiments to impose root temperature treatments on large trees in the landscape. Hence we are forced to make inferences to mature trees in the landscape after characterizing effects of temperature on young plants of the species of interest grown under controlled conditions.

Workers in my laboratory study effects of root-zone temperature on the physiology and development of seedlings or young plants propagated vegetatively. Several years ago, we invested in the construction of special containers in which plants could be grown with precisely controlled root-zone temperatures. The containers were based on concepts published by Graves and Dana (7). Roots of a plant grow in a stainless steel vessel surrounded on its sides and bottom by a polyvinyl chloride (PVC) shell (Figure 2). External electronic water baths ensure that temperature-regulated water is circulated constantly in the space between the outside of the stainless steel container and the inside wall of the PVC shell. The PVC insulates, while the steel transfers heat to the root zone. A different water bath is needed for each temperature regimen in an experiment. The water baths we use can maintain a constant root-zone temperature within 0.5°C (1°F), or they can be programmed to ramp changes in temperature on diurnal cycles to mimic the changes in soil temperature that occur daily in nature. Multiple containers can be controlled by each water bath, and the position of the containers in the greenhouse or growth chamber can be randomized appropriately for various statistical designs. The best way to maintain a uniform root-zone temperature is to grow plants in aerated solution. Alternatively, plants may be grown in solid media in containers designed with bottom drainage holes, but temperature differences exist in various portions of the root zone. We have quantified differences in root system morphology between plants grown in solution and solid media (4), but evi-

PVC shell and ring top
on which steel pot rests

stainless steel pot that is
suspended within the
PVC shell

tubing
through
which water
returns to
circulation
baths

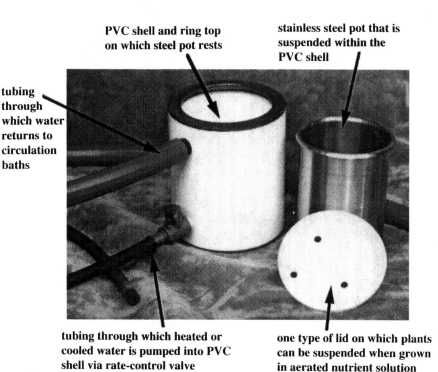

tubing through which heated or
cooled water is pumped into PVC
shell via rate-control valve

one type of lid on which plants
can be suspended when grown
in aerated nutrient solution

Figure 2. A vessel constructed to control root-zone temperature of tree seedlings and plants grown from rooted cuttings. Multiple vessels, each assigned to different temperature regimens, are used in most experiments. Not shown are the electronic water baths to which the vessels are connected. Vessels of this design are particularly effective for growing plants in aerated nutrient solution. Other vessels have been developed to permit water to drain from the root zones of plants grown in solid media.

dence we have obtained to date suggests that the morphological changes do not correlate to physiological differences.

Root-zone temperature effects on numerous tree species have been studied by using this system. Several legumes, including Eastern redbud (*Cercis canadensis*) (2), thornless honeylocust (*Gleditsia triacanthos* var. *inermis*) (11), Japanese pagoda tree (*Styphnolobium japonicum*) (3), and Amur maackia (*Maackia amurensis*) (3), have been included in these experiments. Graves et al. (9) determined how elevated root-zone temperature affected the growth of red maples from Florida, and the effects on seedlings of tree-of-heaven (*Ailanthus altissima*) were described by Graves et al. (10). Graves et al. (11) contrasted the effects of temperature on tree-of-heaven and thornless honeylocust. Cultivars of red maple (*Acer rubrum*) (15), selections of silver maple (*Acer saccharinum*) (5), and cultivars presumed to be hybrids of these species, Freeman maples (*Acer × freemanii*) (15), have been the subject of additional studies. Finally, root-zone temperature effects on two cultivars of apple (*Malus domestica*) were compared by Behboudian et al. (1).

Rather than providing a thorough review of these studies, I will attempt to provide some broad conclusions that address two key questions. First, in what ways do elevated temperatures affect these temperate woody plants? A common goal in many research projects has been to define a critical temperature above which there are negative impacts on plant function. A broad generalization can be made that, under the controlled conditions used in these experiments, constant temperatures up to 32°C (90°F) for several weeks do not appear detrimental. In contrast, root temperatures of 36°C (97°F) reduce root extension, shoot elongation, leaf area, and mass of plants. Such temperatures also have been shown to lower plant water potential, reduce stomatal conductance, reduce chlorophyll concentrations in leaves, and alter the content of numerous essential nutrients in leaves. Thus, the critical range of constant root-zone temperatures consistently has been 32°C to 36°C (90°F to 97°F). Assuming that the responses of mature trees in the urban ecosystem are similar to those of young plants in controlled environments, it appears that when no other stressors are present, the tendency for urbanization to increase soil temperature may be of little consequence for trees if temperatures do not exceed 32°C (90°F) for extended periods.

However, root-zone temperature can exceed 32°C (90°F) at some planting sites in urban landscapes. So a second key question is whether species differ in resistance to elevated root-zone temperature. If resistance is reflected by the capacity of the plant to maintain growth, then the answer clearly is yes. Seedlings of thornless honeylocust have been capable of sustaining high rates of growth with roots exposed constantly to 34°C (93°F) (11) and for up to 6 hours per day at 35°C (95°F) (8). The growth of other species we have studied is curtailed at these temperatures. Direct comparisons of effects of 34°C (93°F) in the root zone on honeylocust and tree-of-heaven provided striking contrasts (11). After 20 days of exposure, stems of tree-of-heaven seedlings had become stunted, root and shoot masses were reduced, leaf area was less, transpiration rates had curtailed, and the hydraulic conductivity of roots was reduced compared to these traits of tree-of-heaven seedlings grown with roots at 24°C (75°F). In contrast, none of these traits differed among honeylocust at the two temperatures.

A slight increase in root-zone temperature to 35°C (95°F) for 24 hours per day, however, caused dramatic effects on honeylocust. Within a few weeks, young, expanding leaves show severe chlorosis (Figure 3). Tissue analysis confirmed reductions in both the manganese and iron content of the leaves. As illustrated in Figure 3, relieving the high-temperature stress resulted in growth of new leaves that were not chlorotic, but the appearance of leaves that had become chlorotic during the exposure of roots to 35°C (95°F) did not change after reducing the temperature. A subsequent study of honeylocust, Japanese pagoda tree, and Amur maackia confirmed that the iron content of leaf tissue declined as the number of hours per day with temperatures of 35°C (95°F) in the root zone increased from 0 to 24 (3). Klock et al. (14) observed decreases in manganese content of honeylocust plants as root-zone temperature increased from 24°C to 36°C (75°F to 97°F). In apple, Behboudian et al. (1) found that 8 hours per day with roots at 35°C (95°F) decreased the iron content of leaves, while exposure for 24 hours per day was necessary to reduce foliar manganese content.

stress relieved

stress initiated

Figure 3. Terminal portion of a shoot of a thornless honeylocust plant that had its roots treated with controlled temperatures. Heat stress began by exposing the roots to a temperature of 35°C (95°F) when the shoot tip was at the position shown by the lower arrow. The stress treatment was relieved when the shoot tip was at the position shown by the upper arrow. Heat caused leaf chlorosis. Leaves formed after the heat treatment were healthy, but foliage formed during heating of the roots did not regain a dark green color after heat stress ended. Treating roots with slightly lower temperatures of 32°C to 34°C (90°F to 93°F) does not cause chlorosis.

Selections within species can vary in the capacity to resist elevated root temperatures. Research with cultivars of red maple and putative Freeman maple has led to the conclusion that 'Indian Summer' Freeman maple and 'Franksred' red maple are relatively sensitive, while 'Jeffersred' Freeman maple and 'Autumn Flame' and 'Schlesinger' red maples are relatively resistant to temperatures of 34°C (93°F) in the root zone (15). The extension of third-order roots, the maintenance of stem elongation, and the mass of plants after treatment at 28°C and 34°C (82°F and 93°F) were among the responses assessed. Later, Zhang et al. (16) studied how the temperature of the rooting medium affected leaf water relations and root development of softwood cuttings of 'Indian Summer' Freeman maple and 'Autumn Flame' red maple. Interestingly, cultivar differences in temperature effects on cuttings were consistent with trends seen in whole plants; the negative influence of heat was more pronounced for 'Indian Summer' Freeman maple than for 'Autumn Flame' red maple. This suggests that stem cuttings could be used to screen genotypes for root-zone heat resistance of whole plants. Recently, Graves and Aiello (5) found that the growth and water relations of genotypes of silver maple from 33°N latitude in Mississippi and 44°N latitude in Minnesota did not differ in response to 35°C (95°F) in the root zone. This indicates that the geographic origin of silver maple should not be used to select genotypes to use for crossing with red maple to develop Freeman maples with superior heat resistance.

Interactive Effects of Temperature and Other Edaphic Factors

Studies of root-zone temperature effects generally have been conducted such that the other environmental conditions to which plants are exposed during temperature treatments do not limit plant function. This may not be an ideal way to assess the impact of elevated root temperatures on urban trees because the influence of temperature likely interacts with other edaphic conditions, including the water content and salinity of the soil. Determination of how the impact of one stressor, such as temperature, is dependent on the severity of another stressor, such as low soil water content, is needed.

Results of recent work in our laboratory illustrate the importance of considering multiple stressors simultaneously. We grew plants of two red maple cultivars in a solid medium in containers that maintained constant root-zone temperatures of 28°C and 35°C (82°F and 95°F). Within both temperature treatments, half of the plants were grown with frequent irrigation to prevent water stress. The soil water content of the other plants at both temperatures was allowed to decline to 15% by volume before plants were irrigated, thus causing periodic drought stress. As will be described in an upcoming research report to be published elsewhere, for certain variables we used as measures of plant development, drought was detrimental only when it was imposed in root zones at 35°C. The implications of such interactions could be very important in the landscape because high soil temperatures might be expected to promote the incidence and severity of drought by increasing the rate of evaporation of water from the soil.

Literature Cited

1. Behboudian, M.H., W.R. Graves, C.S. Walsh, and R.F. Korcak. 1994. *Water relations, mineral nutrition, growth, and 13C discrimination in two apple cultivars under daily episodes of high root-medium temperature.* Plant and Soil 162: 125–133.

2. Graves, W.R. 1988. *Urban root-zone temperatures and their impact on tree hydrology and growth.* Ph.D. dissertation, Purdue University.

3. Graves, W.R. 1991. *Growth and iron content of three legume tree species at high root-zone temperature.* J. Arboric. 17:313–317.

4. Graves, W.R. 1992. *Influence of hydroponic culture method on morphology and hydraulic conductivity of roots of honey locust.* Tree Physiol. 11:205–211.

5. Graves, W.R., and A.S. Aiello. 1997. *High root-zone temperature causes similar changes in water relations and growth of silver maples from 33° and 44°N latitude.* J. Amer. Soc. Hort. Sci. 122:195–199.

6. Graves, W.R., and M.N. Dana. 1987. *Root-zone temperature monitored at urban sites.* HortScience 22:613–614.

7. Graves, W.R., and M.N. Dana. 1987. *A system to control root-zone temperature.* HortScience 22:957–958.

8. Graves, W.R., and L.C. Wilkins. 1991. *Growth of honey locust seedlings during high root-zone temperature and osmotic stress.* HortScience 26:1312–1315.

9. Graves, W.R., M.N. Dana, and R.J. Joly. 1989. *Root-zone temperature affects water status and growth of red maple.* J. Amer. Soc. Hort. Sci. 114:406–410.

10. Graves, W.R., M.N. Dana, and R.J. Joly. 1989. *Influence of root-zone temperature on growth of* Ailanthus altissima *(Mill.) Swingle.* J. Environ. Hort. 7:79–82.

11. Graves, W.R., R.J. Joly, and M.N. Dana. 1991. *Water use and growth of honey locust and tree-of-heaven at high root-zone temperature.* HortScience 26: 1309–1312.

12. Halverson, H.G., and G.M. Heisler. 1981. *Soil temperatures under urban trees and asphalt.* USDA For. Ser. Res. Paper NE-481.

13. Johnson, F.L., D.T. Bell, S.K. Sipp. 1975. *A comparison of urban and forest microclimates in the Midwestern United States.* Agric. Meteor. 14:335–345.

14. Klock, K.A., W.R. Graves, and H.G. Taber. 1996. *Growth and phosphorus, zinc, and manganese content of tomato, muskmelon, and honey locust at high root-zone temperatures.* J. Plant Nutrit. 19:795–806.

15. Wilkins, L.C., W.R. Graves, and A.M. Townsend. 1995. *Responses to high root zone temperature among cultivars of red maple and Freeman maple.* J. Environ. Hort. 13:82–85.

16. Zhang, H., W.R. Graves, and A.M. Townsend. 1997. *Water loss and survival of stem cuttings of two maple cultivars held in subirrigated rooting medium at 24 to 33°C.* HortScience 32:129–131.

Physiological and Horticultural Aspects of the Use of Treeshelters in the California Landscape

D.W. Burger

Seven tree species commonly used in California were grown from liners with or without treeshelters in the landscape for two years. Periodic (approximately every two months) height and caliper measurements were taken and, at the end of the two years, all trees were harvested for fresh and dry biomass determinations. Response to the treeshelter microenvironment was species dependent. Height was greater for sheltered than for unsheltered trees during the first 30 to 250 days for all species. After two years, only *Ginkgo biloba* and *Pinus canariensis* trees grown in shelters were taller than their unsheltered counterparts. Stem caliper was often reduced for sheltered trees. Treeshelters reduced top dry mass of *Fraxinus latifolia*, *Platanus racemosa*, *Quercus agrifolia*, and *Q. lobata* and also reduced root dry mass, root:shoot ratio, total root length, and total root area for all species and cultivars except *Q. agrifolia*. The results are explained on the basis of the microenvironment in and around treeshelters, photosynthetic partitioning, and immobilization of plants growing in shelters. Treeshelters may be useful for tree establishment in the landscape but should be removed once the tree has grown out of it. Staking likely will be required after removal of the treeshelter. Management challenges and potential usefulness of treeshelters in landscape transplanting are also discussed.

Treeshelters are cylindrical or square, translucent, polypropylene tubes of varying heights (60 to 150 cm) originally developed in Great Britain to protect newly transplanted trees from browsing animals. However, it was observed that trees growing in shelters responded with significant increases in height sometimes exceeding 600% that of unsheltered trees (4, 8). These growth enhancements have been attributed to the microenvironment changes around sheltered trees (1, 8, 10). Comparisons between the interior and exterior of treeshelters show the interior environment to have a lower light intensity and a higher temperature, relative humidity, and CO_2 concentration, especially if the shelter is free of any ventilation holes (1, 6). The low-light conditions are known to stimulate stem elongation responses by increasing internodal distances. Other responses such as above-ground biomass accumulation are not al-

David W. Burger, Department of Environmental Horticulture, University of California, One Shields Avenue, Davis, CA 95616-8587.

ways apparent or observed, and the effects of treeshelters on below-ground growth are just beginning to be extensively studied.

Treeshelters have been used to help improve transplanting success of trees in the landscape. Studies over the past decade have shown that treeshelters increase survival (3) and enhance stem growth rates and tree height with relatively little effect on stem caliper and overall biomass (2, 6, 12). Little attention has been paid to the development of roots or dry-matter partitioning of trees growing in shelters. Rendle (15) found that *Quercus robur* trees growing in shelters grew to set heights in shorter periods of time but did not differ in total dry-matter accumulation; however, she did find that dry mass between stems, branches, and roots differed depending on whether treeshelters were used or not. More recently, Svihra et al. (18) found that treeshelters reduced the fresh and dry mass of redwood (*Sequoia sempervirens*) trees that had been growing in the landscape for four years.

Dry-matter partitioning can be an important factor in the early development of trees in the landscape. If root development is inhibited before or during transplantation, a newly planted tree has a lower probability of becoming well established (9). The objective of this two-year study was to determine the effect of treeshelters on root development and dry-matter partitioning of seven tree species common to the western United States.

Materials and Methods
Short-Term Experiments

A randomized, complete block design experiment (six blocks, two replicates per block) was initiated in a container nursery whereby each block contained two trees of each species, one in a shelter (122 cm tall, 10 to 15 cm in diameter, tan Tubex® shelter) and one not in a shelter (control). Seed-propagated liners were used as planting stock, including *S. sempervirens, Q. lobata, Q. agrifolia, Lagerstroemia indica* 'Watermelon Red', *Ginkgo biloba, Platanus racemosa,* and *Fraxinus latifolia.* The trees were grown in 1.8-L (#1) containers filled with UC (University of California) mix (1:1:1, by volume, sand:redwood sawdust:peat moss). Thirty g of Nutricote Total (18-6-8 with micronutrients, Type: 180, PlantCo, Inc., Brampton, Ontario, Canada) were added to the soil surface at planting time. Treeshelters, held upright by one stake, were placed over the appropriate plants after the containers were moved to the nursery bed. The nursery containers were placed on 40-cm centers. An automated irrigation system (spray stakes) was used to add approximately 500 mL of water each day. Half the blocks were harvested after three months and the other half after six months. Measurements of height, caliper, and fresh and dry biomass accumulation were taken at each harvest.

Long-Term Experiments

A randomized, complete block design landscape experiment (ten blocks) was initiated whereby each block contained two adjacent trees of each of the same seven tree species used in the nursery experiments that were planted on 1.8-m centers in rows 1.8 m apart. The trees were irrigated with an automatic drip system distributing approximately 8.7 L every other day for the duration of the experiment. Trees were fertilized once, four weeks after planting, with Agriform 20-10-5 plus minors fertilizer tablets (Grace/Sierra, Milpitas, California). The fertilizer tablets were pressed 8 to 12 cm into saturated soil 6 to 10 cm from each tree immediately after irrigation. After 12 months, height and stem diameter (caliper) were measured and fresh and dry mass were determined for tops (leaves, branches, stems) and roots of trees in half the blocks. Root systems were removed from the ground with a backhoe fitted with a 60-cm-wide bucket. The soil attached to the roots was removed with pressurized water so root fresh and dry mass could be determined. A recently rinsed root system of each tree was shaken to remove excess water, weighed (fresh mass), cut into pieces, placed in a paper bag, dried for at least seven days at 70°C (158°F), and weighed (dry mass). The remaining trees in blocks were harvested after 24 months. Trees were harvested by cutting the trunk at ground level. Twigs with leaves and stems were cut into pieces, weighed (fresh mass), placed in paper bags, and dried for at least one week at 70°C (158°F) to obtain dry mass. Collected biomass data included top (leaves, branches, stems) fresh and dry mass. Root systems were exposed using hydroexcavation techniques (7, 8). Using this technique, undamaged roots as small as 1 mm in diameter were exposed. On deeper, more extensive root systems, hydroexcavation continued until roots as small as 1 cm were exposed. They were then cut at the soil interface before removing the excavated portion from the ground. The root systems were air dried, painted white, suspended above a backlit background, and photographed from

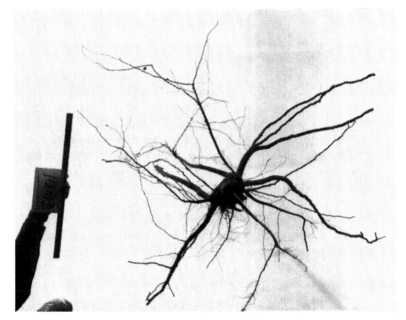

Figure 1. High-contrast photograph of a backlit intact root system extracted from the ground following hydroexcavation. This image was visualized using a video imaging system (AgVision Root and Leaf Analysis) to estimate total root length and total root area.

above using high-contrast black-and-white film. This setup provided excellent contrast between the shadow-darkened root system and the bright background (Figure 1). Once photographed, the root systems were cut into pieces and dried for at least seven days at 70°C (158°F) (for dry mass). The black-and-white photographs were used to estimate total root length and total root area using a video imaging system (AgVision Root and Leaf Analysis, Decagon Devices, Inc., Pullman, Washington). All data for all experiments were analyzed using the General Linear Model (GLM) Procedure of the SAS statistical system (16).

Results

Survival

Unsheltered tree liners (in particular, *Pinus canariensis, L. indica,* and *Maytenus boaria*) were subject to damage or destruction from birds immediately after planting. In these cases, treeshelters were necessary for survival.

Height Increase

All species growing in shelters, except *G. biloba,* showed height increases over control trees, ranging from 62% to 244% after only three months of growth (May to August) (Table 1 and Figure 2). This same result occurred in those tree species measured at six months (Table 1). After one year, *L. indica, Q. agrifolia,* and *Q. lobata* trees growing in shelters were still taller than their unsheltered counterparts, whereas *F. latifolia, G. biloba, P. racemosa,* and *S. sempervirens* trees growing in shelters were no taller than controls. After two years, only *L. indica* and *S. sempervirens* trees growing in shelters continued to be taller than the controls (Table 1). The unsheltered trees of the other five species all had similar heights by then.

Caliper Development

Caliper development was only slightly affected by treeshelters after three months in *F. latifolia, G. biloba,* and *S. sempervirens* (Table 2). At six months, none of the tree species showed differences in caliper, and long-term (one or two years) effects of treeshelters on caliper were observed in *S. sempervirens* and *P. racemosa* (after one and two years) and *F. latifolia* and *Q. agrifolia* (after two years) (Table 2). At no time during this study were caliper differences between control (unsheltered) and sheltered trees observed for *L. indica* or *Q. lobata.*

Top Dry Mass

Top dry mass (TDM) varied in treeshelters during the time of the experiment among most of the species. After 6 months, *L. indica, Q. agrifolia, Q. lobata,* and *S. sempervirens* trees growing in shelters had greater top dry mass than control trees did (Table 3). However, after one year, there was no significant difference between unsheltered and sheltered trees except for *P. racemosa* and *S. sempervirens*: unsheltered trees had higher top dry mass than sheltered counterparts (Table 3). After two years, *F. latifolia, P. racemosa, Q. agrifolia,* and *Q. lobata* trees growing in treeshelters had lower dry mass than did the control trees.

Table 1. Mean height increases of seven tree species over time growing with (+) and without (−) treeshelters (n = 8 for three- and six-month data; n = 20 for one-year data; n = 10 for two-year data).

Species	3 months +	3 months −	6 months +	6 months −	1 year +	1 year −	2 years +	2 years −
Fraxinus latifolia	27 b*	44 a	—	—	162 a	197 a	238 a	233 a
Ginkgo biloba	0 a	0.3 a	1.5 a	4.4 a	13 a	18 a	34 a	51 a
Lagerstroemia indica	27 b	76 a	30 b	76 a	30 b	137 a	98 b	160 a
Platanus racemosa	38 b	64 a	—	—	134 a	173 a	330 a	308 a
Quercus agrifolia	16 b	51 a	27 b	78 a	57 b	144 a	172 a	191 a
Q. lobata	9 b	31 a	19 b	53 a	71 b	200 a	233 a	261 a
Sequoia sempervirens	11 b	25 a	12 b	38 a	85 a	68 a	123 b	213 a

*Values followed by the same letter for each time period are not significantly different from one another at $P = 0.05$ using Scheffe's multiple separation procedure.

Figure 2. Height response after four months of *Fraxinus latifolia* trees growing with (right) and without (left) treeshelters. The treeshelter is 1.2 m tall.

Table 2. Mean caliper increases of seven tree species over time growing with (+) and without (−) treeshelters (n = 8 for three- and six-month data; n = 20 for one-year data; n = 10 for two-year data).

	Mean caliper increase (mm)						
	3 months		6 months		1 year		2 years	
Species	+	−	+	−	+	−	+	−
Fraxinus latifolia	9 a*	6 b	—	—	32 a	27 a	83 a	61 b
Ginkgo biloba	2.0 a	1.3 b	2.6 a	2.2 a	3.5 a	3.2 a	9.1 a	6.4 a
Lagerstroemia indica	4.9 a	4.3 a	5.4 a	5.9 a	12 a	10 a	32 a	23 a
Platanus racemosa	7.0 a	9.0 a	—	—	57 a	36 b	138 a	82 b
Quercus agrifolia	3.4 a	3.1 a	4.1 a	5.0 a	13 a	12 a	31 a	22 b
Q. lobata	1.8 a	2.4 a	2.1 a	2.7 a	16 a	12 a	44 a	32 a
Sequoia sempervirens	3.2 a	1.6 b	4.5 a	5.2 a	24 a	12 b	52 a	36 b

*Values followed by the same letter for each time period are not significantly different from one another at P = 0.05 using Scheffe's multiple separation procedure.

Table 3. Top dry mass of seven tree species over time growing with (+) and without (−) treeshelters. Dry mass data for three months were lost due to a fire in the drying oven (n = 8 for three- and six-month data; n = 20 for one-year data; n = 10 for two-year data).

	Top dry mass (g)					
	6 months		1 year		2 years	
Species	+	−	+	−	+	−
Fraxinus latifolia	—	—	542 a*	463 a	3286 a	2265 b
Ginkgo biloba	3.7 a	3.3 a	11.4 a	6.8 a	23.2 a	17.0 a
Lagerstroemia indica	11.7 b	24.3 a	120 a	177 a	625 a	638 a
Platanus racemosa	—	—	1518 a	720 b	9357 a	3280 b
Quercus agrifolia	22.6 b	48.2 a	113 a	143 a	677 a	533 b
Q. lobata	7.0 b	12.0 a	162 a	96 a	1346 a	925 b
Sequoia sempervirens	16.5 b	31.3 a	386 a	102 b	1125 a	1288 a

*Values followed by the same letter for each time period are not significantly different from one another at P = 0.05 using Scheffe's multiple separation procedure.

Root Dry Mass and Dry-Matter Partitioning

Except for *Q. agrifolia*, all tree species eventually had reduced root dry mass (RDM) when grown in treeshelters (Table 4 and Figure 3). The reduction in RDM occurred most rapidly (three months) for *F. latifolia*, *G. biloba*, and *P. racemosa* and by 6 months for *L. indica*, *Q. lobata*, and *S. sempervirens*. After two years, RDM of sheltered trees ranged from 9% to 71% that of unsheltered trees. Treeshelters reduced the root:shoot ratios of *G. biloba*, *L. indica*, *Q. lobata*, and *S. sempervirens* (Table 4 and Figure 3). Most dramatic was the response observed in *L. indica* and *S. sempervirens*: The root:shoot ratios for the sheltered trees were 11% and 8% that of the controls.

Total Root Length and Total Root Area

Treeshelters reduced total root length by 17% to 39% and total root area by 38% to 89% compared to controls for all tree species except *Q. agrifolia* (Table 5).

Discussion

The reduced root biomass from trees growing in treeshelters was the most striking response observed in this study. Six of the seven tree species showed reductions in root biomass, total root length, and total root area. Some roots from very large root

Table 4. Root dry mass over time and final root:shoot ratios of 7 tree species growing with (+) and without (–) treeshelters. Some roots < 1 cm in diameter remained in the soil after root system excavation (n = 8 for three- and six-month data; n = 20 for one-year data; n = 10 for two-year data).

	Root dry mass (g)						Root:shoot (dry mass basis)	
	3 months		1 year		2 years			
Species	+	–	+	–	+	–	+	–
Fraxinus latifolia	46.3 a*	17.8 b	259 a	147 b	1473 a	1051 b	0.45 a	0.46 a
Ginkgo biloba	5.3 a	4.0 b	6 a	4 a	34	18 b	1.47 a	1.06 b
Lagerstroemia indica	3.3 a	11.3 a	39 a	28 b	1574 a	180 b	2.52 a	0.28 b
Platanus racemosa	40.7 a	27.3 b	673 a	287 b	2394 a	1561 b	0.26 a	0.38 a
Quercus agrifolia	12.2 a	8.4 a	43 a	40 a	165 a	135 a	0.24 a	0.25 a
Q. lobata	12.5 a	13.8 a	91 a	66 b	664 a	316 b	0.49 a	0.34 b
Sequoia sempervirens	7.3 a	4.0 a	64 a	15 b	404 a	37 b	0.36 a	0.03 b

*Values followed by the same letter for each time period are not significantly different from one another at P = 0.05 using Scheffe's multiple separation procedure.

Figure 3. Root development response of *Sequois sempervirens* trees grown with (right) and without (left) treeshelters.

systems associated with control (unsheltered) trees in the landscapes sites were left unexcavated due to their depth and lateral expanse. This means that growth estimates of those root systems are conservative. Still, significant differences were found between sheltered and unsheltered treatments for most of the tree species studied. The reduction in root biomass was likely the result of a reduced overall photosynthate pool (reduced biomass production) and/or a change in photosynthate partitioning between treatments causing a reduction in the root:shoot ratio. Root biomass and

Table 5. Total root length and total root area of trees growing with (+) and without (−) treeshelters after two years. Some roots smaller than 1 cm in diameter remained in the soil after root system excavation (n = 8 for three- and six-month data; n = 20 for one-year data; n = 10 for two-year data).

Species	Total root length (cm)		Total root area (cm^2)	
	+	−	+	−
Fraxinus latifolia	1541 a*	1099 b	1831 a	1034 b
Ginkgo biloba	273 a	166 b	138 a	52 b
Lagerstroemia indica	778 a	636 b	443 a	268 b
Platanus racemosa	2460 a	1713 b	2915 a	1809 b
Quercus agrifolia	485 a	581 a	271 a	276 a
Q. lobata	730 a	605 b	555 a	353 b
Sequoia sempervirens	692 a	539 b	1717 a	195 b

*Values followed by the same letter for each time period are not significantly different from one another at $P = 0.05$ using Scheffe's multiple separation procedure.

root:shoot ratios of trees have been shown to be adversely affected by water and nutrient regimes (5), planting density (14), and light (4), but this is the first report of a long-term reduction in root biomass and root:shoot ratios of several tree species in response to treeshelters. The reduced root biomass found in most of the tree species in this study is most likely due to a combination of environmental factors associated with treeshelters. The light irradiance inside the treeshelter is approximately half that outside the treeshelter (2). This alone would reduce overall available photosynthate.

Top dry mass changes were due either to changes in height or changes in caliper. In no instances were height increases associated with caliper increases and in one case (*S. sempervirens*) increases in height were accompanied with decreases in stem caliper. This is a common occurrence in woody perennials because available photosynthate is partitioned into competing above-ground sinks.

The light environment surrounding a plant shoot can affect its root size and root:shoot biomass ratio and has been widely studied. Individual plant responses are likely under genetic control and "strategies" have been suggested by which a plant invests only enough carbon in roots to support the plant as is develops. Kasperbauer and Hunt (11) found in sweetclover (*Melilotus alba*) that while photosynthesis regulates carbon fixation and biomass production, photoperiod and spectral distribution regulate biomass distribution (partitioning) and new photosynthate. Wilson (19) has also provided a summary of the effects of light and carbon dioxide on the root:shoot ratios of plants. Changes in light, specifically light quality or spectral distribution, could explain why root:shoot ratios differ between sheltered and unsheltered tree species studied here. Tubex® treeshelters used in these experiments were tan in color and have been shown to reduce light irradiance (2). While spectral shift analyses have not been conducted for these treeshelters, it is quite probable the absorption, transmission, and/or reflection of light inside the shelter is substantially different from incident light outside. Analyses such as these will be necessary to support this contention and help provide an explanation for the dramatic root biomass reductions observed in most trees growing inside treeshelters.

Not all trees responded similarly to treeshelters. For some, height was influenced early and the effect diminished over time (e.g., *F. latifolia*, *P. racemosa*, and *Q. lobata*); others were affected for longer periods of time (in this study, two years) (e.g., *L.*

indica and *S. sempervirens*); while others were affected very little (e.g., *G. biloba*). For most tree species in this study, as the tree grew and eventually emerged from the 122-cm treeshelter, the influence the shelter had on growth of the tree diminished. This is to be expected, especially when trees had more than half their above-ground biomass outside the treeshelter (e.g., *F. latifolia, P. racemosa,* and *Q. lobata*). For other tree species, this was not the case. *Lagerstroemia indica* and *S. sempervirens* trees maintained their differences in height even though nearly 50% of the tree was out of the treeshelter. There may be other physiological influences of the treeshelter on lower trunk (that part inside the treeshelter) that have not yet been identified, or the early growth of these tree species inside the shelter may predispose them to longer-term growth enhancements.

The above-ground responses observed in these tree species are similar to those seen by our earlier work and those of others (1, 2, 6, 12, 13, 17). That is, trees grown in shelters are taller, tend to have somewhat smaller stem caliper, and have reduced fresh and dry mass of above- and below-ground biomass. Environmental conditions (reduced light irradiance and increased temperature, relative humidity, and CO_2 concentration) inside treeshelters have been associated with most of these growth responses. Treeshelters should not be left around trees once the tree has grown taller than the shelter. This is especially important in windy areas because trunk deformities result (1). The benefits of treeshelters include enhanced stem height, protection from browsing animals and management practices (herbicide applications), and convenient release of predators inside to control insect pests. The reduction in root mass may not always be a liability to the early development of newly transplanted trees in the landscape depending on the species.

Literature Cited

1. Burger, D.W., G.W. Forister, and P.A. Kiehl. 1996. *Height, caliper growth and biomass response of ten shade tree species to treeshelters.* J. Arboric. 22(4): 161–166.
2. Burger, D.W., P. Svihra, and R. Harris. 1992. *Treeshelter use in producing container-grown trees.* HortScience 27(1):30–32.
3. Costello, L.R., A. Peters, and G.A. Giusti. 1996. *An evaluation of treeshelter effects on plant survival and growth in a Mediterranean climate.* J. Arboric. 22(1): 1–9.
4. Dias-Filho, M.B. 1995. *Physiological responses of* Vismia guianensis *to contrasting light environments.* Rev. Bras. Fisiol. Veg. 7(1):35–40.
5. Fabiao, A. 1995. *Development of root biomass in a* Eucalyptus globulus *plantation under different water and nutrient regimes.* Plant Soil 168–169:215–223.
6. Frearson, K., and N.D. Weiss. 1987. *Improved growth rates within treeshelters.* Quart. J. For. 81(3):184–187.
7. Gross, R. 1993. *Hydraulic soil excavation: Getting down to the roots.* Arbor Age 13:10, 12–13.
8. Gross, R. 1995. Hydraulic soil excavation, pp 177–184. **In** Watson, G.W., and Neely, D. (Eds.). Trees and Building Sites. International Society of Arboriculture, Champaign, IL.

9. Harris, R.W. 1992. Arboriculture: Integrated Management of Landscape Trees, Shrubs and Vines. Prentice Hall, Englewood Cliffs, NJ. 674 pp.

10. Hoagland, D.R., and D.I. Arnon. 1950. The water-culture method for growing plants without soil. Calif. Agr. Expt. Sta. Circ. 347.

11. Kasperbauer, M.J., and P.G. Hunt. 1992. *Root size and shoot/root ratio as influenced by light environment of the shoot.* J. Plant Nutr. 15(6-7):685–697.

12. Potter, M.J. 1988. *Treeshelters improve survival and increase early growth rates.* J. For. 86(6):39–41.

13. Potter, M.J. 1991. Treeshelters. Forestry Commission Handbook 7. HMSO Publications. London, England.

14. Puri, S., V. Singh, B. Bhushan, and S. Singh. 1994. *Biomass production and distribution of roots in three stands of* Populus deltoides. For. Ecol. Manage. 65(2–3):135–147.

15. Rendle, E.L. 1985. The influence of treeshelters on microclimate and the growth of oak. Proc. 6th Natl. Hardwoods Prog., Oxford Forestry Institute.

16. SAS Institute. 1988. SAS/STAT User's Guide, Release 6.03 ed. SAS Institute, Cary, NC.

17. Soffer, H., and D.W. Burger. 1988. *Plant propagation using an aero-hydroponics system.* HortScience 24(1):154.

18. Svihra, P., D.W. Burger, and R.W. Harris. 1996. *Treeshelter effect on root development of redwood trees.* J. Arboric. 22(4):174–179.

19. Wilson, J.B. 1988. *A review of evidence on the control of shoot-root ratio, in relation to models.* Ann. Bot. 61:433–449.

Palm Root Regeneration

Donald R. Hodel, A. James Downer, and Dennis R. Pittinger

Large palms are a conspicuous and important element of the California landscape, especially in coastal areas from San Francisco to San Diego and inland regions of the southern part of the state. They are the signature plant material and are emblematic of the much-popularized California lifestyle. Palms are also important landscape subjects in Florida, Hawaii, and large interiorscapes in colder climates. Because of their woody, monocotyledonous nature, characterized by the production of fibrous, adventitious roots from the base of the stem, even large, mature specimens can usually be transplanted successfully with relative ease and with a small root ball. This relative ease of transplanting gives the palms a distinct economic advantage in landscape development and installation over conifers and woody, broad-leaved, dicotyledonous trees characterized by a branched, woody root system. Unfortunately, many large palms do not survive transplanting or they require an inordinately long time to reestablish. Little is known about palm root distribution and growth and how these factors might affect survivability and reestablishment of large specimens in the landscape.

While many palms are transplanted year-round in California, the general landscape industry rule of thumb has been to transplant palms in late spring or early summer. It is felt that the extended warm period with higher soil and air temperatures following transplanting promote maximum shoot and root growth, thus facilitating reestablishment. There is no rule of thumb for optimal root ball size for successful transplanting. Although common sense would suggest taking a root ball as large as practical, it is a common practice to transplant palms with little or virtually no root ball at all. Recent work in Florida suggests that, in general, the larger the root ball the more successful the transplanting because most palm roots, once cut, do not regrow, and of those that do resprout, the percentage of regrowth increases the farther the roots are cut from the trunk. However, the work also showed that palms have most of their roots within 15 cm (6 in.) of the trunk and, while the percentage of resprouting roots is higher farther from the trunk, the actual number of cut roots resprouting is

Donald R. Hodel is with the University of California Cooperative Extension, Los Angeles County, 2 Coral Circle, Montery Park, CA 91755. A. James Downer is with the University of California Cooperative Extension, Ventura County, 669 County Square Drive, Suite 100, Ventura, CA 93003. Dennis R. Pittenger is with the University of California Cooperative Extension, Los Angeles County, and the University of California Cooperative Extension, Southern Region, Department of Botany & Plant Sciences, University of California, Riverside, CA 92521.

relatively small, thus raising questions about the importance of root ball size in successful transplanting. Perhaps the generation of new roots from the base of the trunk, rather than how many cut roots resprout, is more important.

Methods and Procedures

In June 1997, we began a project at The Arboretum of Los Angeles County in Arcadia, California, to study root distribution and growth in large specimen palms. A narrow trench 6 in. (15 cm) wide, 24 in. (60 cm) deep, and 36 in. (90 cm) long was dug at the base of three specimens each of 16 species using a mechanical trencher (Table 1). Each distance zone was subdivided into two depth zones of 12 and 24 in. (30 and 60 cm), for a total of eight zones in which to quantify root distribution and growth (Figure 1). With two species, *Livistona chinensis* and *Archontophoenix cunninghamiana,* an additional three trenches for each species were hand dug to determine if there would be differences in root regeneration between the hand-dug specimens and those dug with the mechanical trencher. Initial root distribution was determined by percentage of trench surface covered with cut root ends in each of the eight zones. Each trench was backfilled with perlite. The palms were irrigated at 125% of reference evapotranspiration. At three-month intervals for 24 months, each trench in all eight zones was re-excavated and the roots counted, harvested, and weighed. We attempted to correlate root distribution and growth with day length, soil temperature, and distance from the trunk, hopefully enabling us to make recommendations about optimal root ball size and time of year for successful transplanting and rapid reestablishment.

Preliminary Results

Not too surprisingly, most palm species had greatest root densities within the first distance zone of 6 in. (15 cm). Root densities dropped off progressively and steadily in the farther distance zones. In a few species, such as *Caryota mitis, Chamaerops humilis,* and *Rhapidophyllum hystrix,* root densities were more or less the same across

Table 1. Palm species in root regeneration study, 1997–1999.

Species	Common name	Origin
Archontophoenix cunninghamiana	king palm	Australia
Brahea edulis	Guadalupe palm	Guadalupe Island, Mexico
Butia capitata	pindo palm	Argentina
Caryota mitis	fishtail palm	tropical Asia
Chamaerops humilis	European fan palm	Mediterranean
Livistona chinensis	Chinese fan palm	southern China
Livistona decipiens	ribbon fan palm	Australia
Phoenix canariensis	Canary Island date palm	Canary Islands
Phoenix reclinata	Senegal date palm	tropical Africa
Rhapidophyllum hystrix	needle palm	southeast United States
Sabal palmetto	palmetto palm	southeast United States
Serenoa repens	saw palmetto	Florida, Caribbean
Syagrus romanzoffiana	queen palm	Brazil, Argentina
Trachycarpus fortunei	Chinese windmill palm	southern China
Trachycarpus wagnerianus	dwarf windmill palm	Himalayas
Washingtonia robusta	Mexican fan palm	Baja California, Mexico

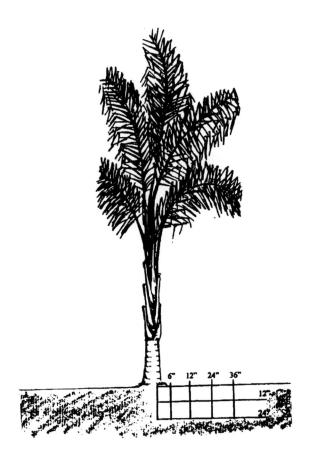

Figure 1. Zones for quantifying palm root regeneration.

all distance zones. All palms had greater root densities in the shallower 12 in. (30-cm) zone than in the deeper 24-in. (60-cm) zone, although root densities for *Butia capitata* and *Chamaerops humilis* were nearly the same in both depth zones.

To date we have counted and harvested roots in two of the three-month intervals, September (late August) and December 1997. Visual observations for all species showed that few, if any, cut roots resprouted at or near the point at which they were cut for any species at any distance or depth zone. Nearly all roots encountered in the trench appeared to originate as new roots from the base of the trunk, although some of these could have been from cut roots that resprouted away from the trench wall and later grew into the trench. Mean root number and dry weight per species are presented in Table 2.

Four species (*Sabal palmetto, Serenoa repens, Syagrus romanzoffiana,* and *Washingtonia robusta*) produced significantly more roots in August than December while two others (*Livistona decipiens* and *Rhapidophyllum hystrix*) produced significantly more roots in December than August.

Table 2. Mean number and dry weight of palm roots for each species, August and December 1997.

Species	Number Aug.	Dec.	Dry weight (g) Aug.	Dec.
Archontophoenix cunninghamiana	18	16	10	16
A. cunninghamiana (hand dug)	22	11	8	8
Brahea edulis	16	32	3	5
Butia capitata	9	23	2	10
Caryota mitis	56	78	8	28
Chamaerops humilis	0	27	0	7
Livistona chinensis	55	97	38	108
L. chinensis (hand dug)	67	75	30 ***	194
Livistona decipiens	84 **	152	30 ***	87
Phoenix canariensis	98	71	41	60
Phoenix reclinata	75	126	9	91
Rhapidophyllum hystrix	24 ***	69	4 *	8
Sabal palmetto	53 ***	19	10	4
Serenoa repens	62 **	7	15	5
Syagrus romanzoffiana	373 ***	100	94 ***	44
Trachycarpus fortunei	95	61	5 **	10
Trachycarpus wagnerianus	136	125	24	33
Washingtonia robusta	27 ***	48	55	21
Soil temperature °F (°C)	70 (21–22)		49–54 (9–13)	

***statistically different at the 0.05 level, DMR.
**statistically different at the 0.07 level, DMR.
*statistically different at the 0.09 level, DMR.

Four species (*Livistona chinensis* [hand dug], *L. decipiens, Rhapidophyllum hystrix,* and *Trachycarpus wagnerianus*) produced significantly more root mass in December than August, while only one species (*Syagrus romanzoffiana*) produced significantly more root mass in August than December.

Interestingly, for *Sabal palmetto, Serenoa repens,* and *Washingtonia robusta,* root mass did not significantly increase from August to December in conjunction with a significant increase in root number, while root mass of *Livistona chinensis* (hand dug) and *Trachycarpus fortunei* significantly increased without a significant increase in root number. These results indicate that the former species produced many small roots when root growth is high, and the latter two species produced larger but not more roots in December than August.

Although not reflected in Table 2, root number and mass were highest close to the trunk and steadily decreased moving away from it in both August and December.

Summary and Preliminary Conclusions

Based on the premise that root growth, regardless of origin, is a significant factor in successful palm transplanting, this very preliminary data suggest that *Sabal palmetto, Serenoa repens, Syagrus romanzoffiana,* and *Washingtonia robusta* have a better chance of survival and reestablishment if transplanted in early summer. Conversely, *Livistona decipiens* and *Rhapidophyllum hystrix* might have a better chance of survival and reestablishment if transplanted in late summer.

However, it might be that these palms could be transplanted successfully in either early or late summer because at this early stage of our work we do not know minimum thresholds of root number and mass necessary for successful transplanting. For example, even though *Syagrus romanzoffiana* produced only 100 roots in December versus 373 in August, it could be that 100 roots are sufficient for successful transplanting.

It might also be that a relatively small root ball, for example from 6 to 12 in. (15 to 30 cm) out from the trunk, is sufficient because root number and mass are much higher close to the trunk. Since it appears that most cut roots do not resprout and a palm must rely on newly generated roots for reestablishment, the root ball's basic function might be simply to protect newly emerging roots in the root initiation zone at the base of the trunk. If so, timing might be critical for successful transplanting, with the optimal time being just prior to or in the early phases of flushes or extended periods of new root regeneration. We hope that by tracking root regeneration at three-month intervals over two years, we will be able to determine the seasonality and nature of palm root growth and answer these questions and others about successful palm transplanting.

Root Growth Control:
Managing Perceptions and Realities

Kim D. Coder

Many infrastructures that concentrate and transport required resources for people are poorly designed and not built to withstand natural processes over time. These engineering flaws are exacerbated by opportunistic tree roots colonizing new resource spaces. To infrastructure managers, blame for failures are delegated elsewhere—in the case considered here, to trees. Tree professionals have been prone to accept this blame and to damage trees to fit them into faulty design, engineering, and maintenance concepts. Predicated upon these areas of concern, professional management of tree root growth is becoming more important. In this context, this paper will review root growth and soil mechanics to clearly identify root-limiting conditions. Additionally, a series of root growth control methods, divided among a number of tool and technique classes, will be presented. Tree-literate management is stressed.

Division of space among the many and varied uses in our communities is highly competitive. The economic, environmental, sociological, and psychological values generated and managed to ensure our quality of life involves an interconnected fabric of biotic and abiotic features. Deeply woven into our developed support systems are natural systems that co-inhabit our usable space. As we concentrate and transport resources to support ourselves, the volumes and surfaces of our spaces become more resistant to the survival of other life forms.

Establishing Blame

The more we sterilize, short-circuit, and usurp natural processes to generate required goods and services, the greater the tendency to relegate remnants of natural systems to nuisance and hindrance. Poorly engineered, designed, and installed resource concentration and use systems are susceptible to chaotic failures and ecological changes generating unanticipated results. Blame for negative events is easily shed from inflexible, ill-considered, and inappropriate human endeavors. There will always be some natural biological system available for receiving transference of human ignorance and failure. We are surrounded by operator error!

Dr. Kim D. Coder, Associate Professor of Forest Resources, School of Forest Resources, University of Georgia, Athens, GA 30602.

Tree roots are commonly part of many of our resource concentration and use structures. Biological illiteracy can be masked for short periods by sheer mechanical prowess in building and maintaining structures. We have been conditioned to blame tree roots for a host of engineering and design failures. Among the scientific community, as other questions are being examined under replicated and controlled conditions, we accept a biased view of cause and effect and often blame tree roots based on circumstantial evidence.

Role of Roots

Roots are not primary causal agents of damage within infrastructures and engineered resource control solutions. Through disregard, tree roots are invited into resource concentration areas in which valuable and abundant resources are available. As with a full cookie jar left open on the floor in the middle of a play room, a child may be blamed (or even punished) for cookie resource indiscretions, but other culprits are often present. The literature is filled with others blaming tree roots for one crime or another. Arborists and community foresters have historically concurred with this blame because of the intimate and structural root contact visible among failed infrastructures. As tree managers, we have sometimes unquestioningly accepted perception spins and have shouldered the blame.

Tree roots control resource volume or space. In most developed-area soils, providing more space for root systems is equivalent to providing more resources for the tree. Roots carefully sense current soil conditions and, in concert with the rest of the tree, exploit resource space. The growth regulation system of a tree, centered between shoots and roots, ensures relatively quick reaction to internal and external environmental changes (11, 13, 14, 15). The role of roots is to colonize and hold resource-containing space. This role requires elongation, radial expansion, lateral development when needed, continual maintenance of an absorbing system, material transport, food storage, element processing, and survival during periods of poor growth or poor resource availability.

Infrastructure Conflicts

The exploration and colonization of resource space put tree roots in seeming conflict with other site uses and structures. Conflicts are most often associated with sewer or septic lines, storm water drains, water supply lines, foundations, sidewalks, streets, parking lots, pavements (floating and with footings), curbs, walls, swimming pools, and structures on dimensionally unstable soils. Many of these conflicts are preventable, with forethought of tree growth over the long-term and with the installation of structures using proper materials and applications. Trees will remain an excuse for poor workmanship, bad development, ignorant designs, and incompetent engineering.

Tree roots contribute to modifying their own environment and developing stress and strain on various types of structures. Sometimes the costs of tree-literate design and engineering are greatly outweighed by the cost of correction and cure. The economics, considering all the indirect and direct costs coupled with benefits over tree life, should be examined closely whenever tree or structural treatments are prescribed.

Here, I will not review the various methods for evaluating managerial actions economically but will examine root control options without cost estimates. I will quickly review the economic perceptions in the literature surrounding tree roots and damage to infrastructure.

Economic Impacts of Damage

A survey of cities estimated that total annual concrete and sewer line repair bills due to tree roots averaged $4.28 (U.S.) per street tree, which amounted to 25% of tree budgets per year on average (34, 35). The same survey found the distribution of repair costs due to tree roots averaged as follows: sidewalks (51%), curb and gutter (17%), and sewers (32%) (35). In a city and county survey, 20% of all tree removals were performed because of infrastructure damage (35). Tree root damage was the main reason given for tree removal and subsequent replacement with another species (4). Another community found 68% of sidewalk damage was adjacent to trees (35). Still another community found 5% of all trees causing sidewalk breaks of at least 2.5 cm (1 in.) in height differential and that 59% of all sidewalk damage was caused by large (76 cm [30 in.]) or larger diameter) trees (35).

In one city, 30% of all surveyed trees were cited for sidewalk damage (of that 30%, 4% were severe damage, 8% were moderate damage, and 18% were minor damage). In that same city, 13% of trees were cited for curb damage (2% were severe damage, 3% were moderate damage, and 8% were minor damage) (57). Of these same trees causing pavement problems, 37% had initiated infrastructure damage at a distance greater than 3 ft (57). One community spent $277.78 per mile of sewer line on root control and associated repairs (52). Average costs of tree-related sewer repair was cited as $1.66 per tree (35). One community used 40% of its annual tree budget for sidewalk repairs stemming from tree root damage (35).

General costs for sidewalk repair because of tree root damage were estimated at $500 per repair, with a life span of the repair estimated at five years if the tree was not removed (53). The most widely used solutions to tree root problems were tree species selection changes, root barriers (only 25% of those surveyed believed they worked), and root pruning (poorly accepted and suspected of increasing structural failures) (35). Tree root growth is considered an expensive nuisance and liability risk in many communities.

Physical Aspects of Damage

Tree roots have been cited as causing increased liability risks, management costs, and maintenance costs. Public concerns and infrastructure manager complaints have included an increased exposure to tree-illiterate, dictated change and symptom treatments (as opposed to treating underlying causes of problems). Some of these quantified values for tree root damage have been cited many times and are cited as established fact in arboricultural literature without regard to source, reporting bias, professional review, or analysis. Note that many of these data have been developed using subjective observations, personal memories, general opinions, and unpublished reports.

Tree roots are directly involved with damage to sidewalks, curbs, gutters, and—to a lesser degree—sewers (35). One community's replacement cycle for sidewalks continually damaged by trees was every five to ten years (35). Tree roots are cited as opportunists, utilizing structural faults in infrastructure to capture essential resources (35). Even small diameter roots are able to cause pavement damage (28). Tree diameter and species are major controlling factors (80% variation accounted) cited for infrastructure damage (34, 35), although managers stated that damage was more site-specific than species-specific (35).

Tree Diameters and Damage

Tree diameter (dbh) is directly related to infrastructure damage. Once trees are well established and begin to exceed 20 cm (8 in.) diameter, damage tends to accelerate (28, 57). Beyond the root plate area of a tree where damage is common, there was little correlation between the amount of damaged caused and how far trees were from roadways and/or how much available rooting volume was provided (28). Larger diameters could be accepted closer to curbs than sidewalks, due to the additional material strength and placement (21) (Figure 1 and Figure 2*).

Where trees were continuing to damage sidewalks, concrete replacement was required on a five- to ten-year cycle whether or not root cutting at the time of concrete replacement was part of the treatment (35). Soil water levels (wet versus dry sites) made no difference in the damage frequency to sidewalks (28). Tree diameter measures and distance of the stem to the infrastructure were part of quantifying damage risks. Unfortunately, seldom are nontree-associated failing infrastructures examined to help visualize the scope of root damage (21).

Infrastructure Damage

Infrastructure age, faults, and deterioration are the sources for root colonization that eventually lead to damage. The materials used in construction can lead directly to failure. Asphalt , which is usually laid down in thinner sheets than concrete slabs and has less tensile strength across the surface than concrete, is prone to show damage more easily than concrete does (57). Concrete is strong under compression but is brittle.

The force required to damage concrete from below can be calculated. For example, take a concrete sidewalk slab that is 10 cm (4 in.) thick, 1.5 m (5 ft) wide, and reinforced with a coarse hardware cloth. The slab lying on the ground can withstand approximately 3,000 psi when loaded from the top if the slab lies flat on a smooth undergrade. This slab can withstand 330 psi if pushed on from the bottom. If a small root elevates the slab, only a small amount (2.5 cm [1 in]) with people continuing to walk on the slab's top surface, only 60 lb of pressure per inch is required to crack the slab. Over time this a relatively small amount of pressure.

For pipes carrying wastewater, older clay and concrete pipes with gasket connections along their length present many avenues for tree roots to colonize over time (35,

---

*All figures and tables are located at the end of this chapter.

45). The pipe bed or underlayment can lead to a proliferation of settling faults. Roots growing along the pipes, and developing mass over time, can exert significant new pressures on pipes. Roots pushing into and around gasket connection points radially expand and break seals. Pipe materials that easily transmit temperature changes to their surfaces can provide areas of fracture pore space and available water condensation around the pipe. New plastic pipe materials, solvent welding systems, and proper installation can help eliminate tree root problems in pipes (45).

Soil Movements

Another infrastructure-damaging event often blamed on trees, and used to destroy valuable trees at large distances from infrastructures, is water-powered soil swell and heave. The expansive clays (montmorillonite and vermiculite), and to a lesser degree unique organic soils, shrink and swell over changing water contents (8, 18, 20). Over 20% of soil areas across the United States contain expansive clays. Without trees present, cracked foundations, broken utility lines, buckled sidewalks, and other damaged infrastructure are the results of volumetric movements of expansive clays (18, 39). Differential swelling and drying in areas around infrastructures lead to major shifting stresses over time (49). Drought periods are especially damaging to structures on expansive clays if the structures are not designed to handle these additional loads (33, 49).

Trees can transpire large amounts of water under good conditions. As water is removed from expansive clay soils, soils shrink. Soil shrinkage from this process occurs wherever roots are concentrated. Soil volume changes—primarily shrinkage—can damage infrastructures not designed or sited properly on expansive clays (20, 30, 44, 49). Most solutions—other than changing design, materials, and their use—are effective only over the short run and usually involve significant damage to any tree involved. Tree removal and abusive, periodic crown pruning practices are inappropriate solutions sometimes used to minimize damage (39).

Growth Environments

Tree roots have specific requirements to grow and survive in a soil area. Eliminating any one of the essential resources will prevent root growth. Roots grow near infrastructures because all the essential resources are present. Thermal changes between materials provide pore spaces at a wall, along a pipe, or under the pavement (28). For example, roots will run linearly along the pore space generated at the interface of the soil and curbing (17). Soil backfill may have a lower bulk density than surrounding soil and may take years to approach surrounding soil limitations in oxygen, water, and pore space resources. Backfilling may result in a process of soil fracturing and channel creation (45). Roots will take advantage of these soil openings and associated resources.

Materials used for underlayment of pavements are usually coarse, well-aerated products, such as sand. The rest of the soil left in position around infrastructure is usually compacted to some degree, with the subsoil or subgrade extensively compacted to bear infrastructure weight. Many dense building materials have enough thermal mass to keep them away from immediate temperature equilibrium with their soil environment. Materials out of thermal equilibrium with neighboring materials lead to water vapor pressure changes and water condensation at the interface (along the surface pore space) (3, 5, 19, 20, 45). Along and under these dense materials, with limited evaporation, the soils can be at or near field capacity for long periods (28, 29).

Pipes made of dense materials have additional thermal interactions with the soil because of liquid temperatures moving inside. The greater the differential of temperatures, the greater chance of pore space development at the soil–pipe interface, of increased maintenance over time, and of water accumulation seasonally or daily. Thermal changes also stress joints, gaskets, and connectors—providing opportunities for roots to utilize additional resource space.

Root Growth

Growth is a permanent increase in whole organism size. Growth in trees may not be a positive increase in living mass but does represent expansion of tissues into new spaces. For roots, the tips elongate and the tissues thicken in diameter. Lateral roots are developed adventitiously and allowed to elongate and radially thicken. Root density, mass, and activity vary with internal and external conditions. Resources required for root growth are summarized in Table 1. An understanding of resource levels that limit root growth means that better methods of controlling growth can be developed.

Roots utilize soil spaces for access to water and essential element resources and to provide structural support. The mineral matrix of the soil surrounds small water-filled pores and larger air-filled pores. Many of these soil pores are continually filling and draining with water and air, depending upon water supplies, water uses, and the atmosphere above. Roots grow following pathways of interconnected soil pores. Pore space can be the result of the space between textural units (sand, silt, and clay particles), between structural units (blocks, plates, grains, prisms, etc.), along fracture lines (shrink-swell clays, frost heaving, pavement interfaces, etc.), and through paths of biological origins (decayed roots, animal diggings, etc.) (46).

Root Locations

Roots survive and grow where adequate water is available, temperatures are warm, and oxygen is present. Roots are generally shallow, limited by oxygen contents, anaerobic conditions, and water saturation in deeper soil. Near the base of the tree, deep-growing roots can be found, but they are oxygenated by fissures and cracks in the soil and around roots generated by the mechanical forces exerted on the crown and stem under wind loads (sway) (22).

Roots proliferate where essential resources are concentrated. Roots will traverse long areas of poor resources, as long as oxygen and moisture are available. Upon sensing (discovery) of organic materials and available resources, absorbing root fans will be generated to colonize and control resource space. Roots under pavements, for example, may grow across an area close to the surface or concrete underside in a relatively unbranched form, only to explode into absorbing root fans on the other side (28).

Root Growth Mechanics

The ability of primary root tips to enter soil pores, further open soil pores, and elongate through soil pores depends upon the force generated by the root and the soil penetration resistance. Root growth forces are generated by cell division and subsequent osmotic enlargement of each new cell (48). Oxygen for respiration and adequate water supplies are required (48) (Figure 3). Tree roots can consume large amounts of oxygen during this process. At 77°F (25°C), tree roots will consume nine times their volume in oxygen each day (17); at 95°F (35°C), roots can use twice that volume. The osmotic costs to cells of resisting surrounding forces and elongating can be significant.

As the diameter of an expanding root increases, its strength to resist structural failure and the expansive force it generates can increase (31). As roots elongate against soil, their ability to resist structural failure depends on root diameter and expansion length (7). The longer the root tip under elongation pressures and/or the smaller in diameter the root, the greater chance that structural failure will occur (7). Short and thick roots generate significant force and minimize structural failure. Radial expansion of the roots immediately behind the tip also helps fracture or reduce penetration resistance in the soil ahead of the elongating root tip (7, 31).

Growth Forces

Roots use the mass of the tissues behind the tip, including root hairs, lateral root formation, and microbial entanglements to minimize the length over which root elongation force is expressed, thus reducing structural failure potential (46). As the root elongates, only root tissue within approximately six root diameters of the tip will be involved with force generation (7). Root tissue further back will act as a anchor or support base in order to push against the soil (7).

If a root is compressed from the sides, it can exert significant force in elongation, depending upon its diameter (31, 37). The greater the diameter, the more force available for elongation (31). The resistance of the soil to allow penetration depends upon the force exerted by the root over its cross-sectional area (7). The bigger the root, the slower the growth for an equivalent amount of force applied, or the greater the force that can be applied (7, 37).

Maximum Forces

The maximum force that roots can exert ranges from 9 to 15 bars (9 to 15 MPa), with 10 bars (10 MPa) being most cited (17, 42, 46). This pressure value is a maximum, with roots instantaneously sensing root tip progression and osmotically adjusting elongation to barely push through soil pore spaces. Tree roots cannot generate enough pressure to push into concrete, pipes, asphalt, wood, most plastics, or most metals. Roots can take advantage of cracks and faults already in materials, or exacerbate cracks and faults by growing root mass within, beneath, or around materials (19).

Because generation of root elongation force requires energy, only as much force as is needed is brought to bear. The foundation force used in elongation arises from osmotic forces using solutes and water. When water is in short supply, or when temperatures increase, the diameter of roots is sacrificed to facilitate more elongation (42). Roots can lose more than one-third of their diameter under dry conditions, leaving roots thinner and elongating at a slower rate (42) (Figure 4). The loss of contact with the soil and the potential for mechanical failure (buckling) of elongating roots can lead to poor tree support.

Morphology Changes

Root thickening, or increasing in diameter, is controlled through growth regulation signals emanating from shoot and root tips and from associated changes in cellulose microfibril angles within expanding cell walls (7). Root radial growth under poor soil conditions is stimulated by small amounts of ethylene. Ethylene is generated by excessive auxin buildup in the roots caused by oxygen shortages, flooding, and hot temperatures. Less than 10 ppm ethylene can stop root elongation and can lead to radially thickened roots (42, 46).

In response to increased compaction, roots thicken in diameter (31, 53). Compaction also forces roots to generate increased turgor pressures concentrated closer to the root tip, to more quickly lignify cell walls behind the growing root tip, and to utilize a shorter zone of elongation (7). Thicker roots exert more force and penetrate farther into compacted soil areas (31). As soil penetration resistance increases in compacted soils, roots thicken to minimize structural failure (buckling), to exert increased force per unit area, and to stress soil just ahead of the root cap to allow easier penetration (31) (Figure 5).

Changing Pore Spaces

Many soils in developed areas are compacted. Compaction is the reduction in size of soil pore spaces by pressure from the surface caused by feet, bikes, vehicles, and vibrations. As soils become more compacted, root growth is modified. The physical features of the soil that impact root growth under compaction are increasing soil strength, increasing soil density, and fewer soil pores.

For effective root growth, pore sizes in the soil must be larger than root tips (17). With compaction in a root colonization area, pore space diameters become smaller. Once soil pore diameters are less than the diameter of main root tips, many growth problems can occur. The first noticeable root change with compaction is morphological: The main axis of a root becomes thicker to exert more force to squeeze into diminished sized pores.

As roots thicken, growth slows and more laterals of various diameters are generated. The diameter of lateral root tips depends on growth regulators and the extent of vascular tissue connections. If laterals are small enough to fit into the pore sizes of the compacted soil, then lateral growth will continue while the main axis of the root is constrained (46). If the soil pore sizes are too small for even the lateral roots, root growth will cease.

Compaction Constraints

To support infrastructures, whether on footings, foundations, or floating on the soil surface, soil is compacted. Compacting soil prevents progressive settling, minimizes soil changes over time, and increases soil strength. Traditional compaction specifications try to attain 96% to 99%, which means that soil strength is maximized and pore space is minimized (25). At the compaction rates used for infrastructures, tree-essential oxygen, water, and pore space are not available and mechanical impedance is great (1, 48) (Figure 6) Water is present but, depending upon soil type, may be held too tightly for tree use.

Oxygen supply to the roots remains a major problem around infrastructure. Accessible pore space for root growth requires low mechanical impedance (for root elongation) and a supply of oxygen. Interacting with these resources are soil microorganisms that use oxygen quickly. In poorly drained or compacted soils, oxygen can be used up quickly and not resupplied (Figure 7). In addition, microorganisms quickly use oxygen for respiration; this oxygen cannot be readily resupplied because of water-filled micropores. Water-filled pores allow oxygen diffusion at a rate 10,000 times less than that of air-filled pores (42). As oxygen drops below 2% to 5% of atmospheric content, root growth and the root's ability to generate elongation force precipitously decline (48).

Need to Breathe

Oxygen is required for root elongation. For respiration to occur, oxygen must move to the living root tissues through the soil matrix. Along any open soil pore path is a myriad of aerobic organisms using any available oxygen. If all of the oxygen is used before it can reach the tree root, changes occur in the root system. For short periods of time with low or no oxygen, trees can generate energy using carbohydrates, but this process is approximately 20 times more inefficient than aerobic respiration (42). The nonwater-filled, larger pores must be able to move carbon dioxide out and oxygen into the root or growth slows. Table 2 summarizes by soil texture class, which is the root-limiting, air-containing pore space in soil (10).

Soil Pore Sizes

As roots elongate, they continually encounter a range of pore sizes. Pore sizes larger than the root tip provide little resistance to elongation. Pore sizes slightly smaller than the root tip provide increasing resistance to root elongation, depending on soil strength and capability of the root to generate force to deform the soil. Soil pores much smaller than the root tip may easily deform with root pressure in weak soils but may be unattainable in strong soils (31, 42, 46).

Roots can not "squeeze" into small, rigid pores where soil strength prevents soil deformation (46). Unless there are fissures, cracks, or other large pore spaces, a strong (compacted) soil will resist roots from expanding and deforming pores (46). Mycorrhizal fungi can assist with proper root functions in compacted soil (16, 47). The fungal hyphae are smaller in diameter than tree roots and can utilize small pore-space areas.

Soil Strength

When soils are purposely compacted for construction, or collaterally compacted around infrastructures, more square feet of soil particle surfaces are present per unit volume, and pore space declines. This process provides more frictional, adhesive, and cohesive forces holding the soil together, or greater soil strength (42). Water movement and aeration pathways are constrained. As water content declines in soil, strength increases and root elongation declines (46) (Figure 8). The mechanical impedance offered by a soil, as given by bulk density measures, is summarized in Table 2 (10). Tree roots can penetrate into soil with mechanical impedance levels of up to 3 MPa (28, 29) (Figure 9 and Figure 10).

Exploiting Space

In and around infrastructures, roots grow and survive where there are adequate resources. Oxygen, water, pore space, and a healthy, ecologically balanced rhizosphere are needed (56). Compacted zones, anaerobic zones, dry zones, and dead zones in soils associated with infrastructure will prevent new root colonization. Depending upon the extent and duration of these anti-root conditions, roots already present can be killed.

As tree roots exploit soil resources, they follow low impedance pathways from a mechanical standpoint and from a water supply standpoint. The paths (corridors) of least resistance through the soil and around small blocking items will be followed, which include staying close to the surface of the soil (28). As water is pulled into the root, the directional aspects of the lowest resistance flow path is sensed, as long as there is a continuous water film in pores and on soil particle surfaces (19, 20, 31). Roots can grow toward available water supplies if plenty of oxygen is available.

Growth Model Beneath Pavements

For traditional paving methods, a root growth model has been proposed (Kopinga model [28]). As root growth occurs, the aerobic conditions and moisture contents under the pavement in coarse textured materials, such as sand, allow for elongation. The moisture is quickly used and not replaced. Roots continue to elongate following an oxygen and moisture gradient that "leads" across the pavement area. Roots grow toward soil volumes with open surfaces where water in soil pore space is replaced and where essential-element supplies and ecologically rich soils are established. Between one side of the pavement and the other, little root branching occurs, unless moisture and essential elements are moving through the pavement and into the soil below. A moisture and oxygen gradient below the pavement keeps roots along the pavement interface. Over time, as new areas on the other side of the pavement are colonized, the transport roots under the pavement will continue to radially expand (28). Pavement damage will be the result.

Root Growth Control Methods

Based upon root growth processes, resource availability, and soil features, there are eight primary forms of tree root growth control. (Table 3). Each primary form attempts to change resource availability, control resource volume (space), or destroy or redirect biological colonization. Under each primary form exists a number of tools and techniques to accomplish root control. Single or compound root control strategies can be used, with combinations presenting the best long-term solutions. Other forms of root growth control exist and can be used. Table 3 is a summary of a wide-ranging area of information and expertise.

Clearly tree-literate design and development processes that minimize material faults and tree accessible space (primary root growth control form #1 in Table 3) are the preferred means for maximizing a tree's, and tree owner's, quality of life over the long-run. Primary root growth control form #8 in Table 3 is simply avoiding problems by keeping large distances between trees and infrastructures. This is probably the most ecological distasteful and socially unacceptable of all forms.

The six remaining primary root growth control forms will be discussed. Remember that many root growth control techniques and tools exist, both outside and inside this particular information organizational system. The most important features of the various forms will be reviewed. Also, cost effectiveness is critical and sometimes "cohabitation and correction" will be the lowest cost option, even though occasional structural repairs are needed. Highly valued trees should not be damaged or removed because of the need to occasionally replace $50 of concrete.

Kill Zones

Kill zones have been used for millennia in agricultural settings. Shelterbelt tree plantings along field edges in the Great Plains of the United States and elsewhere have roots cultivated off with crop care equipment at least once a year and subsoiled periodically. The key result remains that cutting tree roots, as a stand-alone treatment, leads to similar root problems or worse in a short time (35, 45). Cutting too close to the tree can also compromise structural stability (34, 55). In some compacted soils, cutting and cultivating may bring some soil benefits, but roots not cleanly cut, exposed to the air in a damaged state (bent, twisted, torn, broken, etc.), or opened to soil pathogens will cause additional problems (36).

The most common arboricultural practices for generating kill zones for root growth control are trenchers, root saws, rotary pipe knives, and chemicals. With all kill-zone tools, it is critical to calculate how close to the tree to treat, or how much resource and root volume can be removed from the tree before tree health concerns shift from root control to other systemic and structural problems (Figure 11). Trenching has been cited, with increasing root damage severity, as decreasing vigor over longer time periods, constraining twig growth, and increasing twig dieback (36, 56). The temporary nature of the treatment, the sometimes severe residual damage, and the loss of living mass usually suggest other means to accomplish root control.

The two primary chemicals used to generate a kill zone for root growth control are pipe clearance materials (traditional metal salts or herbicides) and in-ground fumigants (soil sterilants). Fumigants used to prevent root grafts can be used to control root growth (26). Both are temporary solutions to a recurring problem. These materials are seeing declining use over time, as more efforts are being made to minimize broad-scale treatments and off-site damage from chemicals. Great care is required around infrastructures and other living things. For example, if a pipe clearance chemical is used with a rotary knife, the assumption is that there are significant pipe faults present or the roots would not be in the pipe. If the pipe is faulty and leaking, any biologically active herbicide or toxin will leak from the pipes and affect other plants in the area (52).

Exclusion Zones

Exclusion zones prevent roots from colonizing soil resource areas due to physical or chemical changes in the three-dimensional soil matrix. From one point of view, urban soils are already root growth exclusion zones. Changing soil structure, pore space volume, or drainage and aeration patterns can generate a soil environment that roots cannot effectively colonize. Additions of physical- or chemical-based soil altering materials (soil-injected clay slurry or concrete solutions) can be effective, at least over the short run if adequate soil volume is treated.

Soil compaction remains the best way to prevent root colonization. With high levels of soil strength and penetration resistance, low oxygen, significant amounts of unavailable water, no air-filled pores, and small-diameter water-filled pores, soil compaction will minimize any root growth. Expansive clay soils, freeze cycles, and biological activities over time can reduce compaction and generate root-accessible pore space.

Addition of nitrogen gas, sulphur (29), sodium, zinc, borate, salts, or herbicides (28) to soil areas or to infrastructure building materials can carry severe environmental costs, have short-term results, and have nontarget damage potential. Other potential treatments, such as electric plasma soil fusion and resin infiltration of soils, are cost prohibitive.

Air Gaps

One of the most effective means of controlling tree root growth is the creation of supporting stone matrices that dry quickly, have extremely large pores filled with air, have poor water-holding capacity, and are impermeable to root penetration. These large air gaps are produced by layers or areas where large gravel (> 2 cm [.75 in.]) and cobble-sized stones are deposited and then paved over. This stone structure reduces rooting significantly (43). Clean, graded, medium-sized rubble (crushed brick remnants) provides an excellent gap material if it is not covered or filled in with sand (28, 29, 41). This construction practice could help recycle old paving and wall materials.

Some communities are experimenting with the use of an air gap left between the soil surface and the pavement (34, 35). A variety of existing soil drain systems (plastic spreaders between geotextile) that yield air-filled gaps can provide root control options along with water drainage control. A reinforced narrow open trench, along with full and rapid drainage, can also be effective. Engineered soils can also provide a variety of root-promoting and root-inhibiting areas with the same basic load-bearing framework. Gaps have been shown to be effective but are rarely used because of builder resistance and lack of demand.

Barriers

Among the easiest and most available materials to control root growth are various types of two-dimensional barriers. A number of commercial products are on the market, some using a herbicide. In a survey of community management programs, 50% of respondents said barriers are considered at least partially effective (24). Survey results indicate that, after species selection and mechanical cutting, barriers represent a more tree-literate approach to root growth control. However, no barrier is completely effective as applied (43).

Many types of barriers have been shown to be effective; a sampling is given in Table 4. Table 4 is not an exhaustive list but is provided to show the diversity of root growth control barriers. There are many "weeding" and mulch fabrics that are not effective for root growth control because they lack fiber-to-fiber strength to resist root elongation or radial expansion (28).

From the sample of effective root barriers listed in Table 4, three barrier types are most common: traps (root engaging and constricting), deflectors (walls), and inhibitors (chemical constraints). No barrier stops all roots under all conditions. Combined features of the barrier, the site, and barrier installation and maintenance are critical to effectiveness (55).

Traps. Screens, welded fiber sheets, and woven and nonwoven fabrics can be considered root traps. The effectiveness of these traps depends on the gap or hole size in the material. Holes in the materials should be large enough to allow root tip growth into or through the material, with materials strong enough to strangle radial growth and girdle roots (28, 50, 55). Smaller holes are more effective than large in limiting root growth (55). Remembering root elongation mechanics, if you keep roots small, they will be able to generate far less force in elongation and radial growth. These permeable materials allow water movement in the vapor and liquid phase and do not constrain gas exchange in the soil.

Good examples of these traps are screen and welded fabrics. Nylon fabric screens with 1/26-in. (1-mm) square openings were found to be effective in controlling root growth, as was copper screen with 1/16-in. (1.6-mm) square openings (55). The smaller holes were considered more effective (55). Weld-woven, synthetic, nonelastic fabrics with the strength to girdle roots growing through openings between 1.3 mm (0.05 in.) and 0.5 mm (0.02 in.) diameter were found to be effective (50).

Deflectors. Deflector barrier types include solid plastic, metal, and wood. Deflectors, when installed correctly, can be highly effective. These barriers attempt to change normal root orientation, to exclude root growth in an area, or to reposition roots to cause less damage. Because these barriers are solid, soil moisture contents and water drainage may be affected (55). In areas where frost heaving and freeze-thaw cycles are present, these deflectors may facilitate additional damage. If drainage is provided around the barrier, roots may take advantage of additional resource space and circumvent the barrier. Barrier thicknesses from 0.15 mm (15 mils) sheets to thicker have been cited as effective. Thicker barriers are easier to install without damage and can handle more intensive site impacts over time (5)

Inhibitors. The last general type of root growth control barrier is an inhibitor. Inhibitor growth barriers use chemical control agents or toxins to constrain root growth. One inhibitor system comes from the nursery production trade. Cupric carbonate ($CuCO_3$) mixed in white acrylic paint at 100 g/L of paint and applied to a solid wall or sheet is effective in controlling roots. Higher rates of 500 g/L were damaging to the whole plant, not just the root tips (2). Other copper-based products have been used as contact herbicides and barrier components. The duration of the root-controlling effect varies depending on soil moisture conditions.

One of the most visible and unique inhibitor barriers is controlled-release herbicide fabric. Depending upon soil temperatures, root growth control can last a long time. One of the most common commercial inhibitor barriers is a herbicide-impregnated, slow-release product developed originally by the U.S. government. The government created three different products using this technology: an anti-root sewer pipe gaskets, geotextile fabric with a herbicide-impregnated nodule barrier, and an anti-root-fouling plastic drip-irrigation emitter (52). All are commercially available.

The geotextile fabric root barrier has been successfully developed, marketed, and used. This inhibitor barrier and its active ingredient will not systemically harm other vegetation, just root tips that come in close contact (52). The herbicide used in this inhibitor barrier is trifluralin (dinitroaniline family), which inhibits cell division in root tips by preventing chromosomal spindle formation. Trifluralin is considered a preemergent herbicide because it inhibits root tip growth from seeds (52). Trifluralin is effective as a contact and a vapor-phase herbicide within the soil. It does not accumulate into higher animal food chains because it is not taken up into the tree (52). Trifluralin is not detectable beyond 10 cm (4 in.) from the barrier into the soil, and so is considered to have no environmental impact beyond the root control area (52). Figure 12 shows herbicide release over time. Figure 13 shows estimated effective lifespans for this type of inhibitor barrier in the soil.

Root Barrier Summary. The advantages and disadvantages of the various root growth barriers are summarized in Table 5. It is clear that the intensity of site usage and installation procedures of any barrier can reduce its effectiveness.

A major concern in root growth control is barrier placement. If long-term tree health and maximizing soil resource volume are critical, barriers should be installed along or around the infrastructure to be protected (3). Placement of barriers should fulfill the objectives of minimizing root-caused damage and maximizing the soil area open for colonization by the tree. Placing barriers along the side of a sidewalk, pavement, foundation, or utility corridor is preferable to placing them near or around the tree base. If containerization of a tree is an objective of using barriers, additional soil resource and tree structural stability issues should be considered.

A second major aspect of barrier placement is root shadow size on the far side of the barrier. The rooting shadow size, shape, and extent depend on soil aeration, soil compaction, and barrier installation procedures. Figure 14 depicts a rooting shadow (Gilman shadow) on the far side of a barrier. After passing beneath a barrier, depending upon soil characteristics, roots again reach the surface (23, 24, 29). The length of soil surface behind the barrier that remains root-free is known as the rooting shadow.

In poorly drained soils, roots can grow back to the surface quickly (within 13 m [4 ft]) (23, 24). In well-drained soils, roots rise more slowly after growing under the barrier (24, 29). If the barrier is deep enough and properly installed to minimize backfill pore spaces, roots will not be able to grow beneath the barrier at all. If the barrier installation trench provides additional pore space and root growth channels, some roots growing beneath the barrier with immediately grow to the surface after passing the barrier (23, 24).

Directed Growth

Roots grow where there are adequate resources, and proliferate where good supplies of resources exist and can be ecologically recycled. Understanding root elongation, colonization, and survival processes allows growth favoring soil layers, corridors, and areas to be designed for directing roots away from infrastructures. Two principal methods are baiting and channeling.

Baiting. Baiting is providing ideal essential resources in healthy soil in some other area, rather than next to infrastructures. Sometimes this process is not possible, but under-soil hydroponics and special in-ground containerization are workable. For practical purposes, an area of open soil surface is identified away from roots impacting infrastructure (Figure 15). These roots are provided with near-optimal resources and additional organic matter. The net result is a much higher survival and growth rate in that part of the root system compared to roots near infrastructures. Near infrastructures, water, growth materials, essential elements, and oxygen should be limited. It is absurd to provide high levels of resources across an entire site and still complain about tree root growth problems.

Channeling. When open surface area is limited or soil resource volumes are small, "shepherding" roots to desirable locations can provide valuable resources for growth. The use of surface or near-surface trenches, channels, layers, and tunnels that are surrounded by root control obstacles, barriers, or resource constraints, can provide needed resources. Growth channels filled with rich, well-aerated, ecologically healthy growth medium will encourage root colonization and survival (35). Using culverts, bridges, raceways, tunnels, and other infrastructure devices can lead roots away from more sensitive infrastructure targets. Under pavements, the use of compacted layers above and below a moist, oxygenated coarse layer (sand) can lead roots under infrastructures and out into open soil surface areas.

Species Selection

Species selection is fraught with problems because of the genetic plasticity of trees under different site conditions, which leads to phenotypic selections without controlled testing, demonstration, and consistent reproduction. The literature seems obsessed with good tree–bad tree lists. You are free to find or prepare your own lists from local and regional sources and your own experience.

A large majority of managers (90% in one survey) believe that by planting particular species and by avoiding others for a given site, infrastructure damage can be minimized (24, 34, 35). Managers develop species preferences over time based upon chance, experience, and perceptions of problems. One reporting system tried to objectively highlight species generating the most infrastructure damage. On a genus basis, *Fraxinus*, *Populus*, *Quercus*, *Robinia*, *Salix*, and *Tilia* were noted for greater than expected incidences of infrastructure damage (20). Planting smaller, less aggressive rooting, and slower-growing species has been recommended, in addition to avoiding specific species–site combinations (54).

Confounding tree species selection is tree size. Different individuals, populations, and species attain different sizes and rooting characteristics depending on soil, site, and environment. Some species grow fast and become large, thereby mechanically and biologically initiating changes in the site and associated infrastructures. Sheer size, rate of growth (size change rate), and mechanical adjustments generated to remain structurally stable interact closely with available rooting volume, soil strength, and distance to infrastructures. Potentially large trees planted in small soil volumes will be quick to exert mechanical forces on surrounding infrastructures.

The size of the root plate, or the zone of rapid taper, varies by genus and species (19). Using root plate or structural rooting distances as a minimum distance to infrastructure is possible. Table 6 shows a means of representing the minimum distance away from a tree stem for use in minimizing root plate interactions. Table 6 represents mechanical functions regardless of species.

The second rooting concern in infrastructure damage is the woody, radially growing, transport roots growing away from the root plate area. Minimum distances that provide adequate resource space and structural support, and that reduce (not eliminate) infrastructure damage can be determined. Table 6 estimates the minimum radius measured from the stem that encompasses the critical rooting area needed for healthy tree survival, which minimizes infrastructure damage and which should not be encroached upon (10). The general values of Table 6 offer rough estimates for planning and designing local, regional, and species-specific guidelines.

For all the preconceived concepts about species, and for all the blame placed on trees for infrastructure damage, the distance to infrastructure and its damage can be structurally related and independent of species (21). It is the physical forces of tree biological colonization and survival, coupled with systemic design and material flaws in infrastructures (without regard to species), that confound tree root growth control.

Conclusions

We have never had more tools available for minimizing infrastructure damage exacerbated by tree root growth. The most important management concept to understand is how we allow tree roots to be associated with infrastructures and colonize faults, cracks, and resource availability areas. Design and engineering mistakes, for which trees are easy scapegoats, tend to be accepted by tree professionals as our failings. It is time to intelligently fight back against the real, demonstrable causes of infrastructure damage, not ignore what we know about tree growth and development. We must not abdicate our professional role in solving tree root growth and infrastructure damage problems. Our responsibilities must lie with creating and using root growth control tools and techniques that are tree literate and do not destroy the many benefits that trees bring to people's lives.

Literature Cited

1. Appleton, B.L., J.F. Derr, and B.B. Ross. 1990. *The effect of various landscape weed control measures on soil moisture and temperature, and tree root growth.* J. Arboric. 16(10):264–268.
2. Arnold, M.A., and D.K. Struve. 1989. *Growing green ash and red oak in CuCO$_3$-treated containers increases root regeneration and shoot growth following transplant.* J. Amer. Soc. Hort. Sci. 114(3):402–406.
3. Barker, P.A. 1994. Root barriers for controlling damage to sidewalks, pp 179–187. **In** The Landscape Below Ground: Proceedings of an International Workshop on Tree Root Development in Urban Soils. Lisle, IL. International Society of Arboriculture, Champaign, IL.
4. Barker, P.A. 1995. *Managed development of tree roots: I. Ultra-deep rootball and root barrier effects on European hackberry.* J. Arboric. 21(4):202–208.
5. Barker, P.A. 1995. *Managed development of tree roots: II. Ultra-deep rootball and root barrier effects on southwestern black cherry.* J. Arboric. 21(5):251–259.
6. Barker, P.A., and P.J. Peper. 1995. *Strategies to prevent damage to sidewalks by tree roots.* Arboric. J. 19:295–309.
7. Bengough, A.G., and C.J. MacKenzie. 1994. *Simultaneous measurement of root force and elongation for seedling pea roots.* J. Exp. Bot. 45(270):95–102.
8. Borden, J.M., and R.M.C. Driscoll. 1987. *House foundations—a review of the effect of clay soil volume change on design performance.* Munic. Eng. 4:181–213.
9. Coder, K.D. 1995. Tree quality BMPs for developing wooded areas and protecting residual trees, pp 111–124. **In** Watson, G.W., and D. Neely (Eds.). Trees and Building Sites: Proceedings of an International Workshop on Trees and Buildings, Chicago, IL. International Society of Arboriculture, Champaign, IL.
10. Coder, K.D. 1996. Construction damage assessments: Trees and sites. University of Georgia Cooperative Extension Service publication FOR96-39. 18 pp.
11. Coder, K.D. 1997. Crown pruning effects on roots, pp 89–98. **In** Proceedings of the Third European Congress of Arboriculture, Merano, Italy. International Society of Arboriculture, Italian Chapter.
12. Coder, K.D. 1997. *Flood-damaged trees.* Arborist News 6(3):45–53.
13. Coder, K.D. 1998. Control of shoot/root balance in trees. University of Georgia Cooperative Extension Service publication FOR98-3. 5 pp.
14. Coder, K.D. 1998. Growth control systems in trees. University of Georgia Cooperative Extension Service publication FOR98-4. 10 pp.
15. Coder, K.D. 1998. Tree growth response systems. University of Georgia Cooperative Extension Service publication FOR98-6. 7 pp.

16. Craul, P.J. 1992. Effects of compaction on root growth, pp 229–232. In Urban Soil in Landscape Design. John Wiley & Sons, New York, NY.
17. Craul, P.J. 1992. Soil conditions and root growth, pp 139–156. In Urban Soil in Landscape Design. John Wiley & Sons, New York, NY.
18. Craul, P.J. 1992. Urban soil stability, pp 110–114. In Urban Soil in Landscape Design. John Wiley & Sons, New York, NY.
19. Cutler, D.F. 1995. Interactions between tree roots and buildings, pp 78–87. In Watson, G.W., and D. Neely (Eds.). Trees and Building Sites: Proceedings of an International Workshop on Trees and Buildings, Chicago, IL. International Society of Arboriculture, Champaign, IL.
20. Cutler, D. 1997. Damage by tree roots and its prevention, pp 39–49. In Proceedings of the Third European Congress of Arboriculture, Merano, Italy. International Society of Arboriculture, Italian Chapter.
21. Francis, J.K., B.R. Parresol, and J.M. de Patino. 1996. *Probability of damage to sidewalks and curbs by street trees in the tropics.* J. Arboric. 22(4):193–197.
22. Gilman, E.F. 1990. *Tree root growth and development: I. Form, spread, depth and periodicity.* J. Environ. Hort. 8(4):215–220.
23. Gilman, E.F. 1995. Root barriers affect root distribution, pp 64–67. In Watson, G.W., and D. Neely (Eds.). Trees and Building Sites: Proceedings of an International Workshop on Trees and Buildings, Chicago, IL. International Society of Arboriculture, Champaign, IL.
24. Gilman, E.F. 1996. *Root barriers affect root distribution.* J. Arboric. 22(3): 151–154.
25. Grabosky, J., and N. Bassuk. 1995. *A new urban tree soil to safely increase rooting volumes under sidewalks.* J. Arboric. 21(4):187–201.
26. Hanisch, M.A., H.D. Brown, and E.A. Brown. 1983. Dutch Elm Disease Management Guide. USDA Forest Service and USDA Extension Service bulletin 1. 20 pp.
27. Kopinga, J. 1991. *The effects of restricted volumes of soil on the growth and development of street trees.* J. Arboric. 17(3):57–63.
28. Kopinga, J. 1994. Aspects of the damage to asphalt road pavings caused by tree roots, pp.165–178. In Watson, G.W., and D. Neely (Eds.). The Landscape Below Ground: Proceedings of an International Workshop on Tree Root Development in Urban Soils. International Society of Arboriculture, Champaign, IL.
29. Kopinga, J. 1997. Special treatments for tree roots: Some considerations on the construction of a growing site for urban trees, pp 77–88. In Proceedings of the Third European Congress of Arboriculture, Merano, Italy. International Society of Arboriculture, Italian Chapter.
30. Lawson, M., and D.P. O'Callaghan. 1995. *A critical analysis of the role of trees in damage to low-rise buildings.* J. Arboric. 21:90–97.
31. Materechera, S.A., A.M. Alston, J.M. Kirby, and A.R. Dexter. 1992. *Influence of root diameter on the penetration of seminal roots into a compacted subsoil.* Plant and Soil 144:297–303.

32. Mattheck, C., and H. Breloer. 1994. Windthrow: Falling without fracturing, pp 66–87. In The Body Language of Trees: A Handbook for Failure Analysis (English trans.). Research for Amenity Trees 4 in a series, HMSO, London. 240 pp.
33. McCombie, P.F. 1995. The prediction of building foundation damage arising from water demand of trees. Aboric. J. 19:147–159.
34. McPherson, E.G., and P.J. Peper. 1995. Infrastructure repair costs associated with street trees in 15 cities, pp 49–63. In Watson, G.W., and D. Neely (Eds.). Trees and Building Sites: Proceedings of an International Workshop on Trees and Buildings, Chicago, IL. International Society of Arboriculture, Champaign, IL.
35. McPherson, E.G., and P.P. Peper. 1996. Costs of street tree damage to infrastructure. Arboric. J. 20:143–160.
36. Miller, F.D., and D. Neely. 1993. The effect of trenching on growth and plant health of selected species of shade trees. J. Arboric. 19:226–229.
37. Misra, R.K., A.R. Dexter, and A.M. Alston. 1986. Maximum axial and radial growth pressures in plant roots. Plant and Soil 95:315–326.
38. Morris, L.A., and R.F. Lowery. 1988. Influence of site preparation on soil conditions affecting stand establishment and tree growth. South. J. Appl. For. 12(3): 170–178.
39. O'Callaghan, D., and M. Lawson. 1995. A critical look at the potential for foundation damage caused by tree roots, pp 99–107. In Watson, G.W., and D. Neely (Eds.). Trees and Building Sites: Proceedings of an International Workshop on Trees and Buildings, Chicago, IL. International Society of Arboriculture, Champaign, IL.
40. Peper, P.J., and P.A. Barker. 1994. A buyer's technical guide to root barriers, pp 186–193. In Watson, G.W., and D. Neely (Eds.). The Landscape Below Ground: Proceedings of an International Workshop on Tree Root Development in Urban Soils. Lisle, IL. International Society of Arboriculture, Champaign, IL.
41. Rendig, V.V., and H.M. Taylor. 1989. Models of root growth (root growth and distribution), pp 74–77. In Principles of Soil-Plant Interrelationships. McGraw-Hill, New York, NY.
42. Rendig, V.V., and H.M. Taylor. 1989. Physical environmental effects (root growth and distribution), pp 74–77. In Principles of Soil-Plant Interrelationships. McGraw-Hill, New York, NY.
43. Reynolds, T.D. 1990. Effectiveness of three natural biobarriers in reducing root intrusion by four semi-arid plant species. Health Phys. 59(6):849–852.
44. Richards, B.G., P. Peter, and W.W. Emerson. 1983. The effects of vegetation on the swelling and shrinking of soils in Australia. Geotechnique 33(2):127–139.
45. Rolf, K., O. Stal, and H. Schroeder. 1995. Tree roots and sewer systems, pp 68–77. In Watson, G.W., and D. Neely (Eds.). Trees and Building Sites: Proceedings of an International Workshop on Trees and Buildings, Chicago, IL. International Society of Arboriculture, Champaign, IL.
46. Russell, R.S. 1977. Mechanical impedance of root growth, pp 169–192. In Plant Root Systems: Their Function and Interaction with the Soil. McGraw-Hill, England.

47. Simmons, G.L., and P.E. Pope. 1987. *Influence of soil compaction and vesicular-arbuscular mycorrhizae on root growth of yellow poplar and sweet gum seedlings.* Can. J. For. Res. 17:970–975.

48. Souty, N., and W. Stepniewski. 1988. *The influence of external oxygen concentration on axial root growth force of maize radicles.* Agronomie 8(4):295–300.

49. Stewart, M., and R. Sands. 1996. *Comparative water relations of trees in clay soils and the potential for building damage.* Arboric. J. 20:313–328.

50. van der Werken, H. 1982. Effects of four root barrier fabrics on penetration and self pruning of roots, pp 292–293. In 27th Annual Report and Proceedings of the Southern Nurserymen's Association Research Conference. Southern Nurserymen's Association, Nashville, TN.

51. van der Werken, H. 1982. Effects of physical and chemical root barriers on growth of *Koelreuteria bipinnata*, p 74. In 27th Annual Report and Proceedings of the Southern Nurserymen's Association Research Conference. Southern Nurserymen's Association, Nashville, TN.

52. Van Voris, P., D.A. Cataldo, C.E. Cowan, N.R. Gordon, J.F. Cline, F.G. Burton, and W.E. Skeins. 1988. Long-term, controlled release of herbicides: Root growth reduction, pp 222–240. In Pesticide Formulations: Innovations and Developments. American Chemical Society, Washington, DC.

53. Wagar, J.A. 1985. *Reducing surface rooting of trees with control planters and wells.* J. Arboric. 11(6):165–171.

54. Wagar, J.A., and P.A. Barker. 1983. *Tree root damage to sidewalks and curbs.* J. Arboric. 9(7):177–181.

55. Wagar, J.A., and P.A. Barker. 1993. *Effectiveness of three barrier materials for stopping regenerating roots of established trees.* J. Arboric. 19(6):332–338.

56. Watson, G.W. 1995. Tree root damage from utility trenching, pp 33–41. In Watson, G.W., and D. Neely (Eds.). Trees and Building Sites: Proceedings of an International Workshop on Trees and Buildings, Chicago, IL. International Society of Arboriculture, Champaign, IL.

57. Wong, T.W., J.E.G. Good, and M.P. Denne. 1988. *Tree root damage to pavements and kerbs in the City of Manchester.* Arboric. J. 12:17–34.

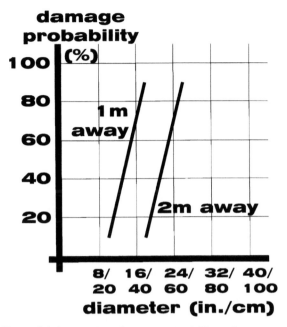

Figure 1. Infrastructure damage potential based on tree diameter and distance from infrastructure for one species (1 MPa = 100 kPa ≈ 1 bar) (21).

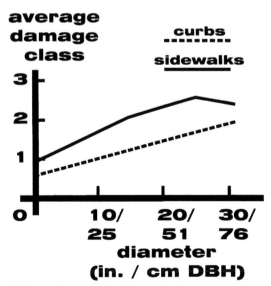

Figure 2. Trunk diameter effects on infrastructure damage (54).

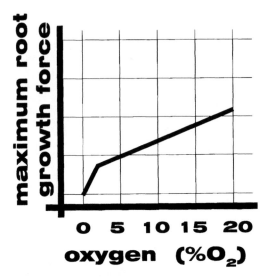

Figure 3. Maximum root growth force expressed by
seedling at various oxygen concentrations (48).

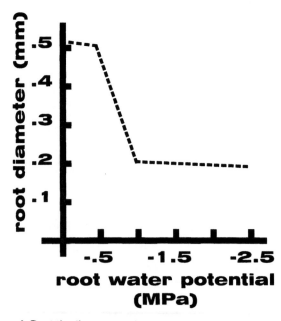

Figure 4. Root tip diameter and root water potential (42).

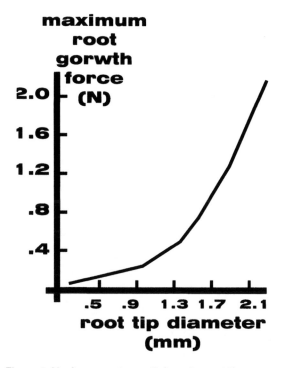

Figure 5. Maximum root growth force by root tip diameter (37).

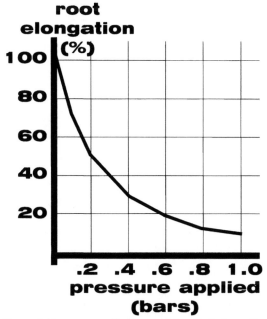

Figure 6. Pressure applied to roots that limit elongation (1 MPa = 100 kPa ≈ 1 bar) (42, 46).

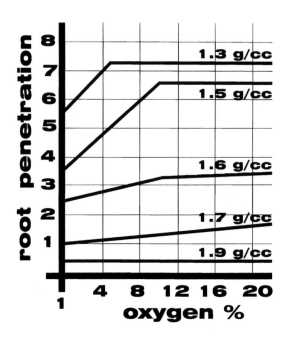

Figure 7. Percentage of oxygen and bulk density
effects on root penetration (42).

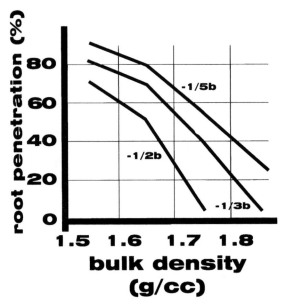

Figure 8. Soil bulk density and water potential effects (in
bars) on root penetration (1 MPa = 100 kPa ≈ 1 bar) (46).

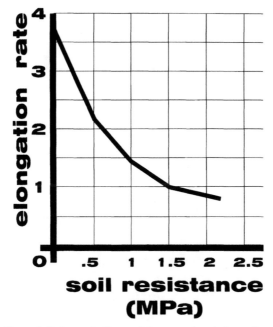

Figure 9. Soil penetration resistance and root elongation rate (1 MPa = 100 kPa ≈ 1 bar) (42).

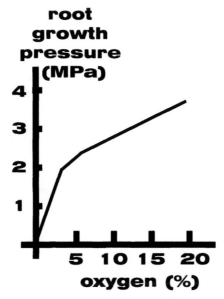

Figure 10. Root growth pressure by oxygen concentration (48).

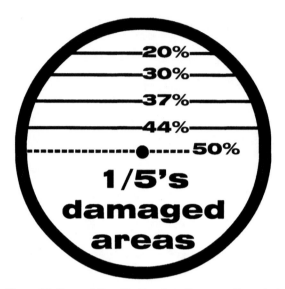

Figure 11. Geometric estimate of rooting area disrupted
by trenching or new infrastructure (10).

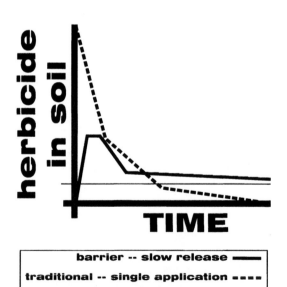

Figure 12. Herbicide release over time (52).

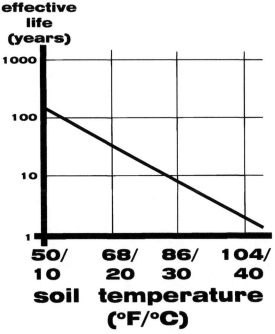

Figure 13. Effective soil life for example slow-release chemical barrier (52).

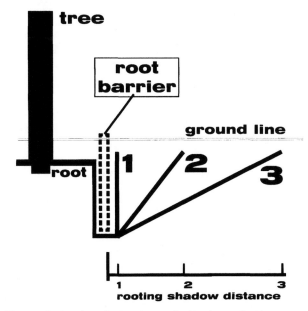

Figure 14. Rooting shadow beyond a barrier under three different conditions. Root #1 escapes up installation trench. Root #2 is in poorly drained soil. Root #3 is in well-drained soil.

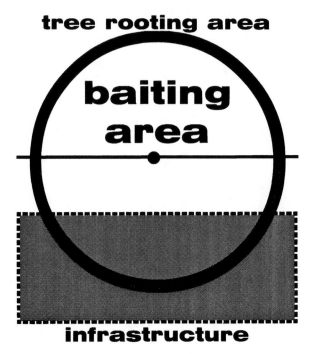

Figure 15. Root baiting area, part of a directed-growth root control technique.

Table 1. Brief list of root growth resource requirements.

	Requirements	
Root resource	Minimum	Maximum
Oxygen in soil atmosphere (for root survival)	2.5% (17)	21%
Air pore space in soil (for root growth)	12% (10)	—
Soil bulk density restricting root growth	—	1.4 g/cc clay (10)
	—	1.8 g/cc sand (10)
Penetration strength (water-content dependent)	0.01 kPa	3 MPa (28, 29)
Water content in soil	12% (17)	40% (17, 27)
Root initiation (O_2% in soil atmosphere)	12% (17)	21%
Root growth (O_2% in soil atmosphere)	5% (17)	21%
Progressive loss of element absorption in roots (O_2% in soil atmosphere)	15% (17)	21%
Temperature limits to root growth	4°C/40°F	34°C/94°F (12)
pH of soil (wet)	3.5	8.2

Table 2. Root growth limiting air-pore space values and bulk-density values, by soil texture (9, 10, after 38).

Soil texture	% of root-limiting pores normally filled with air	Root-limiting bulk density (g/cc)
Sand	24	1.8
Fine sand	21	1.75
Sandy loam	19	1.7
Fine sandy loam	15	1.65
Loam	14	1.55
Silt loam	17	1.45
Clay loam	11	1.5
Clay	13	1.4

Table 3. Primary forms of root growth control: Tools and techniques.

1. **Intelligent development** designs and applications using tree-literate techniques and materials. If you build it correctly, they will not come!
2. **Kill zones** (soil volumes and planes): use of cultivation, cutting, trenching, vibratory plows, and chemicals.
3. **Exclusion zones** (soil volumes): soil structural changes, soil compaction, water/aeration stress, anaerobic conditions, soil injection, soil additives, and chemicals.
4. **Air gaps** (thick plane): designed permanent and temporary air spaces for root pruning or lack of support, coarse stone cobbles, and drain systems.
5. **Barriers** (control plane): commercial traps, deflectors, or containment devices; metals, screens, plastics, paints, and inhibitors.
6. **Directed growth** (ecological island and corridor resource space): systems to concentrate roots elsewhere; guide growth along channels; allow survival in other areas, root culverts, or layers; and engineered soils.
7. **Species selection:** planting trees with lower soil oxygen requirements, improved root morphology and reactivity values, and more effective species and site choices for long-term solutions.
8. **Avoidance:** separate zoning for infrastructure and trees, established biological-free zones, and avoiding problems.

Table 4. Selected list of root growth control barriers found to be effective for various lengths of time.

Synthetic, nonwoven fabric soaked in copper sulfate (51)
Copper screen (55)
Cupric carbonate ($CuCO_3$) in latex paint (2)
Fiberglass and plastic panels
Fiber-welded synthetic fabric or mesh (28)
Galvanized metal screen
Ground-contact preserved plywood
Heavy rigid plastics* (4, 5, 34, 35)
Infrastructure aprons and footings (34, 35)
Metal roofing sheets
Multiple layers of thin plastic sheets
Nylon fabric or screen (55)
Permeable woven fabric sheets (28)
Rock-impregnated tar paper or felt (28)
Slow-release chemical barriers* (34, 35, 55)
Thin layer of asphalt or herbicide mix (43)
Woven and nonwoven plastic sheets (28)

*Common commercial tree growth control products

Table 5. General advantages and disadvantages of root growth control barriers.

General advantages
Effective in trapping and constricting, deflecting, and/or inhibiting root growth (3, 28)
Tree circling barriers inhibit shallow rooting (4)
Roots push to deeper depths (24)
Initiated a greater number of smaller roots (24)
Smaller roots develop; delay onset of infrastructure damage (53)
Can be used in combination with drainage and aeration treatments to control roots (53)
When deeply seated into ground water or anaerobic soil, layers will contain growth (53)

General disadvantages
Roots commonly grow under and over barriers, causing damage (28)
Many barriers are not installed deeply enough (28)
Surface damage to the top of root barriers is common and leads to failure (28)
Thin plastics subject to easy damage along soil surface area (6, 53)
Buried thin plastics failed where punctured or torn during installation (53)
All barriers fail when the top of the barrier is damaged by equipment or traffic (6, 53)
Circling barriers and barriers placed too closely make circling roots a concern (3, 53)
Roots can physically push through thin zones (less than 5 cm) of herbicide or thin plastic (52)
May disrupt water and gas movement (anaerobic conditions and freezing heave) (28)
Deep, tree-circling barriers may compromise structural roots and tree stability (3)
Must break surface of soil and any mulch layer to be completely effective (3, 6, 40)

Table 6. Estimated area of root plate, or zone of rapid taper (10, after 32), and estimated minimum critical rooting area, by tree diameter (10).

Tree diameter (in.)	Structural root distance (ft of radius)	Critical rooting distance (ft of radius)	Tree diameter (in.)	Structural root distance (ft of radius)	Critical rooting distance (ft of radius)
1	1	1	26	10	33
2	2	3	27	10	34
3	2	4	28	10	35
4	3	5	29	10	36
5	3	6	30	10	38
6	4	8	31	10	39
7	4	9	32	10	40
8	5	10	33	10	41
9	5	11	34	10	43
10	6	13	35	10	44
11	6	14	36	10	45
12	7	15	37	11	46
13	7	16	38	11	48
14	7	18	39	11	49
15	8	19	40	11	50
16	8	20	45	11	56
17	8	21	50	12	63
18	8	23	55	12	69
19	9	24	60	13	75
20	9	25	65	13	81
21	9	26	70	14	88
22	9	28	75	14	94
23	9	29	80	15	100
24	10	30	85	15	107
25	10	31	90	16	115
			95	16	120
			100	16	125

Comparison of Root Barriers Installed at Two Depths for Reduction of White Mulberry Roots in the Soil Surface

Paula J. Peper

Three circling root barrier products, DeepRoot®, Tree Root Planter®, and Vespro®, were installed at 30- and 60-cm (11.8- and 23.6-in.) depths and evaluated to determine whether 1) internal vertical ribs prevented circling roots and 2) installation at 30 and 60 cm significantly reduced root biomass and diameter in the top 33 cm (13 in.) of soil. After three growing seasons, 56 white mulberry (*Morus alba*) were excavated and data collected on surface root dry mass, root diameters, and locations. Barriers installed to 30-cm depths did not significantly reduce diameters of roots growing outside the barriers. They did, however, significantly reduce outside surface root dry mass by 31% to 59%. Barriers installed to 60-cm depths reduced surface root dry mass by 85% to 89% and significantly reduced root diameters. Regardless of barrier depth, internal vertical ribs effectively diverted circling roots downward, but more J-rooting was associated with the deeper barriers. Tree growth estimated by measurements of stem diameter, total height, and mean crown width, remained unaffected by treatments.

Damage to urban hardscapes (sidewalks, curbs, gutters, road surfaces, etc.) by tree roots costs California residents at least $62 million dollars annually, either in direct out-of-pocket repair expenses or through tax dollars spent by public works agencies (7). An average 10% of street tree budgets is spent on removing trees that repeatedly cause damage. When these trees are removed, their quantifiable benefits (air pollution removal, carbon sequestration, temperature modification, energy savings) are lost (8, 11).

Damage-prevention efforts have led some cities and counties to install root barriers in new or refurbished landscapes. Although initial research suggested that such methods might divert roots to grow to deeper levels beneath the hardscape, subsequent research has questioned the efficacy of barriers for reducing root biomass in locations with less than ideal soil environments. Gilman (6) found that chemical barriers forced live oak (*Quercus virginiana*) and sycamore (*Platanus occidentalis*) roots

Paula J. Peper, Western Center for Urban Forest Research and Education, Pacific Southwest Research Station, USDA Forest Service, c/o Department of Environmental Horticulture, One Shields Avenue, Davis, CA 95616-8587.

to grow deeper in soil but that many returned to the soil surface within 1.2 m (3.9 ft) of the barrier due to the high water table at the site. High soil bulk densities at deeper soil levels were related to the return of poplar (*Populus nigra* var. *italica*) and ash (*Fraxinus oxycarpa* var. *Raywood*) roots to surface root levels (3). A deeper distribution of roots in the soil profile was found when the soil was cultivated to a depth of 46 cm (18.1 in.), lowering the soil bulk density. Barker (1, 2) also reported that European hackberry (*Celtis australis*) and southwestern black cherry roots (*Prunus serotina* var. *virens*) did not return to soil surfaces within 1 m (3.3 ft) of trees planted in deep, well-drained alluvial soils.

A tree's genetic makeup and the soil environment in which it is grown determine where roots grow and develop. Urban street trees typically grow in poor soil environments; imposing additional restrictions by installing a 60-cm-deep root barrier (a standard depth) may further limit the soil volume necessary and accessible to root growth. Minimal research has been conducted to begin determining optimal barrier depths given varying soil conditions, although Barker's (1, 2) studies at the Solano Urban Forest Research Area (SUFRA) found significant reduction in surface root dry mass for barriers that were only 35 cm (13.8 in.) deep.

This study was established after earlier root barrier experiments using polyethylene rootball casings (35 cm deep) reduced surface root dry mass three- to elevenfold but appeared to encourage circling root growth (1, 2). As a result, the objectives of this study were to: 1) determine if barriers designed with internal vertical ribs would prevent circling roots within barriers and 2) compare root growth responses to barriers installed at two depths, 30 and 60 cm, for significant reduction of surface root dry mass.

Materials and Methods

The study plot was located at SUFRA, on the Solano Community College campus near Fairfield, California. The soil, Class I of the Yolo Series (12), is an alluvial, well-drained, dark brown, generally silty clay loam without mottling. It has a pH range of 6.5 to 7.5 and an electrical conductivity for soluble salts of 300 to 500 μmhos/cm on a dry soil basis. Soil bulk densities are uniform throughout the site, averaging 1.39 g/cm^3 and 1.45 g/cm^3 at 14 and 34 cm (5.5 and 13.4 in) depths, respectively (9).

Two-year-old bareroot seedlings of white mulberry (*Morus alba*) were installed in a randomized complete block design comprising a control and three treatments with two subtreatments (three barrier types installed at two different depths).

The three barrier products tested were DeepRoot® (DeepRoot Partners, LP, Burlingame, California), Tree Root Planter® (Bumble Bee Products, Inc., Signal Hill, California), and Vespro® (Vespro, Inc., San Rafael, California). The barriers, constructed of either polyethylene or polypropylene plastic, consisted of three 60 cm × 60 cm interlocking panels connected by plastic lock strips to form circular barriers with 58-cm (22.8-in) diameters. Standard 60-cm barriers were cut in half to produce the 30-cm depth subtreatment. Internal vertical rib design and spacing constituted the primary difference between barriers. Rib heights for DeepRoot and Tree Root Planter measured 1.5 cm (0.6 in.) with ribs attached at 90-degree angles to the barrier walls. Vespro ribs extended 0.5 to 1.5 cm from the barrier wall in a 90-degree arc. Ribs were evenly spaced on each barrier, but spacing distances ranged from 12 to 17.5 cm (4.7 to 6.9 in.) among the three barriers.

During field preparation the site was disked, ripped to a depth of 60 cm, disked again, ring-rollered, and lastly dragged and leveled with a length of chainlink fence connected to a tractor. Planting holes were drilled 70 cm (27.6 in.) deep using a 60-cm diameter tractor-mounted auger. Holes were then backfilled by hand to 60- and 30-cm depths and root barriers were installed with top edges extending 3 cm (1.2 in.) above ground to deter roots from growing over the tops of the barriers. Ninety-eight trees comprising 14 replications were planted and staked in May 1993. All treatments were maintained in mowed turf, receiving 24 hours of irrigation every 10 to 14 days from April through mid-October.

In spring 1995, squirrels severely damaged tree branches in six of the fourteen blocks while foraging for mulberries; therefore, only the eight unaffected blocks were excavated in 1996. However, two of these blocks were incomplete because three trees died shortly after planting. This reduced 30-cm DeepRoot replications from eight to six and 60-cm Tree Root Planters to seven. Excavation procedures followed those delineated in a previous study (9), removing the same volume of soil from around each tree (1 m [3.3 ft] radius by 33 cm [13 in.] deep). Soil outside of the barrier was removed first, then the roots were measured, cut, bagged, and labeled for further processing at the lab. Barriers were removed and the inner excavation was completed. Inside roots were cut, bagged, and labeled. At the lab, roots were washed, dried at 65°C (149°F) for 72 hours, and weighed.

Data collected included 1) total dry mass of roots inside the barriers, 2) depth of roots at 18 cm (7.1 in.) from the tree bole center, 3) total dry mass of roots outside the barriers, 4) diameters of roots growing outside the barriers, and 5) the distance from the barriers that roots emerged from the floor of the excavation pit. Tree height, crown width, and stem diameters were measured in November of 1994 and 1995.

Analyses of variances (ANOVA) were performed using the following model:

$$response_{ij} = treatment_i + block_j + error_{ij}$$

Block effect was assumed to be random. Bonferroni's multiple t-tests were conducted, testing the control against each of the six treatments ($\alpha = 0.05$). The 30-cm versus 60-cm barrier subtreatments were also tested at $\alpha = 0.05$.

Results

Inside Root Growth

Measurements of root depth at a location 18 cm (7.1 in.) from the tree bole centers were taken on control trees to determine typical depths at which mulberry roots were growing in the soil horizon. Control root mean depth in the top 33 cm (13 in.) of soil was 12.3 cm (4.8) (± 3.6 cm [1.4 in.]). Although barrier treatment roots were not measured for mean depth, they appeared to grow at the same depth as control trees before being diverted by barriers. Interior barrier excavation revealed surface root growth radiating outward from the tree boles, similar to control trees (at approximately 12 cm [4.7 in.] depth) until being diverted down by the barriers (Figure 1). Roots rarely came in direct contact with the barriers; they maintained an approximately 0.5-cm -thick (0.2 in.) "cushion" of soil between themselves and the barriers. The roots appeared to "sense" the presence of the barrier and begin turning downward, forming a 90-degree arc rather than an abrupt angle, before actually reaching the barrier.

As shown in Table 1, inside root dry mass (IDM) and inside root diameters (IRDIAM) for the DeepRoot 60 subtreatment were not significantly different from the control ($P = 0.11$). Only the Tree Root Planter 60 and Vespro 60 subtreatments had significantly less IDM ($P = < 0.01$ and 0.02, respectively) and smaller IRDIAM ($P = < 0.01$ and 0.02, respectively). None of IDMs or IRDIAMs for the 30 cm subtreatments were significantly different from the control.

Nearly half of the barrier-treated trees (21 of 46) exhibited one or more roots that began to circle but were diverted downward by the internal vertical ribs. The distance the roots ran horizontally along barrier edges before ribs deflected them downward was determined by the spacing between ribs. This was 12, 15, and 17.5 cm (4.7, 5.9, and 6.9 in.) for Tree Root Planter, DeepRoot, and Vespro, respectively. Only four of the forty-six barrier-treated trees exhibited circling roots that extended beyond one rib. This occurred twice with the Tree Root Planter and once each with DeepRoot and Vespro. In all cases, the roots were diverted down upon encountering the second rib (Figure 1). The presence of circling roots on no more than two trees per treatment type was not significant because circling roots also were found on two control trees.

Table 1. Means, standard errors (in parentheses), and Bonferroni multiple t-test results for all treatments against the control. The 30- versus 60-cm barriers were also tested for significance.

Treament	Inside root dry mass (kg)	Inside root diameter (cm)	Outside root dry mass (kg)	Outside root diameter (cm)	Distance from barrier (cm)	Stem diameter (cm)	Tree height (m)	Crown diameter (m)
Control	0.392 a* (0.082)	2.60 a (0.292)	0.928 a (0.079)	2.38 a (0.242)	0.01 a (2.092)	5.94 a (0.372)	4.29 a (0.199)	2.70 a (0.206)
DeepRoot 30	0.448 a (0.095)	2.39 a (0.337)	0.643 b (0.091)	2.27 a (0.279)	1.90 a (2.378)	5.92 a (0.422)	3.61 a (0.230)	2.88 a (0.228)
DeepRoot 60	0.282 a (0.082)	2.61 a (0.292)	0.127 b (0.079)	0.80 b (0.242)	17.01 b (2.092)	5.82 a (0.372)	4.37 a (0.199)	2.59 a (0.206)
Tree Root Planter 30	0.447 a (0.088)	2.23 a (0.312)	0.398 b (0.084)	2.09 a (0.258)	0.85 a (2.219)	5.89 a (0.395)	4.14 a (0.213)	2.72 aa (0.215)
Tree Root Planter 60	0.137 b (0.082)	1.53 b (0.292)	0.107 (0.079)	0.72 b (0.242)	18.38 b (2.092)	5.14 a (0.372)	3.82 a (0.199)	2.33 a (0.206)
Vespro 30	0.302 a (0.082)	2.38 a (0.292)	0.380 b (0.079)	1.98 a (0.242)	0.73 a (2.092)	5.21 a (0.372)	4.14 a (0.199)	2.26 a (0.206)
Vespro 60	0.201 b (0.082)	1.98 b (0.292)	0.141 b (0.079)	0.88 b (0.242)	13.81 b (2.092)	5.36 a (0.372)	4.35 a (0.199)	2.33 a (0.206)
30- vs. 60-cm	s	ns	s	s	s	ns	ns	ns

*Treatments followed by the same letter are not significant at $\alpha = 0.05$.
s = significant and ns = not significant at $\alpha = 0.05$.

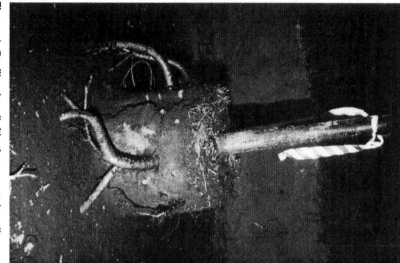

Figure 1. Profile view (left) of excavated mulberry showing roots diverted in 90-degree arc by barrier. Root in foreground had begun to circle but was diverted down by the barrier's internal vertical rib. Even with the barrier removed, roots in the overhead view (right) show its circular configuration. Root on right began to circle before reaching the barrier. missing one rib when growing behind another root. but growing to the barrier edge and being

Outside Root Growth

For 30-cm subtreatments compared to controls, the diameters of roots growing outside the barriers (ORDIAM) and the distance from the barrier (RDIST) at which roots emerged from the floor of the excavation pit were not significant (Table 1). All 30-cm subtreatments significantly reduced mean outside root dry mass (ODM); however, the three subtreatments responded differently. Root dry mass for the Tree Root Planter and Vespro treatments were 43% and 41% of the control ODM, whereas DeepRoot was 70% of the control ODM. Additional t-tests (α = 0.05) contrasting these treatments confirm that the DeepRoot treatments reduced dry mass significantly less than the Tree Root Planter (P = 0.037) and Vespro (P = 0.042).

In contrast, there was no difference in root responses between the three 60-cm subtreatments that reduced ODM from 85% to 88% (Table 1). All three barriers significantly reduced outside surface root dry mass more than the shallower barriers. Similarly, the ORDIAMs were significantly smaller than control and shallower barrier treatments (Table 1). When compared to controls, the deeper barriers reduced ORDIAM 63% to 69%. Additionally, the distance from barriers at which roots of the 60-cm subtreatments grew back up into the top 30 cm of soil were measured. Roots returned to this soil horizon a minimum mean distance of 14 cm (5.5 in.) outside the barriers (Figure 2). With the shallower 30-cm subtreatments, roots typically emerged directly from the bottom of the barriers at a 27 cm (10.6 in.) depth (Figure 3). Root

Figure 2. The first stage of excavation on a 60-cm barrier treatment shows roots re-emerging an average of 14 cm (5.5 in) from the outside of the barrier. These deeper treatments produced significantly less biomass and smaller root diameters outside of the barriers. Roots that were present outside of barriers appeared to grow back up into the surface soil horizon (see roots on right of barrier).

Figure 3. Roots emerged directly from the bottoms of excavated 30-cm-deep barriers as shown in this picture. Although the shorter barriers reduced surface root biomass as a whole, mean root diameters were not significantly different from control diameters. Roots in foreground and on right were growing back toward the soil surface.

depths at fixed distances from barriers were not measured, but roots appeared to be growing back toward the surface soil horizon (Figure 2). The 60-cm barriers exhibited more J-rooting (roots growing under the barriers and abruptly upward). This occurred in one to two roots per tree for approximately 25% of the excavated 60-cm barrier treatments. No one barrier type was more prone to producing J-roots than the next. Barriers tended to be imbedded in the larger-diameter J-roots (≥ 2.0 cm [0.8 in.]), making removal for interior excavations difficult. J-rooting seldom occurred in the 30-cm subtreatments.

Tree Growth

Differences in measures of stem diameter, tree height, and crown diameter between treatment and control trees were not significant (Table 1). The t-tests contrasting 30-cm subtreatments to 60-cm subtreatments also showed no significant difference. Reduction in root biomass in the surface soil horizon did not affect aboveground growth of the trees.

Discussion

Of particular importance are the significant differences in ODM, ORDIAM, and ORDIST between the 30-and 60-cm subtreatments. The exact relationship between increase in root diameter and degree of sidewalk displacement is unknown, but typically, as surface roots grow larger in diameter, more damage is associated with them.

Costello et al. (3) suggest that if root diameter and depth are the same for trees with and without barriers, it seems reasonable that trees with fewer roots are less likely to cause damage. Considering that street tree managers describe multiple incidents of sidewalks being uplifted by a single, aggressive root (4, 5), it may be more reasonable to associate less damage with a reduction both in number of roots or total root biomass and diameter of existing roots in the soil surface layer. In this study, the Tree Root Planter and Vespro 30-cm subtreatments reduced the dry mass of roots growing outside the barriers in the surface 33 cm (13 in.) of soil by nearly 60% (Figure 4a). The DeepRoot 30-cm barriers reduced ODM by about 30%. In this case, a reduction in biomass also equates with a reduction in actual number of roots because root diameters were not significantly reduced. Depending upon barrier type, from 40% to 70% of the mulberry root biomass remained in the surface soil horizon with root diameters not significantly different from control root diameters (Figure 4b). With no reduction in root diameters, this decreases the likelihood that 30-cm barriers will delay the damage caused by roots growing next to sidewalks.

Conversely, the deeper 60-cm subtreatments produced significant reductions in both outside root dry mass and root diameter while also increasing the distance that the barriers diverted roots which re-emerge into the surface soil horizon. The 60-cm outside root dry mass was 11% to 15% of control ODM, and roots in the top 33 (13 in.) cm of soil were roughly one-third the diameter of control roots. Because there are fewer roots and they are of smaller diameter, it is reasonable to assume that the onset of hardscape damage will be delayed.

How much time can be gained before hardscape damage occurs will probably depend upon root growth characteristics of individual tree species and soil conditions. Previous research has demonstrated that different species growing for equivalent times produce substantially different-sized root systems (3, 10). Field observations support this; damage has been associated with sweetgums (*Liquidambar styraciflua*) within 15 years of planting but has not been associated with other species until 30 or more years of age (5). The 60-cm subtreatments in this study may delay the onset of hardscape damage, but additional research is necessary to determine the relationships between root system rates of development (both normally distributed and barrier-diverted) and damage potential.

The J-rooting occurring on one to two roots for one-quarter of the trees planted in the deeper barriers continues to be of concern, although the long-term effects of barriers on the structural stability of trees is unknown. It appears that some mulberry roots are more intolerant to diversion than others, growing beneath the barriers and then returning swiftly returning to a more hospitable environment in the top 30 cm of the soil surface. The level of the roots' intolerance is at some point between 30-cm (no J-rooting) and 60-cm depths in the well-drained alluvial soils at SUFRA. This effect may also help to explain the smaller root diameters and reduced biomass associated with the interiors of the Tree Root Planter and Vespro 60-cm barriers. The reduced mass and diameters may be a result of the roots' physiological response to being diverted to deeper levels. Growth may be going into the length necessary to extend beneath and beyond the barriers instead of into girth (larger inside diameters were associated with 30-cm barriers).

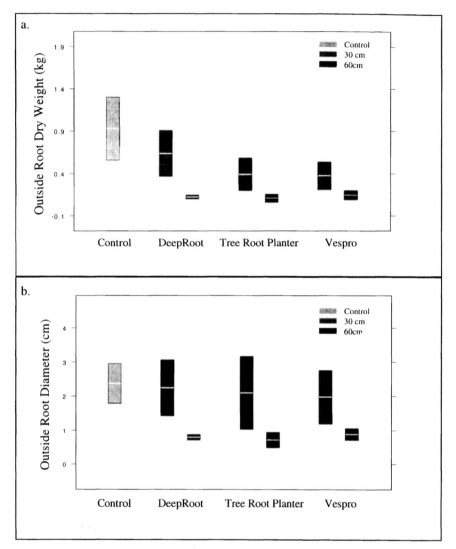

Figure 4. Mean dry mass (a), root diameters (b), and 95% confidence intervals of excavated white mulberry roots for each of the four treatments and the two 30- and 60-cm subtreatments.

While it is doubtful that the minimal J-rooting occurring in this study jeopardizes future tree stability, relationships between soil environment, depth of barriers, reduction of interior biomass, and incidents of J-rooting also require further investigation.

Roots diverted by the 60-cm barriers re-emerged into the surface zone significantly farther (averaging 14 to 18 cm 5.5 to 7.1 in.) from tree boles than control trees, but whether this has any significance in the urban landscape is debatable. Typical street tree planting strip and sidewalk widths in California are each 1.2 m (3.9 ft) (7), and roots would still be emerging within the planting strip if barriers were installed in a circular configuration around individual trees. However, as previously stated, the high reduction of surface root biomass and root diameter associated with these deeper barriers indicates potential for delaying initial occurrences of sidewalk damage. It also appears that the mulberry roots are being diverted to deeper levels (below 33 cm [13 in.]) because above-ground growth was not significantly impacted by the barrier treatments.

Interestingly, ODM reductions for the DeepRoot 30-cm barrier were significantly less compared to the other two 30-cm barrier subtreatments. Variables that could have affected this treatment's responses in comparison to the other two 30-cm subtreatments include differing sample sizes, soil environment, and barrier materials. The DeepRoot 30-cm treatment had a smaller sample size (n = 6 instead of n = 8) because two of the bareroot saplings in the treatment died shortly after planting. However, the variability between samples for this and all treatments was very small and, as indicated by the sample mean, root mass was generally higher per tree compared to the other two treatments. It is doubtful that sample size influenced the response. Similarly, the uniformity of soil type, bulk densities, and irrigation across the site negates soil environment as the cause. The DeepRoot barrier is made of polypropylene, whereas Vespro and Tree Root Planter are polyethylene. However, if something in the plastic materials were accountable, a discrepancy in responses between the DeepRoot 60-cm subtreatments and the Vespro and Tree Root Planter 60-cm barriers would be expected. There was no such discrepancy. The 30-cm DeepRoot response may be an anomaly, but it may also indicate that the outcome of installing barriers at this depth, even in ideal soil conditions and for the same species, is unpredictable. A previous study at SUFRA on Chinese hackberries (*Celtis sinensis*) using 30-cm-deep Tree Root Planter and DeepRoot barriers reduced neither root biomass nor root diameter. In addition, roots returned halfway to the level of control surface roots within 33 cm (13 in.) of the barriers (9).

Conclusions

Reductions of surface root biomass and root diameters were significantly different between barriers installed at 30- and 60-cm depths. There was no reduction in outside root diameters by the 30-cm subtreatments. They did significantly reduce surface root dry mass—but not to the extent of the 60-cm treatments. This result, in combination with results of previous studies, indicates that root response to barriers installed to a 30-cm depth is unpredictable, even when tested in excellent soil conditions. In contrast, the barriers installed to 60-cm depths significantly reduced outside root biomass and root diameter without compromising tree growth. However, noticeable J-rooting was associated with these deeper barriers, indicating that some roots were intolerant of soil conditions at the 60-cm depth. Internal vertical ribs diverted all circling roots within the barriers, regardless of installation depth.

While it could be said that the 60-cm barriers produced more significant reductions in surface root biomass and diameters, increasing evidence indicates that barrier effectiveness depends upon tree species' genetic tolerances to soil environment. In this study, roots of white mulberries (*Morus alba*) in cultivated soil were diverted to at least 60-cm depths and approximately 60% remained at that depth for at least a 1-m (3.3-ft) radius from the tree bole without affecting tree growth. This is similar to Barker's observation (1, 2) that barrier-diverted European hackberry (*Celtis australis*) and southwestern black cherry (*Prunus serotina*) roots did not return to soil surface levels. However, barrier-diverted Chinese hackberry roots returned toward surface levels within 0.66 m (2.2 ft) of tree boles (9). At the same research location, different species have exhibited different responses to barrier treatments installed in the same soil environment. Further investigation on optimal barrier depths in these soils is necessary to develop baseline data on the efficacy of installing barriers in landscapes in which soil conditions are less desirable. If barriers installed at a given depth are not effective in good soil conditions, there is little value to installing them in poorer soils. Conversely, if barriers installed at a range of depths in good soils effectively reduce surface root biomass, testing should continue to determine the relationship between root systems and hardscape damage potential in a variety of soils. Such research must address the long-term effects of barriers on tree health and stability, as well as analyses of the benefits and costs associated with barrier installations, to determine whether they are a cost-effective tool for tree management programs.

Acknowledgments

This project would not have been started, much less completed, if not for Philip A. Barker, USFS Research Horticulturist (retired). Nearly two decades ago, Phil had the foresight to interview street tree managers to determine what research would assist them most in managing the urban forest. He was told repeatedly that their primary concern was how to reduce root damage to sidewalks, curbs, and gutters. The study reported here represents one of the last three root-control studies Phil designed and installed before he retired in 1995. Thank you, Phil, for turning your work over to me. A special thanks to Linda George, Jason Weber, Elinor Tretheway, and the Delta Conservation Camp for their valuable assistance with excavations and data collection.

Use of trade or firm names in this paper is for reader information and does not imply endorsement by the U.S. Department of Agriculture of any product or service.

Literature Cited

1. Barker, P.A. 1995a. *Managed development of tree roots. I. Ultra-deep rootball and root barrier effects on European hackberry.* J. Arboric. 21:203–207.
2. Barker, P.A. 1995b. *Managed development of tree roots. II. Ultra-deep rootball and root barrier effects on Southwestern black cherry.* J. Arboric. 21:251–258.
3. Costello, L.R., Elmore, C.L., and S. Steinmaus. 1997. *Tree root response to circling root barriers.* J. Arboric. 23:211–218.
4. Dunn, L. 1997. Sunnyvale Street Tree Division Manager. Personal interview. 4 Mar.
5. Fitch, M. 1995. Sacramento Street Tree Division Manager. Telephone interview. 16 Mar.
6. Gilman, E.F. 1996. *Root barriers affect root distribution.* J. Arboric. 22(3): 151–154.

7. McPherson, E.G., and P.J. Peper. (Unpublished data). Survey of California cities: Costs associated with street tree damage to sidewalks and other infrastructure elements. US Forest Service, PSW, Western Center for Urban Forest Research, Davis, CA.

8. McPherson, E.G., J.R. Simpson, and K.I. Scott. 1996. "BACT" analysis: Are there cost-effective air quality benefits from trees?, pp 355–359. In Ninth Joint Conference on the Applications of Air Pollution Meteorology with the Air and Waste Management Association. American Meteorological Association, Boston, MA.

9. Peper, P.J., and S. Mori. (Submitted). *Controlled rooting depth of post-transplant trees: Extension casing and root barrier effects on Chinese hackberry.* J. Arboric.

10. Schroth, G. 1995. *Tree root characteristics as criteria for species selection and systems design in agroforestry. Agrofor. Sys.* 30:125–143.

11. Simpson, J.R., and E.G. McPherson. 1996. Estimating urban forest impacts on climate-mediated residential energy use, pp 462–465. **In** 12th Conference on Biometeorology and Aerobiology. American Meteorological Society, Boston, MA.

12. Soil Conservation Service. 1977. Soil survey of Solano Country, California. USDA Soil Conservation Service, Davis, CA. 65 pp.

PART II

MATURE TREE ROOT SYSTEMS

Fill-Soil Effects on Soil Aeration Status

Paula E. Tusler, James D. MacDonald, and Laurence R. Costello

The effect of a fill soil on soil aeration and the efficacy of a subsurface aeration system were investigated. Fill was applied to a depth of 30 cm (11.8 in.) over the root zone (319 m^2 [381.5 yd^2]) of six-year-old cherry trees (*Prunus mahaleb*). Treatments included fill soil with and without an aeration system, and a control (no fill). Oxygen diffusion rate (ODR) and soil moisture content were measured at three depths over a two-year period. Results indicate that fill soil caused a reduction in ODR in underlying soil, but variation within treatment plots did occur. In most cases, the subsurface aeration system did not improve ODR in the underlying soil. These findings lead to the consideration of factors that may contribute to the injury of established trees by fill soils.

Fill soils (or positive grade changes) are commonly found in urban landscapes. Field observations have led to the understanding that fills placed around established trees may cause root injury or contribute to the development of root disease (1, 4, 5). Fill soils are thought to cause oxygen deficits in the root zone of trees (or other vegetation), which result in injury by limiting root respiration. Injury has been noted both in cases for which fill was considered to be the sole cause and for which other factors may have contributed: compaction of the root zone from construction equipment, mechanical injury to roots, and soil-surface sealing resulting from hardscape installation (concrete, asphalt, etc.).

Few studies have attempted to quantify fill-soil impacts on soil aeration status. We have little information regarding the magnitude of impact of fill soil on root-zone aeration, the depth of soil needed to produce an impact, and the physical characteristics of fill and underlying soils that contribute to aeration deficits. Nonetheless, aeration systems are described that are thought to minimize the impacts of fill soils (3). This study seeks to quantify the effect of a fill soil, with and without an aeration system, on the aeration status of an underlying field soil.

Materials and Methods

Six-year-old grafted sweet cherries ('Bing' scion on *Prunus mahaleb* rootstock) growing in an orchard row on the University of California, Davis, campus were selected for fill-soil treatments. *Prunus mahaleb* is reported to be very sensitive to flood-

Paula E. Tusler and James D. MacDonald are with the Plant Pathology Department at University of California, Davis, CA 95616. Laurence R. Costello is with the University of California Cooperative Extension, 625 Miramontes, Room 200, Half Moon Bay, CA 94019.

ing and low aeration levels in the root zone (7, 8). Three treatments were included: 1) fill soil with an aeration system, 2) fill soil without an aeration system, and 3) no fill (control).

The field soil at the study site was 29% sand, 53% silt, and 18% clay, with bulk density (mean of 15 samples) of 1.53 (g/cm³). Bulk density measurements were obtained using a core sampling method: Known volumes of soil were removed using a hand-driven core sampler (A.M.S., American Falls, Idaho) and dried for at least 24 hours in an oven (105°C [221°F]).

Textural analysis of the fill soil was very similar to that of the field soil (26% sand, 48% silt, and 26% clay). Fill was applied on each side of the cherry trees (planted on a berm 30 cm [11.8 in] high), but did not contact the root collars or trunks (Figure 1). The surface of the field soil was lightly scarified before application of fill to minimize boundary interface. Fill was applied over an area of 319 m² (22 m [18.7 ft] long and 14.5 m [11.2 ft] wide) to a depth of 30 cm and settled with water to a bulk density (mean of six samples) of 1.26 (g/cm³).

On half of the fill plot and prior to fill-soil installation, an aeration system consisting of 10-cm (3.9-in.) diameter perforated drainpipe in runs approximately 60 cm (23.6 in.) apart was placed on the field soil (Figure 2). A total of 12 runs of pipe, each 11 m (36 ft) long, was used. The ends of the aeration pipe were vented to the surface via risers in four locations, with the vents facing the prevailing winds and screened off to prevent entry of animals. The locations of the subsurface aeration pipes were marked with flags to identify subsequent aeration measurement sites.

Soil oxygen status was assessed by measurements of oxygen diffusion rate (ODR). ODR is believed to provide a better indication of aeration status than oxygen concentration because ODR measures the rate at which oxygen can diffuse through the soil to a simulated root surface (2). In a previous study, oxygen concentration was found to be relatively high (18% to 20%) in a landscape soil, while ODR was low (6). This result indicated that while oxygen concentration may be satisfactory, soil conditions may limit the diffusion of oxygen to respiring roots.

ODR was determined using an oxygen diffusion ratemeter (Model D, Jensen Instruments, Tacoma, Washington). The meter applies a current to platinum-tipped

Figure 1. Fill applied between berms.

Figure 2. Aeration system.

microelectrodes; the rate at which oxygen is consumed is indicated by changes in current (2).

Five electrodes were placed in a circular arrangement 5 cm (2 in.) apart from one another. For each treatment, three groups of five electrodes were spaced 140 cm (55 in.) apart from one another and aligned in a row. The mean of all fifteen electrodes was recorded as one measurement of oxygen diffusion rate for a particular location and time. ODR was measured at depths of 15 cm (5.9 in.) in the fill soil, 15 cm into the field soil, and 60 cm (23.6 in.) in the field soil, in both treatment and control sites (Figure 3). Measurements were made daily for 12-day periods over the study time (two years). Soil moisture was measured at corresponding depths in both treatment and control sites using tensiometers (Soil Moisture Equipment Corp., Santa Barbara, California). The plot was irrigated with overhead sprinklers as needed.

Data collection began seven weeks after application of fill (to allow time for settling within the fill). To adjust for differences in moisture, ODR data were analyzed (SAS) using analysis of covariance (unequal slopes). Treatment mean effects were compared by using least squares means.

Results
Fill Effects

The fill-soil treatment generally reduced ODR levels in the underlying field soil, but this effect was not consistent for all sampling locations and times. In year 1, the fill-soil treatment (no aeration system) significantly lowered ODR ($P = 0.05$) in the underlying field soil below that of the control at both 15 and 60 cm (Figure 4). In year 2, when electrodes were placed in the same place as year 1, there was no longer a significant effect at 15 cm, but at 60 cm ODR was significantly lower than control levels (Figure 5). After electrodes were repositioned in treatment plots (year 2), ODR at 15 cm in the field soil was found to be significantly lower than the control treatment, but at 60 cm there was no difference.

Aeration System Effects

The subsurface aeration system generally did not increase ODR levels in the underlying soil or within the fill, but as with fill effects, some variation did occur. Comparing the fill-with-aeration treatment with the control, no difference in ODR level was found

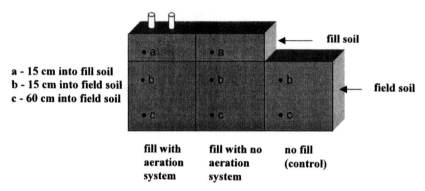

Figure 3. Depth of oxygen diffusion rate (ODR) measurements.

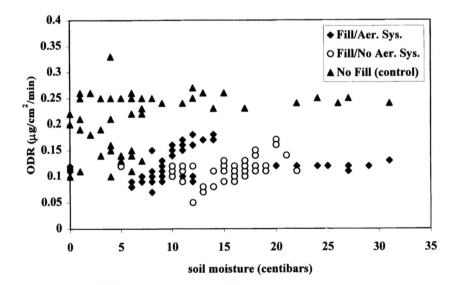

Figure 4. ODR in field soil: 60 cm, year 1, position 1.

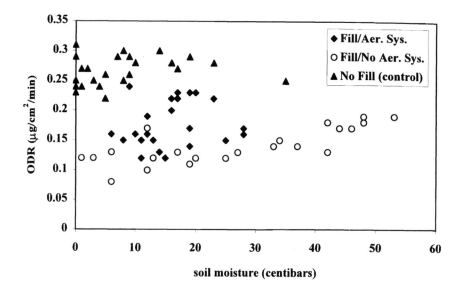

Figure 5. ODR in field soil: 60 cm, year 2, position 1.

at 15 cm in the field soil. At 60 cm however, the fill-with-aeration treatment was found to have significantly lower ODR levels than the control. In year 2, the aeration treatment was found to have significantly higher ODR levels than the control at 15 cm, but at 60 cm ODR was significantly less than the control. After electrodes were repositioned in the treatment plots (year 2), ODR levels were significantly lower in the aeration treatment than in the control at both 15 and 60 cm (Figure 6).

Comparing the fill-with-aeration treatment and the fill-without-aeration treatment, no difference in ODR levels was found in year 1 at 15 cm and 60 cm in the field soil. In year 2, however, fill-with-aeration had significantly higher ODR levels at both 15 and 60 cm. After electrodes were repositioned (year 2), no difference was found between the two treatments at both 15 and 60 cm.

Within the fill itself, ODR levels in the fill-with-aeration treatment were both lower (Figure 7) and higher than the fill-without-aeration treatment, depending on electrode location and measurement time.

Plant Response

Throughout the experiment, no differences in growth, health, or appearance were observed among any of the treatment trees. All trees appeared to be in good condition both before and after fill application. Although trunk diameter and shoot growth measurements were not made, measurements of root growth and location relative to the aeration system will be taken after fill soil has been removed.

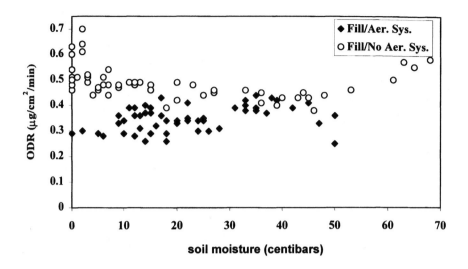

Figure 6. ODR in field soil: 60 cm, year 2, position 2.

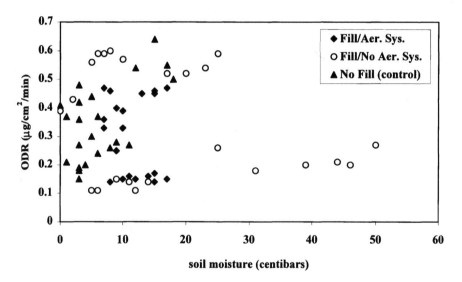

Figure 7. ODR in fill soil: 15 cm, year 1, position 1.

Discussion

In this study, fill soil generally caused a reduction in ODR levels in the underlying field soil, but this effect was variable. ODR was reduced in year 1 at 15 and 60 cm, in year 2 at 60 cm in location 1, and at 15 cm in location 2. We do not know why ODR was not reduced in year 2 at the 15 cm depth (location 1) or at the 60 cm depth (location 2), but it appears that the fill treatment did not have a uniform effect on aeration in the underlying soil. This result suggests that fill may substantially reduce ODR levels in some locations within an underlying field soil, while other locations may be unaffected. Reasons for this effect are likely linked both to the physically heterogeneous composition of many soils (1) and to the actual capacity of a fill to limit aeration.

Throughout the study, no differences in plant growth, health, or appearance resulted from any of the treatments. This finding was somewhat surprising considering the evidence that *Prunus mahaleb* is sensitive to flooding/low aeration injury. An ODR of 0.2 $\mu g/cm^2/min$ is considered to be a critical level (ODRc) for many species: Values less than 0.2 are thought to impair root function (9). In this study, some, but not all, ODR levels were below this threshold. If ODR levels in the root zone of treatment plots were below ODRc throughout the study, then severe plant injury should have been observed. The observation that no visible injury occurred suggests that parts of the root zone were above the ODRc for some period of time during the experiment. This assessment is consistent with the finding that field-soil ODR levels in fill treatments were not uniformly reduced by the fill. Evidently, some areas of the root zone were unaffected by the fill and these were sufficient in number and/or size to maintain adequate root respiration. Whether this occurred as a result of the fill depth, textural and structural characteristics, moisture content, or lateral movement of oxygen within the field soil is not known. We suspect that a combination of factors may have been involved.

No consistent improvement in ODR levels in the underlying field soil resulted from the subsurface aeration system. In most cases, ODR levels were equivalent to those found in the fill-without-aeration treatment. In some cases, ODR levels were either higher or lower than the fill-without-aeration treatment. In previous experiments in the laboratory and greenhouse (unpublished), we have not found a consistent increase in ODR levels resulting from similar aeration or coring treatments. These results agree with observations of corings made in golf greens and of vertical mulches in tree root zones where root development typically occurs within the core-replacement soil. Root growth is not enhanced in the soil adjacent to the core. This suggests that an "aeration-enhanced" zone next to the core may not occur.

On the basis of this study alone, it cannot be concluded that aeration systems are ineffective in improving the aeration status of soils impacted by fill. Our findings cast some doubt on the efficacy of such systems, but more work will be needed for a definitive assessment. Interactions between the field soil, the tree, and the fill are complex and under certain conditions benefits may result from an aeration system. At this point, however, we do not know what those conditions may be.

Our findings suggest that the impact of a fill on the growth and health of a tree is likely to be variable. In some cases, the tree will not show any visible effect; in other cases, it may be injured but not killed; and in other cases, the impact may be fatal. The magnitude of the impact will likely be determined by interactions between the tree, the fill soil, and the field soil. It is likely that soil texture, structure, moisture content, bulk density, and depth of both the field soil and the fill are key elements. For instance, a deep, compact, wet fill placed on a shallow, fine-textured field soil may have a greater impact on tree health than a shallow, low-density, dry fill placed on a deep well-structured field soil. In addition a number of tree-related factors need to be considered: the tolerance or susceptibility of the species to low ODR levels, tree age and health, the portion of the root zone affected by the fill (i.e., the area around the tree covered by fill), and the timing of the fill event relative to the stage of tree development (e.g., dormant season versus the growing season). In addition, whether the fill soil is placed in contact with the tree trunk or root crown may be very important. All these factors related to the tree, fill soil, and field soil (and their interactions) are likely to determine the level of impact of a fill event. Further work is needed to assess the relative contribution of each factor to fill-induced changes in root zone aeration.

Acknowledgments

This research was supported by the Elvenia J. Slosson Endowment Fund for Environmental Horticulture and by a Jastro-Shields Graduate Research Award.

Literature Cited

1. Craul, P.J. 1992. Urban Soil in Landscape Design. John Wiley & Sons, New York, NY.

2. Glinski, J., and W. Stepniewski. 1985. Soil Aeration and Its Role for Plants. CRC Press, Boca Raton, FL.

3. Harris, R.W. 1992. Arboriculture: Integrated Management of Landscape Trees, Shrubs, and Vines (2nd ed.). Prentice-Hall, Englewood Cliffs, NJ.

4. Heritage, A.D., and J.M. Duniway. 1985. Influence of depleted oxygen supply on Phytopthora root rot of safflower in nutrient solution. In Parker, C.A., A.D. Rovira, K.J. Moore, K.J., and P.T.W. Wong (Eds.). Ecology and Management of Soilborne Plant Pathogens. Proc. of section 5 of the Fourth Intl. Congress of Plant Pathology. The American Phytopathological Society, St. Paul, MN. 358 pp.

5. Jacobs, K.A., J.D. MacDonald, L.R. Costello, A.M. Berry, and T. Berger. 1992. The effect of oxygen stress and soil aeration management on susceptibility of oaks to Phytopthora root rot. Report of the Elvenia J. Slosson Endowment for Ornamental Horticulture. (In Press.)

6. MacDonald, J.D., L.R. Costello, and T. Berger, T. 1993. *An evaluation of soil aeration status around healthy and declining oaks in an urban environment in California*. J. Arboric. 19:4:209–218.

7. Perry, R.L. 1987. Cherry rootstocks. In Rom, R.C., and R.F. Carlson (Eds.) Rootstocks for Fruit Crops. John Wiley & Sons, New York, NY.

8. Rowe, R.N., and D.V. Beardsell. 1973. *Waterlogging of fruit trees*. Hort. Abstr. 43:9:533–548.

9. Stolzy, L.H., and J. Letey. 1964. *Correlation of plant response to soil oxygen diffusion rates*. Hilgardia. 35:20:567–576.

Tree Root System Enhancement with Paclobutrazol

Gary W. Watson

Paclobutrazol (PBZ) was applied as a basal soil injection or drench at 2 g a.i. per inch dbh. PBZ treatment was effective in stimulating fine root development of established pin oaks (*Quercus palustris*) and white oaks (*Q. alba*). PBZ treatment may be effective in stabilizing declining trees with insufficient fine root development. Root regeneration of transplanted balled-and-burlapped (B&B) black maple trees (*Acer nigrum*) was increased by PBZ treatment. Root elongation and total root growth were doubled. This could result in faster establishment of transplanted trees. In greenhouse pot tests using American elms (*Ulmus americana*), root-pruned trees responded to lower rates of PBZ, and shoot growth was regulated for a shorter period. Enhanced short-term top growth regulation and root growth stimulation at low PBZ rates would be ideal for treatment at transplanting.

Root development of mature landscape trees can be inadequate to support the crown (16), especially when root space is more constricted than crown space, after root damage, or following transplanting. Root system enhancement and crown size control are two approaches to restoring the balance between the crown and root system.

The growth regulator paclobutrazol (PBZ), a gibberellin biosynthesis inhibitor, has been shown to reduce the shoot growth of many species (4) and is commonly used to control the regrowth of trees under utility lines. This growth regulator has promise for use in the landscape wherever control of plant size is needed. In some situations, it can also increase root growth (1, 2, 4, 14, 17). Reports of the effect of PBZ on root systems often include an increase in the root/shoot ratio (8, 10, 12).

The current commercially available formulation of PBZ (Profile 2SC, Dow AgroSciences, Indianapolis, Indiana) is applied as a basal soil injection or drench. It is relatively inexpensive (less than US$20 for a mature tree) and can be applied rapidly (less than 5 minutes per tree).

Only a few roots at the base of the tree are in direct contact with the PBZ. The PBZ is absorbed by these roots and translocated in the xylem, towards the branch tips (3). The stimulation of root development must be an indirect effect, because the chemical is never in contact with roots more than a 20 to 30 cm (8 to 12 in.) from the base of the tree. Photosynthesis is not reduced by PBZ treatments (6, 9, 15). Increases in root growth may be due partially to increased carbohydrate supply to roots (5, 14). Higher levels of abscisic acid (ABA) often associated with PBZ treatment have been shown

Gary W. Watson, The Morton Arboretum, Lisle, IL 60532.

to maintain growth of roots under drought stress (7). An increase in fine root development implies a more favorable balance between the crown and root system, and less stress in treated trees. Reduced water use and improved water status has been reported after treatment with PBZ (11, 12, 13, 15). Apparent improvements in vigor, color, and drought resistance may be related to a greater capacity of the root system to absorb moisture and mineral nutrients from the soil.

Mature Tree Studies

The paclobutrazol was applied as a basal soil injection within 20 cm (7.9 in.) of the trunk base. A Series 3600 Soil Injection Closed System (Springfield Specialties Co., Springfield, Pennsylvania) was used to inject the diluted (79 mL/L) solution into the soil in 250 mL aliquots for a total of 2.0 g active ingredient (100 mL dilute solution) per caliper inch.

In one experiment, two rows (seven trees each) of pin oak (*Quercus palustris*) trees, between 21 and 27 cm (8.3 to 10.6 in.) dbh were selected from the middle of a large, evenly spaced block of trees on the grounds of The Morton Arboretum. The two rows were separated by a row of unused trees. The trees were in excellent condition. One row of trees was treated with PBZ on August 28, 1989; the other row served as untreated controls.

In September 1992, fine root development was measured using root-density cores. Soil was washed from the roots, and oak roots were separated from other roots and debris by hand. Roots were digitized at 300 dpi resolution, and root surface area was measured with an image analysis system.

PBZ increased fine root density of pin oaks by 92% in the upper 10 cm (3.9 in.) of soil (Figure 1). At approximately 10 cm of soil depth, there was an abrupt change to a more dense and clayey soil horizon. Increases in root density were inconsistent and not significant in this subsoil. This implies that poor-quality soils may have to be improved before PBZ can be effective in improving root development. The visual difference in appearance between treated and control pin oaks was negligible and was limited to a slightly greener leaf color.

In a second experiment, mature white oaks (*Q. alba*) on the grounds of The Morton Arboretum were treated with PBZ. The trees were 50 to 70 cm (19.7 to 27.6 in.) dbh with large, open-grown crowns and located within 500 m (547 yd) of each other. All were in a state of decline as judged by the amount of dieback, tufted growth, and chlorosis in the crown. Four trees were treated and four were untreated controls. Treatment date, rate and method of application, and root sampling procedure were the same as for the pin oaks.

PBZ treatment increased root density of the white oaks from 280 to 460 mm^2 root surface area per cm^3 soil. The first sign of crown improvement (slightly greener color) of the white oaks was observed the second year after treatment. At the time of the root sampling, three full seasons after the treatments were applied, the crowns of the declining white oaks were showing signs of improvement. Color and vigor was improving. Unfortunately, at that time, the majority of the trees included in the study were cut down for reasons unrelated to the study, and too few remained for meaningful

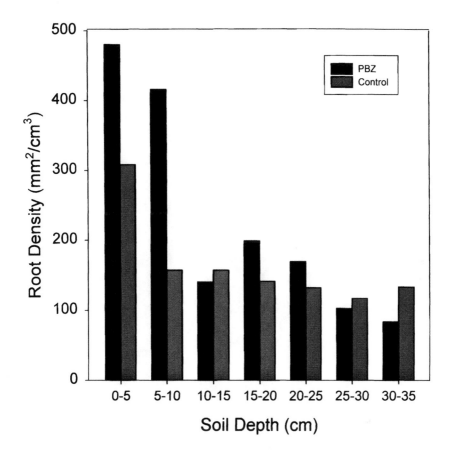

Figure 1. Fine root development of pin oaks after PBZ basal soil injection treatment. Roots were sampled 1 m (3.3 ft) from soil injection site. The greatest root density increases were in the 10-cm-thick (3.9 in.) topsoil layer.

crown growth data to be collected. Of the few trees that did survive, a severely declining tree that was treated with PBZ continued to show crown improvement through 1996, seven years after a single treatment (Figure 2). New growth was deep green and vigorous, and the leaves were not noticeably smaller. In most summers, the leaves were much less scorched by midsummer compared to leaves of a neighboring tree (Figure 3).

In the first two experiments, root development was not assessed until the crown began to show visible signs of improvement, three years after treatment. It is not known how fast the root system responded to the PBZ treatment, or which came first, crown or root improvements. A third experiment has been initiated to answer this question, again using mature white oaks. In the third year, the typical greening usually associated with PBZ treatment could be observed in many trees, but there were not yet any measurable differences in root, twig, or leaf growth. The larger, fuller

Figure 2. White oak treated with a PBZ basal soil injection. Photos were taken prior to treatment (top) and seven years after treatment (bottom).

crowns of this group of oaks may account for the slower response (more chemical must be moved a greater distance).

Growth regulator treatment is not a quick cure for mature declining trees. It will take several years for any visible crown response to develop. Rapidly declining trees could die before the treatment would have a chance to stabilize them. PBZ treatments may prove to be more useful on trees in the very early stages of decline, or as preventive maintenance on mature, but still healthy trees.

Transplanted-Tree Studies

The sampling method used in the studies with mature trees could not distinguish between possible increases in root branching and/or elongation. Visual observation suggested that the fine roots were more profusely branched (Figure 4). Knowing the specific effect of PBZ on root growth and morphology is important in relation to future applications of this technology in the landscape. In situations such as transplanting, where roots have been severed and must grow long distances to reestablish the original root spread, a rapid elongation rate is important, perhaps more important than increased fine root proliferation. Several studies have been initiated to provide this information.

Ten 7-cm (1.6 in.) caliper black maples (*Acer nigrum*) were transplanted in late fall of 1996. Ten trees were not transplanted. Half of each group were treated with PBZ as a basal soil drench at 2 g a.i. per inch caliper prior to budbreak the following

Figure 3. Leaves of white oak trees treated with PBZ (right) showed less marginal and intervenal leaf scorch than untreated controls.

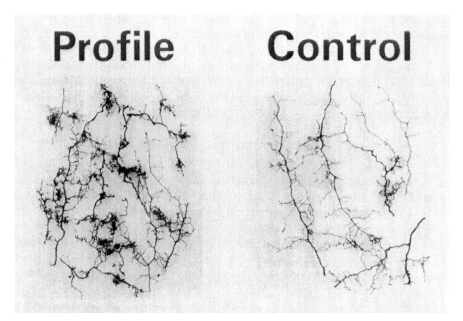

Figure 4. Pin oak fine roots from a tree treated with PBZ (left) and an untreated control (right). PBZ was applied as a basal injection and roots were sampled 1.5 m (4.9 ft) from trunk.

spring. The four treatments (five trees each) were: transplanted + PBZ; nontransplanted + PBZ; transplanted without PBZ; and nontransplanted without PBZ (control).

In September 1997, root regeneration was measured by harvesting all of the roots growing from a 30-cm-wide, 20-cm-deep section of the rootball. Roots of nontransplanted trees were also severed in this same area to observe root regrowth. This small amount of root damage (less than 10% of the rootball circumference and less than one-third of the depth of a standard rootball) was not enough to cause stress, and provided a good comparison of root regeneration potential between vigorous nontransplanted trees and stressed transplanted trees. The longest root from each tree was measured, and all roots were oven dried and weighed after harvesting.

PBZ increased root dry weight in both the transplanted and nontransplanted trees (Figure 5). The longest roots of transplanted trees treated with PBZ were up to 90 cm (35.4 in.). Without PBZ, the longest root of transplanted trees was 45 cm (17.7 in). In both transplanted and nontransplanted trees, root dry weights were approximately doubled by the PBZ treatment.

Both root elongation and branching appear to be increased by PBZ treatment. It usually takes a transplanted tree several years to regrow the normal spreading root system that was lost during harvest. Increased root elongation would result in faster replacement of the normal spread of the root system. Increased branching would mean faster proliferation of fine roots into the enlarged soil volume occupied by the root system of PBZ-treated trees. Based on the first year data from these maples, it is possible that transplanted trees could become established in half the normal time after PBZ treatment. Additional work is continuing to confirm these early results.

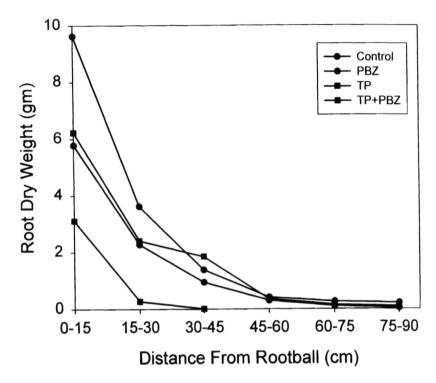

Figure 5. Root regeneration of B&B black maples during the first season. The maximum length of regenerated roots was twice as long as for the transplanted trees after PBZ treatment. PBZ treatment doubled the total regenerated dry root weight.

If shoot growth regulation persists too long, PBZ treatment may not be of much practical value for transplanted trees. Vigorous growth is expected to return once the tree is established. Greenhouse pot experiments using elm seedlings showed that shoot growth of root-pruned plants (analogous to root loss from B&B transplanting) was regulated at a lower rate than nonroot-pruned plants (analogous to nontransplanted trees), and the growth regulation lasted for a shorter period of time (Figure 6). Top-growth regulation of the "transplanted trees" at the lower rate was greatest up to formation of the seventh leaf (indicated by more negative values), and then began to lessen. At the higher rate, in both "transplanted" and "nontransplanted" trees, shoot growth was more regulated, but almost equally so. If this holds true in field tests with larger trees, very low rates of PBZ applied at planting time could be very effective without the prolonged effects that would slow shoot growth after the tree is established.

Conclusion

Paclobutrazol treatments can increase root growth and show promise for use as a treatment for trees under stress resulting from underdeveloped root systems. Trees showing early signs of stress and decline may benefit the most. The response is prob-

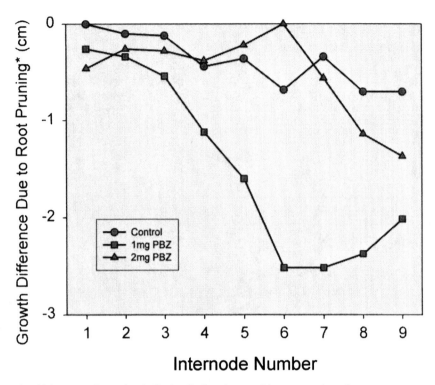

* a higher negative value indicates that root pruned trees grew less than
  non-root pruned trees treated at a similar rate

Figure 6. Shoot growth of root-pruned, container-grown elms (like B&B transplanted trees) was regulated at a lower rate of PBZ than nonroot-pruned elms (like nontransplanted trees). At this low rate, the shoot growth regulation began to decrease in the last third of the experiment.

ably not rapid enough in large trees to be useful as a treatment for rapidly declining trees. Trees that have restricted root environments may benefit, especially when treatment is combined with mulching or other procedures that improve the root environment. Transplanted trees, or trees that have lost large portions of their root system from construction activities, may regenerate the lost roots faster and be stressed for a shorter period if treated with PBZ. Treatment as part of a Plant Health Care program may also prove beneficial in maintaining a high root/shoot ratio and high vigor. Much more research is needed to understand the potential benefits of paclobutrazol treatments in enhancing root development.

Literature Cited

1. Ashokan, P.K., W.R. Chaney, and G.S. Premachandra. 1995. *Soil-applied paclobutrazol affects leaf water relations and growth of American elm* (Ulmus americana L.) *seedlings.* Plant Growth Reg. Soc. Amer. Quar. 23:1–12.

2. Bausher, M.C., and G. Yelenosky. 1986. *Sensitivity of potted citrus plants to top sprays and soil applications of paclobutrazol.* HortScience 21:141–143.

3. Couture, R. 1982. *A new experimental growth regulator from ICI.* Proc. Growth Regulat. Soc. Amer. 9:59.

4. Davis, T.D., N. Sankhla, R.H. Walser, and A. Upadhyaya. 1985. *Promotion of adventitious root formation on cuttings by paclobutrazol.* HortScience 20:883–884.

5. Davis, T.D., G.L. Steffens, and N. Sankhla. 1988. Triazole plant growth regulators. Hort. Rev. 10:63–105.

6. DeJong, T.M., and J.F. Doyle. 1984. *Leaf gas exchange and growth responses of mature 'Fantasia' nectarine trees to paclobutrazol.* J. Amer. Soc. Hort. Sci. 109:878–882.

7. Kozlowski, T.T., and S.G. Pallardy. 1997. Growth Control in Woody Plants. Academic Press, New York, NY. 641 pp.

8. Marquard, R.D. 1985. *Chemical growth regulation of pecan seedlings.* HortScience 20:919–921.

9. Rieger, M., and G. Scalabrelli. 1990. *Paclobutrazol, root growth, hydraulic conductivity and nutrient uptake of 'Nemaguard' peach.* HortScience 25:95–98.

10. Ruter, J.M. 1994. *Growth and landscape establishment of* Pyracantha *and* Juniperus *after application of paclobutrazol.* HortScience 29: 1318–1320.

11. Ruter, J.M., and C.A. Martin. 1994. *Effects of contrasting climate and paclobutrazol on the growth and water use of two container-grown landscape plants.* J. Environ. Hort. 12:27–32.

12. Swietlik, D., and S.S. Miller. 1983. *The effect of paclobutrazol on growth and response to water stress of apple seedlings.* J. Amer. Soc. Hort. Sci. 108:1076–1080.

13. Wample, R.L., and E.B. Culver. 1983. *The influence of paclobutrazol, a new growth regulator, on sunflowers.* J. Amer. Soc. Hort. Sci. 108:122–125.

14. Wang, S.Y., and M. Faust. 1986. *Effect of growth retardants on root formation and polyamine content in apple seedlings.* M. Amer. Soc. Hort. Sci. 111:912–917.

15. Warren, S.L., F.A. Blazich, and M. Thetford. 1991. *Whole-plant response of selected woody landscape species to uniconazole.* J. Environ. Hort. 9:163–167.

16. Watson, G.W. 1991. *Attaining root:crown balance in landscape trees.* J. Arboric. 17:211–216.

17. Watson, G.W. 1996. *Tree root system enhancement with paclobutrazol.* J. Arboric. 22:211–217.

Planning Installation of Underground Services

Dealga P. O'Callaghan

In Britain, all essential services have been underground for many years, and street trees have accommodated to the situation. The threat to street trees has therefore been from maintenance rather that installation. However, during the early 1990s the arrival of cable television resulted in hundreds of thousands of kilometres of cable being placed underground in urban areas. This led to a public outcry, confrontations with municipal arborists, and a lot of acrimony. Developments have led to a partial solution. The problem is assessed against the legal framework governing the regulation of trees and the environment in Britain; a way forward, which has been demonstrably successful in other areas of conflict, is proposed.

In the United Kingdom, the tendency has been to locate all essential services underground whenever possible. This has been the case for many years and, in most towns and cities, what will strike the North American arborist is the total lack of overhead lines, except for some telephone distribution lines in the older residential areas. All other services—electricity, gas, water, telecommunications, and most recently, cable television—are below ground.

Because services such as telecommunications and electricity (normally found aboveground in other countries) have largely been below ground for so long in Britain, the urban tree population has accommodated to these services. The main threat to urban trees has not been the installation but rather the maintenance of services. However, in the early 1990s the equilibrium was upset by the arrival of the cable television revolution. Almost overnight, whole streets were being opened to install the new cables; the roots of many street trees, and those in private gardens adjacent to the streets, were cut. The reaction from the public was initially mixed as they balanced the "benefits" of cable television with the damage to the trees, but within 18 months or so, the balance tipped in favour of the trees as the magnitude of the project became evident.

Providing cable television to all major cities and towns in Britain is a monumental task. In the city of Liverpool (a major provincial city with approximately 650,000 people) and the surrounding urban communities of Sefton, St. Helens, Knowsley, and Wirral, this involved hundreds of thousands of kilometres of cable. The cost for the

Dealga P. O'Callaghan, Managing Director and Principal Consultant, Environmental Consultants International Ltd., Suite 328, Queens Dock Commercial Centre, 67 Norfolk Street, Liverpool L1 0BG, England.

Liverpool installation alone was some £16 million (US$25 million). The costs for major cities such as London and Birmingham can only be guessed. As demand for cable television grew in response to advertising, there was urgency about the work, and care was not always taken by the contract crews. Inevitably, conflicts arose between the arboricultural officers in the municipalities, who are charged with managing the urban tree population, and the cable companies who were anxious to get customers on line as quickly as possible.

This controversy had the effect of focusing the minds of arboriculturists and engineers alike on the issue of the proper planning of underground installation and the protection of tree roots. How this evolved (and was to some degree resolved) must be viewed within the context of the legal framework that regulates both tree work and engineering work in the United Kingdom

The Environmental Legal Framework

Trees are heavily regulated in Britain and have been since 1947 when the first of the Planning Acts of the postwar era was passed. Although the concept of protecting trees by means of tree preservation orders (TPOs) has existed since the 1930s, it was the 1947 Town and Country Planning Act that created TPOs as we know them. This legislation has been consolidated and strengthened over the years and is currently contained within the 1990 Town and Country Planning Act (1) at Chapter 8, Part VIII—Special Controls, Chapter 1, Trees, Sections 197–214.

Essentially, at Section 197, the act places a statutory duty upon local authorities (municipalities) to protect trees and, at Section 198, provides them with the power to create tree preservation orders to accomplish this. In addition, local authorities have the power to impose conditions for the protection of trees on any planning permit granted for development of any kind. The 1991 Planning and Compensation Act provides the courts with the power to impose fines of up to £20,000 (US$32,000) or twice the value of the tree, whichever is the greater, per tree, for violation of a TPO or for a breach of planning conditions.

As the legislation currently stands, utilities can override local planning restrictions when the restrictions would interfere with their statutory duty to provide a supply, although this is to be changed by the current Parliament. However, cable television is not seen as a utility because it is not an essential service such as water, gas, electricity, or telephone and as such does not have the benefit of the exemption.

In addition to the Town and Country Planning Act, other acts of Parliament relate directly to the protection of trees and the environment, for example, the Countryside and Wildlife Act of 1981, the Food and Environment Protection Act of 1985, and the Forestry Acts (as amended), (1). As if this were not enough, there are also European directives (European Community laws) covering similar aspects, for example, the Environmental Assessment Directive (85/335/EEC), the Habitat Directive (92/43/EEC), and the Electricity Deregulation Directive (96/92/EC) (4). The latter may seem out of place, but this directive ranks environmental protection equally with security, regularity, and continuity of supply, which are major public service obligation placed upon utilities. A summary of the legislation is set out at Table 1.

The Engineering and General Legal Framework

Quite apart from the environmental laws, there are other acts of Parliament that impact utilities (Table 2). For example, regional electricity companies (RECs) are governed by the Electricity Act of 1989. At Paragraph 9 of Schedule 4 to this Act, it is clearly stated that:

> (7) Where a license holder exercises any powers conferred under sub-paragraph (4) or (6) above, he shall:
>
> (a) cause the trees to be felled or lopped or their roots cut back in accordance with good arboricultural practice and so as to do as little damage as possible to trees....

Table 1. Summary of environmental and environmentally related legislation.

Act of Parliament/directive	Main functions
The Electricity Act, 1989	Paragraph 9 of Schedule 4: "All work to be done in accordance with good arboricultural practice ..."
European Directive 96/92/EC	Directs that all work must be undertaken with due regard for the environment; and that environmental issues rank equally with Security & Regularity of Supply.
The Town & County Planning Act, 1990	Legislates for Tree Preservation Orders (TPO), Conservation Areas, and other designations, such as AONB, SSSI, etc.
The Countryside & Wildlife Act, 1981	Protects flora, fauna, habitats, etc.
The Food & Environment Protection Act, 1985	Provides for labeling and control of pesticides, etc.
The Forestry Acts (as amended)	Provides for felling licenses, etc.
European Directive 85/337/EEC	Legislation requiring Environmental Impact Assessments for large-scale projects.
European Directive 92/43/EEC	Habitat Directive: Legislates for the protection of habitats and scheduled species.

Table 2. Acts of Parliament that concern utilities.

Act of Parliament	Purpose, industry, and company
Telecommunications Act, 1984	Privatization of British Telecom and opening of market to competition.
Gas Act, 1986	Privatization of British Gas; followed by opening the market to competition.
Electricity Act, 1989	Privatization of Electricity Boards and setting up of regional electricity companies, generators, and transmission companies, and introduction of competition.
Water Industry Act, 1991	Privatization of Water Boards and opening the market to competition.

It is significant that this is the only area in the law where mention is made of "good arboricultural practice" and where roots are specifically mentioned. Nonstatutory standards and guides are available to assist utility companies in meeting their obligations under the 1989 act, for example, the British Standards Institute's Guide to Trees in Relation to Construction (BS 5837) and its "Recommendations for Tree Work" (BS 3998) (2), which is currently being revised and will include utility arboriculture as a separate section. There is, therefore, no excuse for damage being caused to trees by utilities in either aboveground or underground operations.

All industries in Britain, including the utilities, are bound by the Health and Safety at Work Act of 1974 and associated regulations (1). As with the Electricity Act, there are numerous nonstatutory guides and codes governing work in the utility sector. The most significant of these as related to arboriculture are the Electricity Association Technical Guide (G55/1) of 1997 (3) and the Health and Safety Guidance Note (GS48) (5). These are set out at Table 3.

Table 3. Nonstatutory guidance notes, codes of practice, and standards.

Source and title	Purpose/relevant content
NJUG 10, *Guidelines for the Planning, Installation & Maintenance of Utility Services in Proximity to Trees*	Guidelines and methodologies primarily for the installation of underground cables in locations close to trees. Little guidance on over-ground utility work close to trees.
Electricity Association Engineering Recommendation G55/1, Issue 1, 1997, *Safe Tree Working in Proximity to Overhead Electric Lines*	Code of practice requiring utility arborists to be competent and properly certified. Also contains extensive guidelines.
Health & Safety Executive Guidance Note GS48, *Training & Standards of Competence for Users of Chainsaws in Agriculture, Arboriculture & Forestry*	Defines the criteria for training and competencies required for safe use of chainsaws.
British Standards Institute (BSI) publications BS 3998, *Recommendations for Tree Work* BS 5837, *Guide for Trees in Relation to Construction*	Equivalent to ANSI. Equivalent to ANSI A300. Specific guidance on all aspects of trees and the construction process; a very thorough document.

The New Roads and Street Works Act of 1993 governs the requirements for training and competence, notification, road closures, signage, etc. for contractors working on public highways. As such, it relates directly to the installation of underground of utility services and is a severe piece of legislation. It is designed to protect the public and any operatives and to minimise disruption.

Summary of Legal Framework

In short, the utilities find themselves within a complex framework of legislation, regulation, and licensing and have had public service obligations placed upon them in an increasingly competitive environment. They function in a complex environment and few have taken the step of employing professional arboriculturists or environmentalists to assist them in meeting their obligations. The complexity of the situation is represented at Figure 1.

The green industry is also remiss in not representing itself in a professional manner to the utilities. Therefore, when advice is sought by utilities on the matter of dealing with tree roots and underground services, it has been invariably from the wrong profession. More often than not, it has been sought from landscape architects or related environmental professionals who deal mostly with environmental impact statements at macro levels and are inexperienced in dealing with the problems of

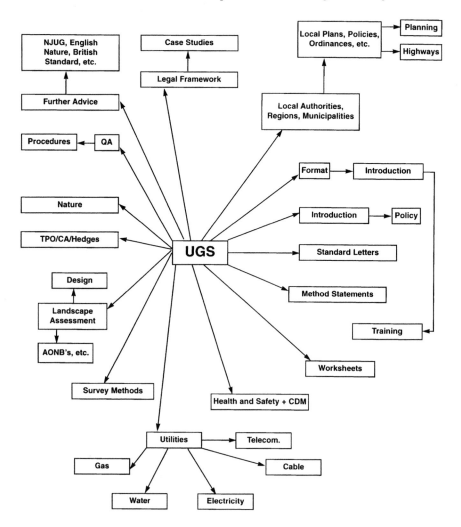

Figure 1. Spider diagram illustrating the complexity of legislation/regulation and controls that affect underground operations.

implementation faced by the utilities. The end result has been conflict, confrontation, and loss of trees due to root damage.

Recent Developments

Stemming from the public outcry and the confrontations between the cable television industry and local authorities, some initiatives have evolved. For example, one of the London boroughs initiated a study of the effects of trenching upon the health and stability of street trees. Most significantly perhaps, the National Joint Utilities Group (NJUG), a representative body for utilities, produced a technical publication (6) dealing specifically with installation and maintenance of utility services in proximity to trees.

This technical publication, known as NJUG 10, deals primarily with the installation of underground services and provides detailed information on how roots are damaged and methodologies for their protection. It also provides a basic legislative framework. The publication also provides a series of recommendations for use when special precautions are required when trenching close to trees (Figure 2). These NJUG recommendations are considered a "rule of thumb" approach which, although better than nothing, does not have any scientific basis. However, the recommendations do convince contractors to take some care. A serious drawback to NJUG 10 is that it is a voluntary guideline and contractors are not bound to adhere to it, although local authority arboricultural officers can insist on its application when trees are the subject of statutory controls (i.e., TPOs and planning conditions) or are within Conservation Areas or other designated areas such as sites of special scientific interest, Areas of Outstanding Natural Beauty, National Parks, and the like.

Another problem with the NJUG guidelines is that they were introduced well after the cable television was being installed. At the time, many contracts had been let out by competitive bid, and the requirements for the protection of roots (i.e., hand digging, trenchless technology) had not been factored into the work specifications under which the contracts had been awarded. The implication of the guidelines was a significant increase in price after the contract had been awarded and, in some instances, started. Many contractors were understandably reluctant to implement the guidelines because of costs and delays in completion.

NJUG 10 Is Only a Partial Solution

Although well intentioned, and in many ways and a significant step forward, the NJUG guidelines fell far short of being effective. The main reason for this was that NJUG 10 did not provide any guidance as to how the guidelines could be implemented within the legislative framework. The technologies for protection of roots have been available for many years. However, contractors will always take the line of least resistance—and this has traditionally involved using mechanical excavators to open trenches quickly and efficiently, even though NJUG 10 provided a model for the layout of underground utility services (Figure 3.)

Some of the lead bodies in the green industry (e.g., the National Urban Forestry Unit [NUFU], the Arboricultural Association [AA], and the International Society of

PROTECTING ROOTS
(1)   Establish a protection zone around each tree:

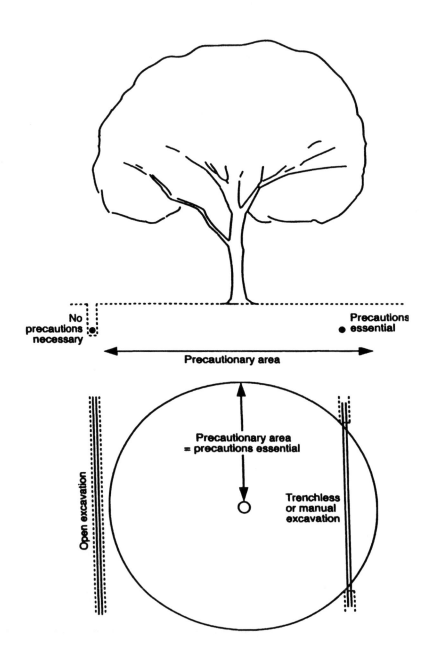

Figure 2. From NJUG 10.

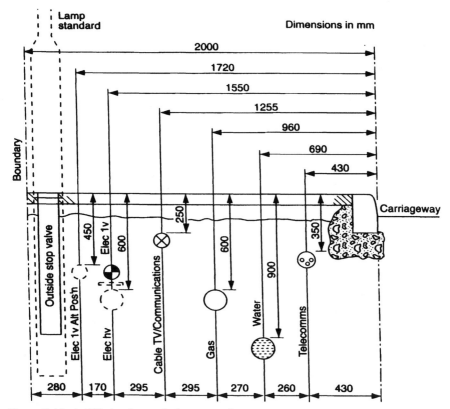

Figure 3. Ideal utility landscape below ground.

Arboriculture [ISA]) published material in both written and video form, explaining the techniques in some considerable detail. NUFU organised a series of technical workshops in an effort to spread the tree root protection message. However, the effects of these initiatives have been negligible and trees continue to be damaged.

What is missing from the initiatives to date is a proper, planned approach to the installation of underground services. It is ironic that all the elements of how to install underground services without damaging tree roots are in place but there has been no initiative until now to integrate these elements into the framework of legislation, regulations, guidelines, and codes of practice.

The Way Forward

What is proposed to advance the situation is the use of a standard *pro forma* approach to the problem. The planning legislation provides a workable framework into which the pro forma approach can easily be fitted. Indeed, this has already been accomplished for the protection of trees on construction sites (7). This system utilises all the existing planning legislation, planning regulations, and government advice and empowers local authorities to ensure the complete protection of trees on construction sites. Furthermore, the success of the approach lies not just in a user-friendly approach for local authorities, but more significantly that it is equally user-friendly for building contractors.

The same approach is being developed for the utility sector as a joint venture between Environmental Consultants and O'Callaghan Associates. This approach provides a Supplementary Planning Guidance note (SPG) that details how local authorities will seek to regulate the installation of underground services near trees under their jurisdiction and contains, but is not limited to, notification procedures, survey requirements, required survey drawings, required tree details, details of routes to be followed, selection procedures for contractors, training requirements, required specifications, preferred technologies, required worksheets and site notes, and recordkeeping requirements.

By spelling out in detail what is required, the local authority can exert a great deal of pressure upon the utilities and their contractors to follow the system. The effect of the SPG is to remove confrontation from the process and to make it more economic for both sides to work together.

The local authority SPG note or *pro forma* packet contains a checklist of requirements to be met by the utility, a model method statement, a series of standard letters covering the various notifications, a cross-reference to statutory controls and policies, an inspection and policing procedure, and an enforcement procedure

The utility/contractor *pro forma* packet contains a checklist of requirements to satisfy the local authority, model survey sheets, a method statement template, guidance for selection of contractors, foreman/team leader model worksheets, model specifications, site inspection records, model compliance certificates, and a model personnel training and competency record.

The information is supplied in digital form as well as hard copy. A guidance booklet accompanies each packet purchased by the utilities. This procedure will be part of ISA's Sustainability of Resources Programme (SORP), and training in its use is an integral part of the product.

To date, a number of areas of work in which protection of trees is involved have been developed using the *pro forma*/template format and are being used successfully, especially in the creation and administration of tree preservation orders (8), the protection of trees on construction sites, (7) and in mortgage risk assessment. All are part of the SORP Programme.

Conclusions

The success of the *pro forma*/template approach in addressing problems with trees in urban situations lies in the fact that it is very user friendly and has built-in checks and balances. It is nearly impossible to go wrong, as the process is logical and in a step-by-step format.

There is every reason to be optimistic that this approach, demonstrably successful in other applications, will be successful when applied to the installation of underground services near to trees. Once the procedure is in place, it becomes almost impossible not to use it because it makes life easier for all involved and removes the confrontational aspects that have plagued this area of tree protection.

Perhaps the most attractive aspect of the approach is that it utilises existing legislation and regulations and integrates the components so that all concerned are empowered to work together to protect the trees. Economically, it is attractive to utility companies and their contractors because it removes the delays and expenses that result from confrontational impasses which have, until now, dominated this industry.

Most important, the process is infinitely variable. As new technologies and methodologies are developed, they can be assessed, tested, and integrated into the programme. Because of this aspect, the SORP programme, like all the others, is updated regularly.

The way forward is clear—a *pro forma*/template approach will protect and preserve tree roots from the work of contractors.

Literature Cited

1. **Acts of Parliament (1974 through 1991)**
    The Health & Safety at Work Act, 1975
    The Forestry Act, 1979 (as Amended)
    The Countryside & Wildlife Act, 1981
    Telecommunications Act, 1984
    The Food & Environment Protection Act, 1985
    The Gas Act, 1986
    The Electricity Act, 1989
    The Town & Country Planning Act, 1990
    The Planning & Compensation Act, 1991
    The Water Act, 1991
    HMSO Publications
2. **British Standards Institute Publications**
    BS 3998:1989, Recommendations for Tree Work
    BS 5837:1991, Guide for Trees in Relation to Construction
    BSI Publications UK
3. **Electricity Association Engineering Recommendations G55/1, Issue 1, 1998**
    Safe Tree Working in Proximity to Overhead Electric Lines
4. **European Directive 85/337/EEC (1985)**
    On the Assessment of the Effects of Certain Public and Private Projects on the Environment
    European Directive 92/43/EEC (1992)
    On the Conservation of Natural Habitats and Wild Flora & Fauna
    European Directive 96/92/EC (1996)
    Concerning the Common Rules for the Internal Market in Electricity
    EU Publications
5. **Health & Safety Guidance Note GS48 (1997)**
    Training & Standards of Competence for users of Chainsaws in Agriculture, Arboriculture & Forestry
    HMSO Publications

6. National Joint Utility Group (1995)
    Guidelines for the Planning, Installation and Maintenance of Utility Services in Proximity to Trees.
    NJUG Technical Publication No. 10.
7. O'Callaghan, D.P., and M. Lawson. 1995. Trees and development conflicts: The importance of advance planning and site control in tree preservation plans. **In** Watson, G.W., and D. Neely (Eds.). Proceedings of the Trees and Buildings Conference. International Society of Arboriculture, Champaign, IL.
8. SORP. 1997. Tree Preservation Orders PGS/QA. International Society of Arboriculture, Champaign, IL.

Tree Roots and Infrastructure

Örjan Stål and Kaj Rolf

Tree roots that penetrate sewer pipes and disrupt their function can have serious economic consequences. Agencies or persons responsible for sewer systems could reduce or avoid root intrusion by siting pipes away from existing mature trees, by reducing the number of pipe joints, and by ensuring that pipes are properly installed. Agencies or persons responsible for parks and public gardens can also minimize or prevent root intrusion by planting only slow-growing species with nonaggressive root systems near sewers.

Both living and nonliving installations are necessary in urban environments, but these two features occasionally come into conflict, creating difficult economic, technical, and ecological problems. Common examples (9) of conflicts arising between infrastructure and vegetation are

- tree roots that grow into sewer pipes, impair their function, and reduce their effective lives
- tree roots that deform gas and water pipes
- plant roots that disrupt paved surfaces (including tramlines) and reduce their lifetimes
- tree root systems that cause subsidence damage to houses and buildings on clay soils
- excavations near existing trees (damage to root systems, lowered water table)
- reduced volume of soil and reduced availability of water to trees
- transport of heavy machinery outside paved areas, leading to soil compaction, which creates conditions unfavorable for root growth
- effects of pollution (road salt, chemical herbicides) on vegetation

It has become apparent in recent years that tree roots penetrating into sewers and disrupting their function (sewer blockages and basement flooding) are a more serious problem than was previously suspected. The results from a survey (7) carried out between 1993 and 1995 showed that practically all urban areas of Sweden were affected by root intrusion into sewer pipes. The annual cost of repairing root damage to the sewer system by pipe clearing or replacement was an estimated US$ 7.4 million. However, this must be regarded as an underestimate because few municipalities had a projected repair policy and because the survey was based only on publicly owned

Kaj Rolf and Örjan Stål, Swedish University of Agricultural Sciences. Department of Agriculture Engineering, Section of Horticultural Engineering, P.O.Box 66, S-230 53 Alnarp, Sweden.

sewer systems. A large number of sewer systems are privately owned and were not included in the data. The results imply that root damage to sewer systems is a considerable economic problem. Urban councils regarded the problem as one of moderate to serious importance and deemed the extent of the damage in the last three to five years as unchanged or increasing.

Root intrusion tends to occur primarily on older pipes, but this investigation has shown that tree roots also penetrated the more modern types of sewer pipes. Of the Swedish municipalities surveyed, 37 of them recorded 63 cases of root intrusion into pipes installed after 1979. In half of the 63 cases mentioned, information on the internal condition of the affected pipes was documented through closed-circuit video inspection, still photographs, or written descriptions. Of the urban councils surveyed, 59% could provide no explanation for the occurrence of tree root damage to their sewer systems, while 27% believed that the damage was due to faulty installation practices (10).

The main factors determining the extent of tree root intrusion into new sewer systems could be summarized as follows:

- Trees in the vicinity of the damaged pipes were most likely to be willow or poplar.
- The pipes were mainly small (225 mm [8.9 in.]) concrete pipes joined by a rubber joint seal with a convex cross section. Some cases of root intrusion into PVC pipes have also been reported.
- Pipes installed in shallow, clay soils were most likely to be damaged.
- The affected pipes were installed between 1979 and 1985, and root intrusions were discovered in most instances after 1985.

Documentation of root damage to sewer systems in many cases was unavailable or incomplete. This is probably because many of the individuals or agencies responsible for municipal sewer systems are not aware that root damage can occur even in relatively new sewer pipes. This problem should be brought to their attention as soon as possible because it is likely to become even more serious with time, as pipes age and as tree root systems expand. It will then be possible, we hope, to prevent the extensive damage seen in older pipes today.

Root intrusion is most likely to occur at the following sites:

- connections between two different types of pipe (e.g., concrete and PVC)
- connections between pipes, manholes, and inspection chambers
- joints between chamber rings and manhole covers and frames

Newly installed sewer pipes should be both filmed and tested before the local authorities assume responsibility from the contractor because it has been shown that pipe defects are most likely to arise during installation.

Why Do Roots Grow into Pipes?

Roots grow into pipes when the pipe joints are unable to withstand root pressure. Pipe manufacturers make pipe joints that are sealed to avoid water leakage; the seals are not made to withstand roots because of the limited knowledge about the roots' ability to penetrate different materials. Researchers have shown that certain plant root tips can develop an axial pressure of up to 2.6 MPa (12). Measurements of the ability to develop axial pressures have almost exclusively been done on seedlings of annual plants. Pfeffer (2) conducted the only known experiment on tree roots. On a horsechestnut seedling with a root tip diameter of 2.5 mm (0.1 in.), an axial pressure of 0.67 MPa was measured. The sealing pressure for sewer pipes varies between 0.3 and 1.0 MPa, depending on the type of pipe material and construction.

Technical developments take place without knowledge of the biological mechanisms of root development. Roots have the capability of changing shape through a radial expansion when there is a resistance (1). Roots expand to release pressure on the root tip, get thinner, and then expand again. This has been observed in the research using geotextiles as root barriers (6, 13). In these experiments, roots have a very small diameter when penetrating the geotextile root barriers. There is a lack of knowledge on what effect this strangulation has on further root development and root functions. We do know that plants with strangulated roots have a decrease in stem diameter growth compared to plants without strangulated roots (Stål and Rol, unpublished).

Soil conditions around pipes are favorable for root growth. The backfill creates good drainage conditions, water is available around the pipe, and nutrients are in the pipe. If a root reaches a pipe, there is a risk that the root will penetrate a joint or crack in the pipe.

Sewer Damage Control and Its Economic Consequences

The most common methods of removing roots from sewer pipes are root cutting, high-pressure flushing, or—in the most serious cases—pipe relining or replacement (Figure 1). Of the 242 councils replying to the survey (7), only 39 (or 16%) had a policy of surveying the extent of damage and setting forth specific measures to deal with it. The majority of urban councils simply apply emergency remedies when the damage becomes acute. These measures address only the results of the damage, not its cause.

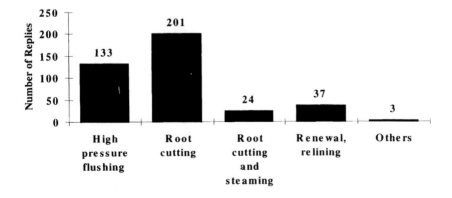

Figure 1. The most common methods of removing roots that have penetrated sewers in Sweden's municipalities (8).

Strategies for the Sewer Manager

When root intrusion has been identified in a stretch of pipe, the area should be thoroughly investigated with respect to the following technical, economic, aesthetic, biological, and cultural viewpoints. Based on this investigation, plans should be drawn up for dealing with the problem. The choices are either pipe-centered or vegetation-centered.

- Evaluate the vigor and the ecological, aesthetic, and cultural worth of the trees in relation to the damage they cause (5).
- Consider replacing certain trees or altering the landscape if the trees are relatively unimportant and the pipes are in good condition, apart from the damage by roots. Trees causing damage which are in themselves in poor condition (old, diseased, or damaged) should be replaced by more suitable species with a slow growth pattern; this will increase the aesthetic, ecological, and cultural value of the area. Replacing the vegetation in problem areas is often considerably less expensive than renovating or replacing pipes. If sewer and park authorities cooperate on the above strategies, the former could reduce their repair costs while the latter could obtain the funds to renew or adapt existing urban landscape areas. A current research project in Sweden is analyzing how freed economic resources can be divided between sewer and park authorities.
- If tree roots from valuable trees cause damage, these trees should be preserved and pipe replacement should be considered. If trees have to be removed, it is important that the replacement trees be provided with good soil conditions so that they can develop normally without posing a future threat to the sewer system.
- Where a change in land use is possible, creation of an ecological stormwater handling system, instead of stormwater pipes, should be considered. If an open reservoir were made, the trees and bushes would become a resource rather than a problem (11).
- Replacing trees of low worth that have caused damage to sewer pipes or storm drains should be the responsibility of, and funded by, the sewer authority. However, the park authority should carry out maintenance of these trees.

Strategies for the Vegetation Manager

- Before choosing trees to be planted in crowded urban environments in the vicinity of mechanical installations, determine the soil space available. Quick-growing trees and bushes should be avoided in restricted areas. Slow-growing species and those with less active, nonaggressive root systems are more suitable (3).
- Avoid square planting pits, which provide only a limited amount of growing space for the rootball. Rectangular trenches are preferable because they allow the root system to grow and develop normally in at least one, and preferably two, directions.
- Loosen compacted soil before planting and ensure that the soil is well drained.
- A plant-bed alternative, which can be used when trees are planted in a traffic area, is to create a load-bearing soil. This consists of a well-graded skeleton

material of crushed rock or lava mixed with soil and compacted so that it is stable and can carry light traffic. The skeleton material bears the load while remaining permeable to water and air, thus providing good soil drainage and aeration. Load-bearing soils have proven successful in trials in Holland, England, Denmark, Norway, and Sweden (4).

• Another technique is to install a root barrier around the rootball. This can be used at planting or installed later to existing trees. However, root barriers should never be used to justify planting large trees in confined areas or for laying pipelines close to trees. Several studies have shown that a root barrier is ineffective when sited too near a tree: The roots can descend to considerable depths to go under the barrier, or they can grow over it if it does not extend sufficiently above the soil surface. Materials suitable as root barriers are a thick polythene (0.5 to 1.0 mm), which is also impermeable to water, or a geotextile (fiber matting) if a water-permeable root barrier is required. However, none of the geotextiles currently available are completely resistant to root penetration, although the thicker, thermal-treated types have performed best in trials (6).

Conclusion

Excavation and trenching for pipes, roads, and other infrastructures can cause considerable damage to highly valued trees in urban areas. The development of techniques and methods to solve these problems has often been governed by short-term economic interests.

Acknowledgments

Research on trees and sewers was funded by the Swedish Council for Building Research (BFR) and by Swedish Water and Wastewater Works Association (VAV, VA-FORSK), whose contribution the authors greatly acknowledge.

Literature Cited

1. Hettiaratchi, D.R.P. 1990. *Soil compaction and plant root growth*. Phil. Trans. R. Soc. London. B 329, 343–355.

2. Pfeffer, W. 1893. *Druck und arbeitsleistung durch wachsende Pflanzen*. Abhandlungen der Koniglich Sachsischen Gesellschaft der Wissenschaften 33:235–474.

3. Rolf, K., Ö. Stål, and H. Schroeder. 1995. Tree roots and sewer systems, pp 68–77. **In** Watson, G.W., and D. Neely (Eds.). Trees and Buildings Sites: Proceedings of an International Workshop on Trees and Buildings, Chicago, IL. International Society of Arboriculture, Champaign, IL.

4. Rolf, K., and U. Moback. 1991. *Trädgropar i gatumiljö*. Utemiljö, Gröna Fakta nr 4:1991. (In Swedish.)

5. Rolf, K., and Ö Stål. 1994. *Tree roots in sewer systems in Malmö, Sweden*. J. Arboric. 20(6):329–335.

6. Stål, Ö. 1995. *Rotspärrar håller rötterna i schack*. Utemiljö, Gröna Fakta nr 2:1995. (In Swedish.)

7. Stål, Ö. 1996. *Rotinträngning i avloppsledningar. En undersökning av omfattning och kostnader i Sveriges kommuner. (Root intrusion in sewer pipes: A study of the extent of root intrusion in Swedens's municipalities.)* Svenska Vatten och Avloppsverksföreningen. VA-FORSK Rapport Nr 1996–02. (In Swedish, with English summary.)

8. Stål, Ö. 1997. How to solve the problem with interactions between trees and sewers. **In** Pathways to Sustainability: Local Initiatives for Cities and Towns. International Conference, Newcastle, Australia, June 1–5, 1997. 285 pp.

9. Stål, Ö. 1998. *Utveckling av vakuumtekniken som schantningsmetod.* Bygg och teknik. 1 (Jan.):53–63. (In Swedish.)

10. Stål, Ö., and J. Rosenlöv. 1995. *Trädrötter och avloppsledningar. En fördjupad undersökning av rotproblem i nya avloppsledningar.* Svenska Vatten och Avloppsverksföreningen. VA-FORSK Rapport nr 1995-11. (In Swedish.)

11. Stål, Ö., and B. Mattsson. 1996. Alternative methods to avoid operational and maintenance problems with tree roots in storm water sewer pipes, pp 453–461. **In** Niemczynowicz, J. (Ed.). Integrated Water Management in Urban Areas: Searching for New Realistic Approaches with Respect to Developing World. Proceedings of the International Symposium, Lund, Sweden, Sept. 1995. NESCO-HIP.

12. Taylor, H.M., and L.F. Ratliff. 1969. *Root growth pressure of cotton, peas, and peanuts.* Agron. J. 61(May–June):398–402.

13. Wagar, J.A., and A.P. Barker. 1993. *Effectiveness of three barrier materials for stopping regenerating roots off established trees.* J. Arboric. 19(6):332–338.

Tree Root Failures

E. Thomas Smiley, Thomas R. Martin, and
Bruce R. Fraedrich

Tree failures occur when a stressing force such as the wind pushes against the leaves, branches, and trunk of a tree (sail effect) and there is a weakness in the tree or soil. When winds exceed 50 or 60 mph, the weakness can be relatively minor yet the tree will fail. For lower-velocity wind or simple gravity to cause failure, the structural weakness must be more extensive. This study was conducted to develop methods of predicting which trees will fail at relatively low wind velocities, so that remedial action can be taken before tree failure.

The structural failure of trees during Hurricane Fran resulted in losses of human life, houses, and vehicles, as well as a disruption in the electrical and transportation infrastructures in the central piedmont area of North Carolina on September 6, 1996. The Raleigh, Durham, and Chapel Hill areas experienced sustained winds of 45 mph with gusts to 79 mph. Rain accumulation immediately preceding and during the storm was 9 in. (22.5 cm). Greensboro, 48 miles west of Chapel Hill, experienced sustained winds of 34 mph and gusts to 48 mph with 4 in. (10.2 cm) of rain.

Trunk breakage and root plates sizes were studied after previous hurricanes (1, 3, 6). The information collected has lead to several methods of quantifying tree structure. A study of giant sequoia (*Sequoia gigantea*) failures found that root decay was a major predisposing factor in 19 of 22 root failures studied (4). There are no other published studies comparing the extent root decay to tree failures.

The typical pattern of root decay is from the tip of the root toward the trunk and from the bottom of the root upward (5). This makes detection difficult. One practical way to detect decay is by probing roots in the transition area between trunk and horizontal roots (2). Tate (7) found that 14.4% of urban trees in the New York City area have trunk decay. The number of urban trees with root decay is unknown. As with trunk decay, it is expected that a small amount of root decay will not predispose a tree to failure, but when decay is extensive the tree will be more likely to fail. The difficulty is determining the point at which decay becomes too extensive.

This study compares data for trees that survived Hurricane Fran and those that failed during the storm in an attempt to develop a set of criteria that can be used to predict which trees will fail in lower winds and in future storms. In addition, a general model of tree failure is presented.

E. Thomas Smiley, Thomas R. Martin, and Bruce R. Fraedrich, Bartlett Tree Research Laboratories, 13768 Hamilton Road, Charlotte, NC 28278.

Materials and Methods

Trees that failed during Hurricane Fran in Greensboro, Raleigh, Durham, and Chapel Hill, North Carolina, were examined September 8 and 9, 1996. A population of trees that survived the hurricane was examined on November 12 and 13, 1996. This "control" population was located on the campus of the University of North Carolina, Chapel Hill, the location of a large number of failures during the storm. Standing trees with signs or symptoms of root rot or root damage were preferentially selected for the control group.

Tree characteristics examined were diameter at 4.5 ft (1.4 m) above the soil line (dbh), crown spread, tree height, species, condition, depth of soil over the main buttress roots, amount of sound wood in the roots, number of roots with decay present, the type of failure (either root or soil), and site characteristics. Sound wood in the root system was measured by probing with a 1/8-in. diameter drill bit or, when cracks or breakage was present, by directly measuring the wood thickness.

Results

Seventy-four windthrown and 39 surviving trees were examined in the Raleigh, Durham, and Chapel Hill areas. Tree loss was minor in the Greensboro area. Both failed trees and survivors had relatively large diameters with medium to high crown density (Table 1). The majority were oaks, as would be expected in an area where the native climax forest is of the oak-hickory type (Table 2).

Table 1. Range and average characteristics of the study trees that failed or survived Hurricane Fran in and around Raleigh, North Carolina.

Characteristic	Failed (average)	Survived (average)
Dbh, in.	12–70 (26.5)^z	17–52 (37.5)
Crown diameter, ft	20–80 (40)^y	25–80 (52)
Height, ft	8–100 (70)	40–100 (75)
Number in study	74	39

^{z}To obtain centimeters, multiply inches by 2.54.
^{y}To obtain meters, multiply feet by 0.303.

Table 2. Percentage of tree species that failed and survived after Hurricane Fran in and around Raleigh, North Carolina.

Tree species	% failed (n = 74)	% survived (n = 39)
Acer rubrum	5	0
Liriodendron tulipifera	5	10
Quercus alba	10	25
Q. phellos	17	30
Q. rubra	26	15
Q. stellata	7	8
Ulmus	7	3
Other	23	9
Total	100%	100%

Table 3. A comparison of nine threshold guidelines against tree failures and survivors of Hurricane Fran in the area around Raleigh, North Carolina. Guidelines are composed of a percentage-of-roots-with-decay factor and a depth-to-decay factor expressed as a percentage of dbh. If the threshold value is exceeded, remedial action is recommended.

		% correctly predicted	
≥ % of roots decayed	≤ % of dbh thickness	Failed	Survived
20	15	44	92
	20	77	64
	25	88	35
33	15	44	100
	20	77	64
	25	88	64
50	15	22	100
	20	55	78
	25	66	71

Two-thirds of the tree failures were soil failures. Poor soil drainage highly corresponded to this type of failure. Roots that were broken were in the diamter range of 0.75 to 1.5 in. (1.9 to 3.8 cm). Breakage most often occurred at a wound or other weak area in the root.

One-third of all failed trees had fill soil above the buttress roots. This compares to only 8% of the control group. Root rot was present in 13% of the failed and 38% of the surviving trees examined. The average amount of sound wood above the decay on failed trees was 5.3 in. (13.5 cm) on 64% of the root system; for surviving trees there was an average of 7.8 in. (19.8 cm) of wood above decay on 16.5% of the root system.

To predict failures associated with root decay, threshold levels for decay were chosen and tested. Values were assigned with a depth-to-decay component and a percentage-of-roots-with-decay component. Data collected in this study were applied to these tests (Table 3).

Discussion

When hurricane-force winds are preceded by heavy rain, it can be expected that large numbers of trees will be windthrown. In general, the trees that fail will be large with a full crown and growing in poorly drained areas. Trees with fill soil over the root system will be much more likely to fail than those without. However, beyond these few qualitative factors it is difficult to predict whether a specific tree will survive or fail.

Trees with root decay are much more likely to fail under nonstorm as well as storm conditions, possibly even from the weight of a climber or the shock load of a limb being lowered. Quantitative threshold value formulas were presented and tested against the data collected in this study. As with previous above-ground stem breakage threshold tests (6), our goal was to predict about 50% of the decay-related failures under hurricane-force winds while minimizing the number of surviving trees that exceed the threshold. These prediction values can be found in at least two places on Table 3, with > 33% roots decayed to < 15% of dbh, and with > 50% roots decayed to < 20% of dbh. The > 20% root decay data were thought to be unreliable due to the low number of trees included. Therefore, the more roots that have decay, the more solid root wood is required to keep the tree upright. For example, a tree of 30 in. (76.2 cm) dbh, would require more than 4.5 in. (11.4 cm) of solid wood on three of ten roots for it to be below the threshold value. If the same tree had decay in five of ten roots, it would require more than 6 in. (15.2 cm) of solid wood to be below the threshold value. When trees exceed the threshold value, removal or other remediation is recommended. Threshold values may need to be lowered for higher value target and compounding circumstances such as leans, cavity openings, cracks, etc.

Using the information from this study as well as previous work, a generalized model for tree failures was developed (Figure 1). This model consists of three parts: 1) a stressing force such as wind, 2) the tree's resistance to the force—commonly referred to as the "sail effect"—the importance of which may be increased by a leaning condition, and 3) a weakness. The weakness may be one or a combination of many factors including inherently weak wood, saturated soil, decayed roots or stems, cracks, and weak branch attachment.

When wind velocities exceed 50 mph and trees have moderate to large crowns, relatively minor weaknesses (e.g., wet soil) can bring about the failure. This is the "hurricane" model (Figure 2). It was demonstrated in the comparison between Raleigh-area failures and the lack of failures in Greensboro where winds did not exceed 48 mph. If, however, the sail effect of the trees was reduced by pruning or other means, the tree may survive higher wind velocities.

On the other hand, the type of failure most feared by arborist is the "weak-tree" model (Figure 3). In this case, the weakness is so extensive that even a minor force from gravity or the weight of a climber may bring the tree or limb down. It is this weak-tree scenario that should be easiest to predict using threshold values for decayed wood in trunk, limbs, and roots.

Much more work needs to be done with windthrown trees to accurately predict which trees will fail in high winds. This project is intended as a starting point for arborists to discuss root-related failures. We encourage others to test these values for root decay and to expand on these models of other soil, stem, and root weaknesses. The ultimate goal is to have the ability to prevent the catastrophic losses associated with failure of large trees.

Literature Cited

1. Cutler, D.F. 1991. *Tree planting for the future: Lessons of the storms of October 1987 and January 1990.* Arboric. J. 15:225–234.
2. Matheny, N.P., and J.R. Clark. 1994. A Photographic Guide to the Evaluation of Hazard Trees in Urban Areas. (2d ed). International Society of Arboriculture, Champaign IL. 85 pp.
3. Mattheck, C., K. Bethge, and D. Erb. 1993. *Failure criteria for trees.* Arboric. J. 17:201–209.

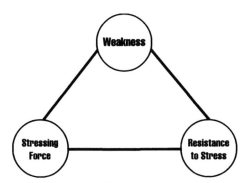

Figure 1. A model for tree failures, showing that three primary factors are involved: a weakness, a stressing force such as wind, as a resistance to the stress (the "sail effect").

Figure 2. The "hurricane" model: When the wind exceeds 50 mph, it becomes the predominant stressing force, able to topple trees with only minor defects.

Figure 3. The "weak-tree" model shows that if the weakness is extensive, such as decay in trunk or roots, even the ever-present force of gravity may cause tree failure.

4.   Piirto, D.D., W.W. Wilcox, J.R. Parmeter, Jr., R.L. Gilbertson, and I. Tavares. 1984. Causes of uprooting and breakage of specimen giant sequoia trees. Univ. Calif. Div. Of Agric. Natr. Res. Bull. 1909. 14 pp.

5.   Shigo, A.L., and J.T. Tippett. 1981. Compartmentalization of decayed wood associated with *Armallaria mellea* in several tree species. USDA For. Ser. Res. Paper NE-488. 20 pp.

6.   Smiley, E.T., and B.R. Fraedrich. 1992. *Determining strength loss from decay.* J. Arboric. 18:20–204.

7.   Tate, R.L. 1986. *Stem decay in street trees in New Jersey and park trees in Central Park, New York.* J. Arboric. 12:73–74.

Acknowledgements

We would like to thank the following people who contributed to this project: Frank McKeever, Kirk Pelland, Joe Bones, Walt Dages, and Lynn Roberts.

Photo 1. The failure of this elm was predisposed by soil over the root system and on the root collar.

Photo 2. Soil failures, the leading type of failure found after Hurricane Fran.

Photo 3. Root decay played a part in the failure of 13% of the failed trees that were studied.

Photo 4. Surviving trees were probed to determine the extent of root decay.

PART III

URBAN SOILS

Simplified Soil Testing

James Urban

Ninety percent of all plant problems are soil related, but significant soil testing is not included in the design fees for most landscape architects and the costs of significant modification to the existing soils are not figured into the typical owner's planting budget. The typical design project is a small site where the natural soil profiles have been previously disturbed. They often show up on USDA soil maps as only one soil type. Such areas have likely been heavily graded since the maps were made, or the soils are not classified. The cost of hiring a soils consultant is not included in the budget, and local Extension staff are often not trained in urban soil problems. What do you do? Ignoring the situation or writing some vague specification that requires the contractor to fix problems that are "discovered" during the construction process are not the right answers, although they are the default approach on far too many projects. The site designer has an explicit obligation to know what the conditions are and to design the plan to reflect them. Far too many landscape architects and site designers do not have the skills or knowledge to undertake soil analysis.

The designer can learn a lot about the soils very quickly during the initial site visit by purchasing (at less than US$200) and learning to use a few simple tools. Having reliable soils information may also help expand the budget for soil improvement by demonstrating to the client where specific problems exist and that the money will be well spent.

Tool #1: A Hand Soil Sampler

This is a metal, T-shaped sampler that is pushed into the soil to extract soil cores (1 in. [2.5 cm] diameter and 12 in. [30.4 cm] long). Many models are on the market, but buy a good, solid one. A cheap, lightweight one will be difficult to use in hard soils. Each soil core can be examined in seconds, and samples from many locations can be extracted from across the site in minutes. Most of the samples are discarded after examination, while some may be kept in plastic sandwich bags for further analysis. In existing urban areas, take some samples directly adjacent to the pavement to look at the soil beyond the existing plant beds. If possible, take some samples diagonally underneath the existing pavement. The cores reveal information about several aspects of the soil.

James Urban, ASLA, 915 Creek Drive, Annapolis, MD 21403

Soil Profile

Has there been soil disturbance? Undisturbed soils normally have a dark black or brown organic layer (O horizon) or a root mat layer in heavy sod. A topsoil layer of dark to light brown or reddish brown humus soil (A horizon) is below the O horizon. Lower yet is a lighter-colored subsoil layer (B horizon). All three layers frequently appear in the first 12-in. probe in most soils. A deeper probe of the second 12-in. layer of soil should be extracted if you suspect problems or disturbance. The transition between each layer should be gradual. A sharply defined transition often indicates soils that have been disturbed and that additional probing is necessary.

Take some sample cores in the areas where the grass or plants at the site are the greenest and some in the areas where the grass or plants are thinner or less green. Take samples in the area where there are large existing trees and compare them to the soil color in the grass areas. The soil underneath large trees is more likely to be the natural soil profile. If there are no large existing trees at your site, take some cores at the largest trees closest to the site to determine what the natural profile might have looked like. Take samples at the top and bottom of steep slopes to determine if the slope is a natural condition or a deep cut from previous construction. Natural slopes will be darker at the bottom, while construction cuts are normally lighter or grayer in color at the bottom. Take some cores in the wettest parts of the site and at the driest.

Soil Texture

Examine each core, squeezing each layer in your fingers to determine the relative amounts of sand and clay (Figure 1). By spending a little bit of time in good soils that are of known textures, you can quickly learn to identify the extremes of heavy clays and light sands. Try not to sample in extremely dry conditions because dry soils are more difficult to visually identify. Use the following descriptions to determine soil texture.

- Sandy soils feel gritty, are not moldable (cannot be formed into a cohesive ball), and do not feel sticky
- Silty soils feel like flour or talcum powder when dry, and are somewhat sticky and moldable when wet; dry clods are somewhat difficult to crush.
- Clay soils are very moldable and sticky when wet; dry clods are extremely difficult to crush.

Most soils are a mixture of various amounts of clay, silt, and sand, which makes then more difficult to classify in the field. A more exacting method for examining soil texture by feel is in the appendix to this chapter.

These simple site test are simply looking for problem soils and changes in soil patterns that can help you determine how the soils at the site are related. The more you probe soils throughout a given region, the more easily you will be able to identify good and bad soils.

Soil Moisture and Drainage

Find out when it last rained in the area, or when the site was last irrigated, then feel how much moisture is in the soil. Do your fingers get muddy even though the surface

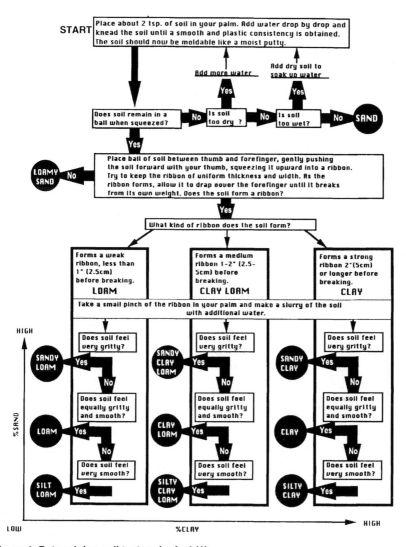

Figure 1. Determining soil texture by feel (1).

is dry? Is the soil dry several inches down even though it just rained? Next, smell the soil. To learn what good soils smell like, grab a handful of good garden soil or pull back some dry leaves in a forest and take a handful of the damp humus. What you are smelling is the odor of aerobic microbes digesting the organic matter in the presence of oxygen. If there is oxygen there is drainage. You can smell it even in winter. If it smells more like the trap in your kitchen sink or the black leaves you pull out of that place in a ditch that never quite drains, you are smelling anaerobic microbes digesting organic matter without oxygen. No oxygen means poor drainage. Soils that have little or no odor are either very low in organic matter or are overly dry. Soil color is also a good indicator of previous drainage rates. Gray soils generally are poorly drained, while light brown to red-brown soils have good drainage.

Soil Compaction

How hard is it to insert the probe and how deep can you push it into the ground? Again, a little testing in your own lawn and garden and in some other soils will teach you the fundamentals. If you cannot insert the probe, you can be sure that roots won't grow there. Look for hardpans and compacted layers below the first several inches— it may indicate previous construction activity or soil disturbance. Very wet soils may feel quite soft even if they are compacted. Lightly compacted soils may feel very stiff if they are overly dry. Get to know the relationship between soil moisture, soil type, and compaction. Take a clue from the existing vegetation as well as the soil probe. Remember, you are looking for extremes to find the problem soils not necessarily trying to determine absolute levels.

Tool #2: A pH Meter

The most significant chemical determinant in plant failure after soil texture and drainage is pH. A handheld pH meter can give you a reasonable look at this factor in a short amount of time. The Kelway meter is popular, easy to use, and readily available. Inserted in the ground, it must be left in place for several minutes and the ground moisture must be at a level to permit correct readings. This type of meter can give varied results depending on soil moisture and its chemical makeup, but it is very useful for quickly identifying problem soils and extremes. Read and follow the instruction manual. An amplified pH meter (such as the Piccolo pH meter) gives much more accurate readings but requires mixing a soil sample with distilled water and letting the sample sit for at least an hour. The Piccolo meter is useful if you are planning to use pH-sensitive plants such as azaleas or other ericacious plants and need a more precise Ph reading.

Soil pH is very difficult to permanently change to any great extent. Do not rely on simply telling the client to add a little sulfur or lime to permit a special plant pallet to survive. Design within the pH range you find at the site.

Tool #3: A Bucket and Towel

Any planting design, especially for a client who is not going to actively garden, must reflect the other chemical components of the soil. While extensive additional soil testing may be beyond your reach financially, a series of simple tests for nutrient and trace elements should be considered at some point in the design process. Most state Extension services perform these analyses at very low cost, and you should consider having them done early in the project. Soil analysis typically costs around US$100 on a typical residential project.

So, add a small bucket and trowel to your small collection of tools. Use the trowel or your soil probe to collect a separate series of samples from each soil type. Mix the samples from each soil in the bucket to get an average sample of soil for that soil type (be sure to wipe out the bucket after each sample). Use sealable sandwich bags to store the soil. Include the the soil-analysis results in the project bid documents so that the contractor will know exactly what kinds of modifications to the nutrient levels will be required. Writing specifications that leave the testing and modifications to the contractor after the bid only invites problems, such as the contractor underbidding this portion of the work or ignoring it altogether.

Conclusion

With a few simple tools, an amazing amount of information can be gathered very quickly and cheaply. An accurate site analysis can be completed, and many of the problems of planting can be avoided. Corrections can be suggested that will be specific to actual identifiable problems, increasing the chances of including the cost of soil modifications in the budget. Specific solutions should be developed based on local experience and the project budget. Modifications to soil structure can be expensive; therefore, modifying the design to reflect the existing soil conditions is usually the most economical solution and often the best for the client.

Acknowledgments

This article is based in part on a lecture by Dr. Frank Gouin, Professor Emeritus, Department of Natural Resources Sciences and Landscape Architecture, University of Maryland.

Literature Cited

1. Watson, G.W., and E.B. Himelick. 1997. Principles and Practices of Planting Trees and Shrubs. International Society of Arboriculture, Champaign, IL.

Appendix

Product Sources

Soil Sampler (Ben Meadows Co., 800/241-6401)

Oatfield Soil Sampler Model A, with auger and extensions for dense soils	$180.00
Oatfield Soil Sampler Model B, compact with extensions	$70.00

Kelway Soil Tester pH meter. (A.M. Leonard, Inc., 800/543-8955) (useful for quick, rough, field measurements)	$90.00

Piccolo pH Meter (Ben Meadows Co., 800/241-6401) (requires the soil be mixed with distilled water)	$128.00

Note: The above products are available from several sources. This supplier list is not an endorsement for any company and is included for convenience of the reader only.

Soil Compaction on Construction Sites

Thomas B. Randrup

Soil compaction was estimated on 17 construction sites randomly selected in the suburbs of Copenhagen, Denmark. Bulk densities were measured from the soil surface to depths of 1 m, at 0.1 m intervals, using a nuclear moisture/density probe. Sampling sites were located in and outside construction areas, respectively. Soil on construction sites was heavily compacted at depths from 0.3 to 0.8 m, but unexpectedly, no significant differences regarding soil compaction were found between types of contracting, whether landscape architects were involved or not, or between different qualities of work specifications. That no differences were found is believed to be caused by unintended soil compaction. Unintended soil compaction is a result of construction site traffic occurring on areas not meant for traffic, i.e., areas meant for planting.

Soil compaction on construction sites is a well-known problem. Alberty et al. (1) described the relation between soil compaction occurring on construction sites and its effects on woody plants. Bulk density readings in the construction zone were within the range of what had been found to restrict growth of woody plants. Pfieffer et al. (15) analyzed landscape design and maintenance requirements in four urban parking lots. Soil compaction and inadequate irrigation appeared to have the greatest impact on plant survival and vigor.

Lichter and Lindsey (10) evaluated how effective five different surface protective treatments were in preventing soil compaction. The five treatments were mulch, gravel, mulch/geotextile, mulch/grid, and plywood. No material proved to be effective in preventing compaction. Instead, the conclusion was that the best treatment would be to involve all members of the development team in securing as little grading and construction traffic as possible in future tree root zones. Day and Bassuk (4) reviewed the effects of amelioration treatments and concluded similarly to Lichter and Lindsey (11) that soil compaction is a serious problem for the landscaping industry and will continue to be so long as modern construction techniques are used.

Once soil compaction has occurred, it can be regarded as permanent, as the natural drying and freezing cycles presumably have been overestimated in respect to loosening compacted soils (8). Both Rolf (20) and Håkansson and Reeder (8) said that alleviation of soil compaction is only a minor aid to the natural processes of retaining a natural structure of the soil. Thus, reestablishment of the original soil structure is almost impossible.

Thomas Barfoed Randrup, Ph.D., Senior Consultant, Landscape Architect, The Danish Forest and Landscape Research Institute, Hoersholm Kongevej 11, 2970 Hoersholm, Denmark.

In Denmark most building activity is on former farmland. The landscaper's main concern is to protect the soil from compaction during construction. Topsoil, with a content of organic material of approximately 4% to 5%, is not suitable as a construction material. Therefore, in Danish construction sites, the topsoil is always stripped before the actual building process begins.

All involved in landscape construction and the landscape deal with the same dilemma: soil compaction is a problem for plants but is often required for site stabilization. Let us denote deliberate soil compaction "intended soil compaction" (as seen in fill areas under mounds, etc.), as opposed to "unintended soil compaction" originating from inadvertent vehicular traffic from contractors. In the present study, unintended soil compaction is investigated in relation to the planning, design, and building processes within construction sites. The purpose of this work is twofold: 1) to see how widespread soil compaction is on construction sites and 2) to see if planning and design can prevent unintended soil compaction.

Materials and Methods

Construction sites were studied in three counties in Denmark: Frederiksborg, Roskilde, and Copenhagen. The exact locations and detailed descriptions of the individual construction sites are provided by Randrup (17). The typical soil texture in these areas is glaciated clay soils, which is likely to be compacted if the soil is exposed to a load force (9).

To secure the areas for the planned investigation, the following requirements were imposed.

1. The Danish quality assurance reform was introduced in January 1987 (13). This reform orders developers in public-funded construction projects to carry out quality assurance tests in new construction situations. The aim is to ensure a minimum of construction failures in buildings and in the surrounding landscape. Thirteen of the construction sites were publicly funded. To give contractors bound by the quality assurance orders time to adapt to new habits, work specifications were not required for at least two years after the quality assurance reform was introduced.

2. The construction sites had to be on previously open farmland in order to be certain that the source of a compaction would originate from the building process.

3. The sites should have at least 2,000 m^2 (21,500 ft^2) of open and unpaved space to enable the study of construction traffic patterns.

These restrictions yielded a "population" total of 47 construction sites in the three counties. From this population, a sample was randomly chosen for analysis. The technique of subsampling was applied (2). The primary units were construction sites, and 17 sites were established. To determine construction effects on compaction levels, a sample site (control) outside each of the nine construction sites was selected. These control sites were in adjacent farmland unaffected by construction.

The secondary units were 1 m^2 areas. At the construction sites, the squares were not randomly chosen but were selected to avoid planned storage areas, areas planned to be exposed to grading, planned building process roads, and planned underground utility lines. Such areas are intentionally compacted and are not suitable for this analysis. Areas that had been planted were ignored in order to avoid soil loosened during the planting process. For practical reasons, the number of secondary units per construction site varied from one to four. Within the secondary units, three points forming an isosceles triangle with approximately 1 m side lengths were selected for soil density measurements.

All sites were farmed prior to construction. All soils were clayey glaciated soils (15% to 70% clay + silt), and all construction was completed one to five years before the study. Six sites were commercial developments with a few large buildings on the sites. Eleven sites were residential developments with dense housing covering 30% to 40% of the site.

Bulk densities were measured on 35 test areas in all and on all nine control areas. Measurements were made from the soil surface to depths of 1 m (~3 ft) at 0.1 m intervals (~4 in.). To obtain a fair representation in the expected layered and unhomogeneous soils (6), bulk densities were estimated three times at every depth in every test area. The number of subsamples at each depth is shown in Table 1.

The measurements were taken by a gamma-ray single probe. With the single-probe method, it was possible to make measurements at greater depths than seen previously. The method is described in detail by Gardner (5) and Saare (21). The instrument measures transmission or scattering of gamma radiation. When calibrated, these transmissions measure the bulk density of wet soil. The moisture content of the soil was measured by a neutron source in the instrument. The dry bulk density was calculated by deducting moisture content from the wet soil density.

An aluminum tube was inserted into the soil before any measurements were made. The radiation sources were lowered into this tube. Great care was taken not to disturb the soil around the tubes during insertion.

A relationship between wet bulk density (core sampling) and transmission counts per minute was made using 21 different test sites. The sites varied in soil type (from

Table 1. Results of soil compaction on construction site measurements, shown as average bulk densities from surface to 1 m (18).

	Construction sites			Controls		
Depth	n	mg/m³*	std.	n	mg/m³*	std.
0.1 m	93	1.65	0.22	23	1.72	0.18
0.2 m	93	1.61	0.27	27	1.76	0.17
0.3 m	93	1.77	0.28	27	1.81	0.23
0.4 m	93	1.91	0.28	27	1.77	0.25
0.5 m	93	1.96	0.24	27	1.73	0.23
0.6 m	92	1.95	0.23	27	1.77	0.24
0.7 m	87	1.91	0.22	27	1.78	0.23
0.8 m	84	1.88	0.18	27	1.85	0.25
0.9 m	71	1.84	0.23	26	1.91	0.21
1.0 m	31	1.79	0.24	23	1.96	0.19

*An overestimation of approximately 0.10 to 0.15 mg/m³ is assumed to be due to local compaction around the aluminum installation tube.

pure sand to 50% clay + silt), moisture content (from 0% to 31% H_2O by volume), measurement depth (from 10 to 60 cm [4 in. to 2 ft]), distance between radiation source and soil sample (from 0.2 to 30 cm [1.5 in. to 1 ft]), and counting rate (from one to four minutes). The number of core samples varied between three and eight at the individual locations. In general, an overestimation of approximately 0.10 to 0.15 mg/m^3 on all measurements may be due to local compaction around the aluminum tube. This, however, has to be studied in detail.

For each construction site, selected planning and design-related matters were assessed: 1) the extent to which landscape architects and 2) gardeners were involved in the implementation of the landscape design, 3) how contracting was organized, 4) the quality of work specifications, and 5) whether specifications for soil loosening were given (Table 2). Grouping within one of these classes was carried out on a basis of existing work specifications and following systematic interviews (24) of developers, technicians, and contractors. The extent of work specifications for planting areas varied from a few drawings to approximately 40 pages. They were often grouped into separate soil and planting specifications. Therefore, the Danish Building Planning System No. 74 (12) was applied to group the specifications in a standardized way and to evaluate the quality of the specifications.

To determine if the groupings within these planning and design-related classes influenced soil compaction, a hierarchical model with both fixed and random effects was applied as described by Randrup and Dralle (19).

Table 2. Results of the analysis of organization and design of construction sites in relation to soil compaction, expressed by bulk densities (19).

Class	Description	Treatment	Number of construction sites	Corrected mean* mg/m^3	Standard deviation mg/m^3
a		i	j	$u + a_i$	s_{ai}
Control	Reference sites	0	9	1.76	0.03
Landscape architect	Design and individual inspection	1	6	1.94	0.03
	Design only	2	6	1.93	0.03
	Not involved	3	5	1.94	0.02
Landscape gardener	Soil handling and planting	1	5	.92	0.02
	Planting only	2	12	1.96	0.02
Type of contracting	Turnkey and general contracts	1	11	1.91	0.02
	Individual trade contracts	2	6	2.00	0.03
Quality of specifications	Sufficient to comprehensive	1	12	1.95	0.02
	Insufficient to lacking	2	5	1.90	0.03
Soil loosening specified?	Yes	1	12	1.94	0.02
	No	2	5	1.94	0.03

*Average bulk densities are corrected according to unequal variances.

Results

The bulk densities in the top 0.3 m of the soil were lower inside the construction sites than in the control locations. Bulk densities at depths of 0.4 to 0.8 m were higher inside the construction sites than on the controls. Below 0.8 m, bulk densities inside the construction sites were lower than the controls. Outside the construction sites (on the controls) the bulk densities were similar at all depths.

Because compaction at the construction sites occurs mainly in the top 0.3 m of the subsoil (Table 1), comparative analyses were restricted to this fraction of the soil (i.e., 0.1, 0.2, and 0.3 m depths below the topsoil). The corrected mean bulk density for control sites was 1.76 mg/m^3, while inside construction sites the corrected mean was 1.94 mg/m^3. This difference is statistically significant on a 0.1% level. The level outside the construction sites was unexpectedly high. However, the general levels are not of major importance in analyzing the effects of treatments within the construction sites.

Results of the analysis of treatment effects are listed in Table 2. No significant differences were found between treatments in either of the cases.

Discussion

In the top layers of a Danish clay soil exposed to annual farming, soil bulk densities of about 1.55 to 1.65 mg/m^3 are considered normal. In this survey, higher bulk densities were found both inside and outside the construction sites (Table 1). Bulk densities above normal were also found by Hansen et al. (6), who estimated bulk densities between 1.59 and 1.72 mg/m^3 at depths of 0.1 to 0.9 m in a similar Danish agricultural field with clay soil. Typically, bulk densities in a range from 1.5 to 1.7 mg/m^3, on soil types similar to those presented, inhibit root penetration (3). However, local conditions, such as cracks, hydrology, and species, influence the actual threshold level for root growth.

The relatively high bulk densities found in this study may be due to the measurement technique used. In the clay moraine glaciated soils, which were often dry and stony, a gentle insertion of the measurement aluminum tube proved to be difficult. Therefore, an overestimation of approximately 0.10 to 0.15 mg/m^3 on all measurements could be due to local compaction around the aluminum tube.

Construction practice in Denmark commonly involves stripping and stockpiling the upper 0.1 to 0.5 m of soil during grading. Following grading and construction, the soil is replaced. Because this was the case on the sites examined, the higher bulk densities seen at a depth of 0.4 to 0.9 m should be the result of unintended compaction.

Even if the bulk densities were overestimated by 0.1 to 0.15 mg/m^3, the subsoil was still compacted at depths of approximately 0.3 m (1 ft). The compaction level found at these depths must be regarded as detrimental to root growth (14, 23, 25, 26). The decrease in porosity occurring from compaction (7) will in many cases also slow drainage. A zone of saturated soil could develop just above the subsoil, also reducing plant growth.

When compaction is found at depths below the subsoil, equipment used to alleviate compaction must operate at great depths, especially if the loosening procedure is carried out from the topsoil surface. In this study, the soil had been loosened in 12 of the 17 cases, according to the contractors. Positive soil loosening effects could be found occasionally, but in the overall results as shown in Table 1, no effects were found. Previously, several people have stated that alleviating soil compaction is difficult and usually not successful (8, 16, 20, 22).

Håkansson and Reeder (8) said that if machines weighing more than 14 metric tons were used on clay soils, compaction to depths of 0.6 m (2 ft) and lower could be expected. On Danish construction sites, machinery weighing from 17 to 25 tons is generally used (17). Dozers, scrapers, and motorgraders of the same size (and probably even larger) are used worldwide today.

Unexpectedly, no differences among the treatments of the construction sites were found. Neither the involvement of landscape architects or landscape gardeners, nor the type of contracting (major turnkey contracts or individual trade contracts), nor quality of work specifications had an effect on compaction levels (Table 2). These treatments were used to explain the influence of planning and design on soil compaction on construction sites. The nonsignificant differences between treatments is believed to be caused by unintended soil compaction.

Conclusions

Because modern building processes are practiced under circumstances that do not match the intentions of the work specifications and because no differences were found among the treatments on the construction sites, it is recommended that design and work specifications be developed according to a specific evaluation of the actual building site. From this study, it is suggested that the entire construction area be divided into 3 zones: a building zone, a working zone, and a protection zone. Zoning will control the construction traffic patterns more efficiently and therefore limit unintended soil compaction.

The building zone areas are covered with buildings, roads, and pathways. Areas very close to buildings are also included in this category. Any future planting on these areas should be designed with the expectation that soil compaction occurred during construction. Therefore, no attempts at prevention or preservation should be conducted in these areas. Instead, work specifications should concentrate on how the areas should be treated after the building process, in order to make them suitable for planting. These include use of new soil, appropriate soil-loosening aggregates, and optimal soil loosening depths.

Working zones most often function as storage areas, driveways, etc. during the construction period. This study proves, unfortunately, that the majority of planned planting areas are used as work zones. As with the building zone, any future planting should be designed with the expectation that the soil will be compacted during construction. If high soil porosity is required on areas within the working zone, the specifications should focus on how these areas should be protected or how soil loosening may be carried out.

No building structures and no traffic should be permitted in the protection zone. Protection can only be achieved by fencing to completely avoid inadvertent construction traffic. In peripheral areas, heavy traffic often occurs unnecessarily; these areas should be protected, too.

More detailed descriptions on how exactly to establish the three zones cannot be given in this context because the zones must be planned according to the design and structure of the buildings and the open areas at each site. On many low and dense-type construction sites, there are no protection zones: the building and work zones cover the entire area.

Acknowledgments

This research was founded by The Royal Veterinary and Agricultural University, Denmark, and The Danish Forest and Landscape Research Institute. Dr. Kim Dralle is gratefully acknowledged for carrying out the statistical analysis and for careful reading of the manuscript.

Literature Cited

1. Alberty, C.A., Pellett, H.M., and D.H. Taylor. 1984. *Characterization of soil compaction at construction sites and woody plant response.* J. Environ. Hort. 2(2):48–53.

2. Cochran, W.G. 1977. Sampling Techniques. John Wiley & Sons. New York, NY.

3. Craul, P.J. 1992. Urban Soil in Landscape Design. John Wiley & Sons, New York, NY. 396 pp.

4. Day, S.D., and N.L. Bassuk . 1994. *A review of the effects of soil compaction and amelioration treatments on landscape trees.* J. Arboric. 20(1):9–17.

5. Gardner, W.H. 1986. Water content, pp 493–544. In Klute, A. (Ed.). Methods of Soil Analysis, Part 1. Physical and Mineralogical Methods. American Society of Agronomy, Agronomy Monograph No. 9 (2d ed.).

6. Hansen, S., S. Storm, and H.E. Jensen. 1986. Spatial Variability of Soil Physical Properties. Theoretical and Experimental Analyses. I. Soil Sampling, Experimental Analyses and Basic Statistics of Soil Physical Properties. Research Report No. 1201. Dept. of Soil and Water and Plant Nutrition. The Royal Veterinary and Agricultural University, Copenhagen, Denmark. 54 pp + appendices.

7. Harris, W.L. 1971. The soil compaction process, pp 9–44. In Barnes, K.K., W.M. Carleton, H.M. Taylor, R.I. Throckmorton, and G.E. Vanden Berg (Eds.). Compaction of Agricultural Soils. An American Society of Agricultural Engineers Monograph, St. Joseph, MI.

8. Håkansson, I., and R.C. Reeder. 1994. *Subsoil compaction by vehicles with high axle load—extent, persistence and crop response.* Soil Till. Res. 29:277–304.

9. Jones, C.A. 1983. *Effects of soil texture on critical bulk densities for root growth.* Soil Sci. Am. J. 47:1208–1211.

10. Lichter, J.M., and P.A. Lindsey. 1994. *The use of surface treatments for the prevention of soil compaction during site construction.* J. Arboric. 20(4):205–209.

11. Lichter, J.M., and P.A. Lindsey. 1994. Soil compaction and site construction: Assessment and case studies, pp. 126–130. In Watson, G.W., and D. Neely (Eds.). The Landscape Below Ground: Proceedings of an International Workshop on Root Development in Urban Soils. International Society of Arboriculture, Champaign, IL.

12. Mølgaard, K., Langford, K., and K.J. Christensen. 1992. BPS: Typiske beskrivelsesafsnit anlægsgartnerarbejde—vejledning. [Building planning system: Typical specification sections, Landscape construction work, Recommendations.] BPS Publication 74, 2d rev. ed. August 1992. Danish National Housing and Building Agency, Copenhagen. 160 pp. (In Danish.)

13. National Housing Agency. 1986. Kvalitetsikring [Quality Assurance]. Publication No. 90, Copenhagen, 44 pp. (In Danish.)

14. Patterson, J.C. 1977. Soil compaction—Effects on urban vegetation. J. Arboric. 3(9):161–167.

15. Pfieffer, C.A., Wott, J.A., and J.R. Clark. 1987. Analyses of landscape design and maintenance requirements in urban parking lots. J. Environ. Hort. 5(4): 188–192.

16. Pittinger, D., and T. Stamen. 1990. Effectiveness of methods used to reduce harmful effects of compacted soil around landscape trees. J. Arboric. 16(3): 55–57.

17. Randrup, T.B. 1996. Plant Growth in Connection to Building Activity: The Influence of Planning and Design on Growth Conditions of Lignoses in Unintended Compacted Soils. Ph.D. thesis. The Royal Veterinary and Agricultural University, Copenhagen Denmark. (In Danish with English summary). 308 pp.

18. Randrup, T.B. 1997. Soil compaction on construction sites. J. Arboric. 23(5): 207–210.

19. Randrup, T.B., and K. Dralle. 1997. Influence of planning and design on soil compaction in construction sites. Landscape Urban Plann. 38:87–92.

20. Rolf, K. 1994. Recultivation of Compacted Soils in Urban Areas. Report No. D6:1994. Swedish Council for Building Research/Department of Agricultural Engineering, University of Agricultural Sciences, Alnarp, Sweden. 68 pp.

21. Saare, E. 1963. Gammastrålning för bestämning av volymvikt. [Gamma radiation for determination of bulk density.] Grundförbättring. 16:233–243. (In Swedish.)

22. Smiley, T., G. Watson, B. Fraedrich, and D. Booth. 1990. Evaluation of soil aeration equipment. J. Arboric. 16(5):118–123.

23. Veihmeyer, F.J., and A.H. Hendrickson. 1948. Soil density and root penetration. Soil Sci. 65:487–493.

24. Yin, R.K. 1989. Case Study Research: Design and Methods. SAGE Publications. London, UK.

25. Zimmerman, R.P., and L.T. Kardos. 1961. Effect of bulk density on root growth. Soil Sci. 91:280–288.

26. Ziza, R.P., H.G. Halverson, and B.B. Stout. 1980. Establishment and Early Growth of Conifers on Compact Soils in Urban Areas. US Forest Service Research Paper NE-451. 8 pp.

Soil Mixes for Urban Sites

Patrick Kelsey

Constructed soils or soil mixes have a variety of applications in the urban environment. Initially, they were created for use in prescription athletic turf. Today, they are used in planters at grade and above, in planting beds, and as replacement soils in parkways adjacent to and under structural sidewalks (4, 6). Soil mixes are created to serve different purposes; each mix will be a unique combination of materials designed to fit the specific objectives of the planting site. Designing the appropriate soil mix is as important as the design of the hardscape associated with the landscape to be installed. Correct construction and installation of engineered soils are vitally important for the proper function of the soil (9). This paper describes effective techniques for the design, construction, and installation of engineered soils by looking at the components used and design concepts associated with their utilization. Constructed soils are made from a mix of mineral soil materials, organic matter, and chemical additives for the purpose of providing rootable space for landscape plants outside the nursery production industry. They differ from nursery mixes in that they are designed to be maintained without volumetric loss for an extended length of time.

Soil Particle Sizes and Texture

Several standards exist for the determination of particle sizes in a soil. The two most common are the ASTM and USDA classes. Typically, ASTM classes are used for civil engineering and architectural specifications, while USDA classes are used in forestry, horticulture, and landscape architecture. The particle size components for these two systems are shown in Table 1. The large variation in size for classes with the same names often leads to confusion in the development and installation of soil mixes because arboricultural professionals and designers are using the same terminology for different size classes.

For example, in the ASTM classification, medium sand ranges from 2.000 to 0.42 mm in diameter, while in the USDA system, the particle size class ranges from 0.50 to 0.25 mm (2). Thus, the ASTM classification will produce a much more poorly graded product than the USDA system if medium sand is specified. Herein lies the problem: Many soil specifications list sand amendments as well as mix components by name and not by the desired particle size class. Additionally, if the soil specifications are

Patrick Kelsey, Research Soil Scientist, The Morton Arboretum, 4100 Illinois Route 53, Lisle, IL 60532.

Table 1. Comparison of ASTM and USDA particle size classes.

Class	ASTM	USDA
Gravel	4.76 mm	2.00 mm
Very coarse sand	—	1.00 mm
Coarse sand	2.00 mm	0.50 mm
Medium sand	0.42 mm	0.25 mm
Fine sand	0.074 mm	0.10 mm
Very fine sand	—	0.050 mm
Silt/clay	< 0.074 mm	< 0.050 mm

based upon roadway subgrade classes, then the underlying standard is most likely ASTM. Without numeric specification, the mix produced may be made with medium sand and still be poorly graded.

The size of the silt and clay fraction also needs to be assessed in constructing fill materials. The maximum size limit for the silt fraction is 25% larger in the ASTM classification (Table 1). The very fine sand of the USDA system is largely considered silt by the ASTM method (3). The reason for this is that materials of this size exhibit cohesive properties similar to silts and clays.

The Value of Understanding Soil Texture

Much emphasis has been placed on soil texture. In constructed soils, the actual texture is less important than the particle size distribution of the individual particles. The importance of texture is the underlying interpretation associated with other soil properties and attributes. Figure 1 shows the percentage limits for soil textures of horticultural and arboricultural importance. These limits were derived by evaluating the physical characteristics of hundreds of urban soil profiles and their relationship to tree and shrub growth. Interpretations were developed and published by reference in Watson and Himelick (16). The interpretations have been modified with the addition of new information and reflect changes made to the particle size limits for the textural classes. The limits for clay in each of the soil texture classes have been lowered to coincide with The Morton Arboretum Soil Characterization Laboratory recommended limits for clay contents in urban soils and soil mixes. Table 2 shows interpretations of soil properties for the horticultural textures that have been established by the lab.

In addition to texture, the total clay content impacts the ability to use a soil in an urban site. By evaluating the growth and health of new tree plantings in urban soils, we have established guidelines for clay contents in urban soils. Fifteen percent clay is

Table 2. Soil interpretation for horticultural texture groups.

Characteristic	Clay	Silt	Sand	Coarse loam	Fine loam
Air exchange	poor	poor	very good	good	good
Drainage	poor	poor	very good	good	good
Infiltration	very slow	very slow	rapid	moderate	moderately slow
Compactability	high	very high	low to moderate	moderate	moderate to high
Nutrient storage capability	very high	very high	low	moderate	moderate
Tilth	poor	poor	very good to fair	very good	good

the maximum limit for optimal soil quality in a planter soil. Twenty-seven percent clay is regarded as the maximum clay content that should be allowed in any constructed tree soils, even those that are predominantly the local topsoil. Thirty-four percent clay is the point at which very significant losses can be expected due to poor soil conditions related to soil texture (Table 3).

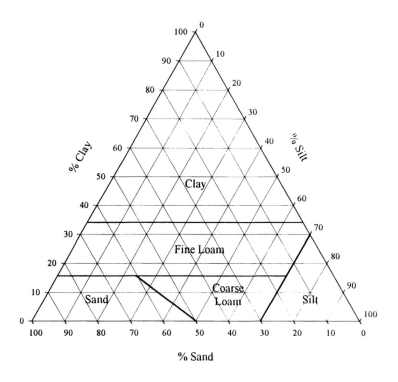

Figure 1. Textural limits for urban horticultural practices.

Table 3. Transplant survival in tree planter soils. Data include a variety of species.

Soil clay content (%)	Total planters	Total survivors	Transplant survival (%)
0 to 10	16	15	94
11 to 15	51	51	100
16 to 27	42	22	52
28 to 34	29	3	10
> 35	18	3	17

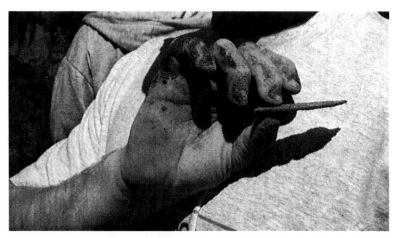

Figure 2. Platy structure developed from the cementation of sand particles by fine clays made of calcium carbonate.

Soil Structure

Properly constructed soil mixes typically have either single grain structure or weak granular structure (5). Both of these aggregate types allow maximum water infiltration. Soils constructed with significant amounts silts and clays typically develop a platy structure as a result of soil cementation and compaction during installation (Figure 2). Once created, this structure is difficult to reverse. In 20-year-old planting beds at The Morton Arboretum, a platy structure was created when sand was added to clayey topsoil. Tillage has been used with chemical treatments in an attempt to overcome the problem with little success. Spomer (13) gives recommendations for the volumetric addition of sand to amend topsoil.

Soil Mixes

Constructed soils have seen widespread use in the development of prescription or athletic turf. Significant use of these soils has recently begun in the landscape industry. The use of a soil mix in the landscape shares many similarities with that of prescription athletic turf (PAT), yet the differences merit attention. Soil mixes used in planters must provide stability to the plant materials to prevent windthrow. The rooting medium must out of necessity be deeper and resistant to subsidence. Typically, the surface course of PAT is less than 6 in. (15.2 cm) in depth. Commonly, planter soil mixes are 24 to 42 in. (61 to 106.7 cm) deep, although they may be deeper in grade-level plantings. Structural soil mixes are used where pavement constraints exist and there is a need to provide soils of load-bearing capacities (4, 6). This paper does not include information concerning structural soils.

Soil mixes specified for constructed landscapes commonly contain locally derived topsoil mixed with peat moss with or without sand (1). These mixes have no uniformity, are poorly graded, and are subject to subsidence as the peat moss decomposes. Chemical and physical limitations associated with these soils are detailed in Kelsey

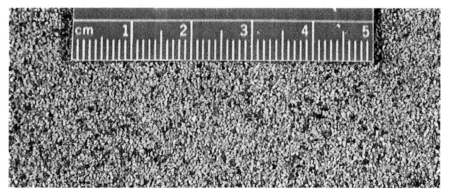

Figure 3. Uniform medium sand is the base material for many soil mixes.

(8) and Kelsey and Rieger (9). An effort was undertaken to create a soil mix with adequate drainage plus good moisture and nutrient-holding capacities that could be leached of unwanted constituents, such as deicing salts, for use in urban planters and planting sites where soil replacement is warranted. As part of this work, mix components were evaluated for their physical and chemical properties.

Mineral Components

A soil mix must have as its basis a noncompressible mineral material. A well-graded, medium sand (0.50 to 0.25 mm) provides a good base (Figure 3). The sand should be angular. Sand that is rounded or subrounded will have the highest packing density, thereby reducing rootable space and water-holding capacity and becoming more susceptible to shear while increasing the penetration resistance. The medium sand should be a minimum of 90% by volume of the total mix.

The sand should be thoroughly washed before use in any soil mix. The silt and clay fraction of angular torpedo or "horticultural" sand commonly contains a large percentage of cementing agents (Figure 4). Silt and clay contaminants may account for as much as one-quarter of the weight of unwashed torpedo sand. The data in Figure 4 show that, on average, 27% of the materials present in ten subsamples of torpedo sand were silt and clay. Of that percentage, more than 70% of the contaminants were clay-sized calcium carbonate particles and silica particles (Figure 5). Both of these agents are primary components of portland cement. Thus, to reduce the possibility of surface crusting of the soil mix, the silts and clays must be washed out.

Organic Matter

Organic matter attributes vary with the size of the particle much in the same way as mineral materials. Coarse organic matter is generally greater than 5 mm in diameter. Fine organic matter ranges from 5 mm to 0.002 mm, and colloidal organic matter is less than 2 microns (0.002 mm) in diameter. Coarse organic materials are characterized as having small surface-to-volume ratios, large macropores including

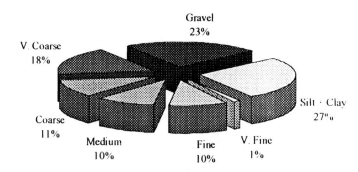

Figure 4. "Horticultural" or torpedo sand particle size distribution.

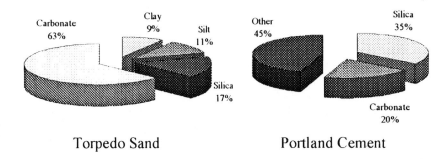

Torpedo Sand   Portland Cement

Figure 5. Cementing agents in unwashed torpedo sand found in the silt + clay fraction.

internal macropore space, and low nutrient exchange capacity. Fine organic matter has an intermediate surface-area-to-volume ratio that increases dramatically below 1 mm. Macropores are smaller in size and there are fewer internal macropores to the organic matter particles. Cation and anion exchange are highly variable, although exchange capacity generally increases with decreasing particle diameter (14). Colloidal organic matter provides microbial habitat, has moderate exchange capacities, and generally acts similar to clay particles. Colloidal organic matter often repels water and may line the interior surfaces of macro- and micropores, thereby reducing the movement of materials into and out of the pores. This may cause a reduction in air exchange as well as a loss of water movement.

Numerous sources of organic matter are available for use in soil mixes. Coarse organic matter sources include wood and bark chips, tub grindings, brewer's waste, and wood shavings. Fine organic matter includes composted leaf molds, manure, mushroom compost, and sawdust. Organic matter sources commonly contain colloidal materials (less than 2 microns) that, when present in large quantities, may cause problems with the soil mix.

Few micromorphological studies of urban soils have been conducted. Most of the work done at the Center for Urban Ecology (now closed) in the National Capital Parks Region focused on the micromorphological evidence of compaction (12). However, a growing body of experience suggests that colloidal organic matter migrates along pores clogging them, particularly if they are small pores (Patterson, personal communication). The process of organic matter movement and subsequent lining of pores is well documented in natural soils (15). Colloidal materials that line pores may seal them, reducing both the exchange of air and water. Many composted organic materials are water repellent (14). The combination of water repellency and particle migration may have a negative impact on the drainage of constructed soils if the colloidal organic matter content is too high. Further investigation of these processes is necessary to determine the potential level of risk in soil mixes.

Organic matter contents of soil mixes should not exceed 5% by weight. There should be a mix of coarse and fine materials. Efforts should be made to minimize the amount of colloidal humus that is initially put into the mix. As decomposition occurs, humus will form naturally.

Soil Drainage

Soil mixes are typically constructed in two layers: a coarse-textured subsoil and a topsoil layer that is typically higher in organic matter (Figure 6). This method of soil building may mimic the natural horizonation of soils, but it creates a number of problems for root system growth. Bisequal soils have an inherent interface that must be overcome by roots and water moving through the profile. Four constructed soils were evaluated for the influence of lithologic discontinuity, or textural interface, on the rootable volume of the soil as controlled by saturation due to a high water-table condition (Figure 7). The greatest rootable volume was present in soils in which uniform soil mixes were present. The interface showed little effect on the capillary fringe in any of the soils. Water tables will persist in stratified materials for a longer period of time than in uniform soils. Even when drainage is optimized in the soil, localized anaerobic conditions may develop or persist as the result of accelerated decomposition that occurs in areas with high moisture content, even in unsaturated soil (Figure 8). Thus, the evaluation of saturation should always be coupled with a measure of anaerobic conditions. Simple methods such as the steel rod procedure detailed by Hodge (7) are excellent for addressing the aeration status of high organic-matter-content soils. This technique is less effective at organic matter contents below 2%.

Irrigation

The single greatest limitation to the use of soil mixes in planters is managing the water needs of the plants. Several investigators have produced methods of estimating the water needs of plants in confined spaces (10, 11). The water-holding capacities of uniform soil mixes vary with the amount and type of fine-textured materials, particularly clay. Increasing amounts of fines will increase the overall water-holding capacity but may not increase the available water. Nonirrigated planters on Lake Shore Drive in Chicago, Illinois, had no more visible signs of moisture stress than did irri-

Figure 6. Typical planter soil installation in separate layers. The approach creates an interface on which water perches, thereby reducing the rootable space.

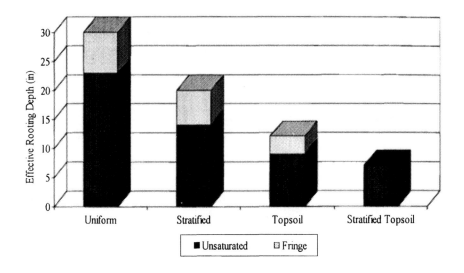

Figure 7. Effect of soil stratification on rooting space in urban planters.

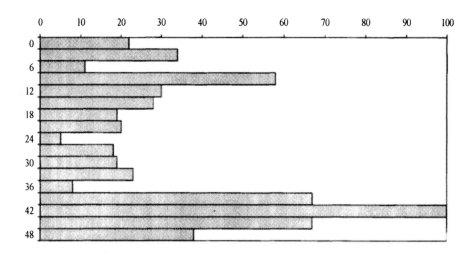

Figure 8. Soil-reduction patterns in urban planter soils.

gated planters at the same location during the period 1992 to 1994 (9). However, the soil mixes in these planters were highly variable and contained more silts, clays, and colloidal organic matter than is typical of a constructed soil mix.

Planter Considerations

While soil mixes can be used in planting beds and parkways, they are typically used in at-grade or above-grade planters. Planters provide a unique environment in that plants are essentially growing in a permanently confined space. As has been shown above, the rootable space can be restricted in soil mixes just by stratifying the soil layers. If planter conditions are not conducive to good drainage, water will perch in the planter even if bottom drainage is installed. Figure 9 shows the design of above-grade planters in use in Chicago that were designed in consultation with The Morton Arboretum Soil Characterization Laboratory. This planter design utilizes a sloped soil surface, vertical side wall drains, and a vitreous clay bottom drain to provide maximum relief from saturation. Because the soil used is a uniform, coarse-textured mix, infiltration and percolation rates are high, thus allowing for a sloped surface. The soil mix covers the vertical drains at the edge, which reduces the potential for surface runoff to directly enter the tile system. Most of the time this system is installed with irrigation. When irrigation is installed, it can be used in the spring to flush deicing salts from the planters when they are used in roadway medians.

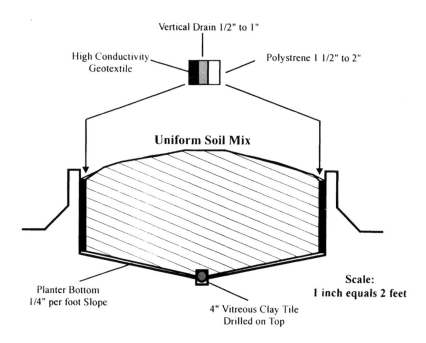

Figure 9. Chicago planter design. This planter is designed to optimize aeration and reduce the period of saturation.

Conclusions

The use of constructed soil mixes is an effective means of increasing the rootable area in urban sites with limited space. The design of the soil mix must be tailored to the specific site and to the proposed plant materials. The base material for installation should be composed of uniform, medium sand with not more than 5% coarse and fine organic matter by weight. The sand should be thoroughly washed of silts and clays that may contain cementing agents such as silica and calcium carbonate. The organic matter used should not be subject to rapid decomposition so that subsidence is avoided. The soil should be uniformly mixed to avoid the effects of layering and the occurrence of a perched water-table condition. Fertility levels should be tested and evaluated at the time of installation and adjusted accordingly. Small amounts of topsoil containing less than 15% clay might need to be added to provide adequate nutrient exchange sites. The total topsoil added should not exceed 10% of the soil mix by weight.

Literature Cited

1. American Institute of Architects. 1993. MASTERSPEC. Section 02900, pp 1–29. American Institute of Architects, Chicago, IL.
2. American Society for Testing Materials. 1989. Standard test method for classification of soils for engineering purposes. D2487. Annual Book of Standards 4.08: 288–297. American Society for Testing Materials, Philadelphia, PA.
3. American Society for Testing Materials. 1989. Standard method for particle size analysis of soils. D422. Annual Book of Standards 4.08: 86–92. American Society for Testing Materials, Philadelphia, PA.
4. Couenberg, E. 1994. Amsterdam tree soil, pp 24–33. In Watson, G.W., and D. Neely (Eds.). The Landscape Below Ground: Proceedings of an International Workshop on Tree Root Development in Urban Soils, Lisle, IL. International Society of Arboriculture, Champaign, IL.
5. Craul, P. 1992. Urban Soil in Landscape Design. John Wiley and Sons, New York., NY. 396 pp.
6. Grabosky, J., and N. Bassuk. 1995. *A new urban tree soil to safely increase rooting volumes under sidewalks.* J. Arboric. 21:187–201.
7. Hodge, S., R. Boswell, and K. Knott. 1993. *Development of the steel rod technique for the assessment of aeration in urban soils.* J. Arboric. 9:281–288.
8. Kelsey, P. 1994. 1994. Maintaining tree health: Soil chemical perspectives, pp 211–218. In Watson, G.W., and D. Neely (Eds.). The Landscape Below Ground: Proceedings of an International Workshop on Tree Root Development in Urban Soils, Lisle, IL. International Society of Arboriculture, Champaign, IL.
9. Kelsey, P., and R. Rieger. 1996. Evaluating the effectiveness of deicing salt mitigation strategies on Lake Shore Drive, Chicago, Illinois. The Morton Arboretum Contract Report. 53 pp.
10. Kopinga, J. 1991. *The effects of restricted volumes of soil on the growth and development of street trees.* J. Arboric. 17:57–63.

11. Lindsey, P., and N. Bassuk. 1991. *Specifying soil volumes to meet the water needs of mature urban trees and trees in containers.* J. Arboric. 17:187–201.
12. Patterson, J.C., and C.J. Bates. 1994. Long term, light-weight aggregate performance as soil amendments, pp 149–156. **In** Watson, G.W., and D. Neely (Eds.). The Landscape Below Ground: Proceedings of an International Workshop on Tree Root Development in Urban Soils, Lisle, IL. International Society of Arboriculture, Champaign, IL.
13. Spomer, A. 1982. Amending landscape soils with sand. Horticulture Facts LH-6-82. Univ. of Illinois Coop. Ext. Serv. 4 pp.
14. Stevenson, F.J. 1986. Cycles of Soil. John Wiley and Sons, New York, NY. 380 pp.
15. Vepraskas, M. 1992. Redomorphic features for identifying aquic conditions. Tech. Bull. 301. North Carolina State Univ. 33 pp.
16. Watson, G.W., and E.B. Himelick. 1997. Principles and Practice of Planting Trees and Shrubs. International Society of Arboriculture. Champaign, IL. 199 pp.

Soil Compaction at Tree-Planting Sites in Urban Hong Kong

C.Y. Jim

Various soil limitations commonly influence the performance of landscape plants in cities, with physical problems often neglected. This study evaluates the compaction of soils at tree sites in urban Hong Kong at both roadside and park habitats. Field and the laboratory studies evaluated selected physical properties of 100 samples, including structure, texture, consistence, bulk density, and porosity. A large proportion of the soils are excessively coarse textured and stony, with widespread structural degradation and compaction. Two-fifths of the samples have bulk densities above the 1.6 Mg/m^3 threshold, with some exceeding 2 Mg/m^3. An increase in particle packing results in collapse of interstitial voids and shifts in pore-size distribution. The causes and consequences of compaction are discussed in relation to tree growth. The findings indicate an association between soil texture and compaction, with the sandy nature of the soils checking the extent of compaction and its negative impacts on root development. The results yield useful management implications for adoption in the local urban tree program.

Humankind as an agent of soil formation has long been recognized by soil scientists. Whether the impacts are regarded as modifications of natural factors, namely climate, organism, relief, and parent material and time, or as an independent sixth factor leading to meta-pedogenesis, the important role played by humankind has been widely expounded. The study of soils in relation to agriculture and forestry, vis-à-vis that of natural soils, is implicitly or explicitly focused on the effects of various activities on this vital resource. A plethora of imprints, both positive or negative, is left in soils as evidence of the pervasive and profound changes.

Soils in human settlements are especially subject to drastic and intensive disturbances due to the addition, removal, mixing, and transformation of soil constituents. Such unnatural processes, inimical if not arresting to normal pedogenesis and soil horizon development, furnish an extraneous suite of pedoturbations. With different modes and magnitudes of impacts, urban soils are characterized by exceptional variabilities. A continuum from natural to disturbed and to entirely reconstituted, manufactured soils could be identified.

As a planting medium, the highly heterogeneous technogenic or damaged soils are often beset with multiple physical and chemical limitations. The accidental or intentional actions have led to altered materials in terms of composition and organization,

C.Y. Jim is Professor and Head, Department of Geography and Geology, University of Hong Kong, Pokfulam Road, Hong Kong.

properties, and behavior. The resulting soils have to support the landscape plants that are demanded in cities. Urban trees, with greater and longer-term soil needs for water, nutrient, and anchorage than other growth forms, are particularly affected by edaphic problems. Soil quality to a large extent determines the growth rate, health, vigor, establishment, and long-range welfare of urban trees and is generally regarded in arboriculture as the fundamental stress factor of woody plants.

The accurate detection and diagnosis of soil problems should be the initial step in tree planting that ultimately affects the success or failure of an urban greening program. Unfortunately, the significance of soil evaluation has not been matched by appropriate attention; indeed, it is widely neglected by researchers and practitioners. Efforts are concentrated on species-cultivar selection and the subaerial environment, with the substrate factor too often taken for granted. Recent advances in urban soil science should provide a secure platform to rectify this longstanding oversight, so as to make more rational use of the resources earmarked for urban forestry.

Physical soil restrictions are more permanent and difficult to ameliorate than chemical ones. Deleterious properties such as undesirable texture, damaged structure, compaction, sequestered rootable volume, lithologic discontinuity, and inert materials are not easy to correct or remove once trees have been planted. Chemical limitations, besides the accumulation of a high level of toxic pollutants, are more amenable to curative measures. Despite their importance, physical constraints have received comparatively less attention (if not been completely overlooked) in arboricultural practice and landscape horticulture in general.

Of the different forms of physical soil limitations related to urban tree growth, soil compaction is a commonly encountered difficulty. Compaction is a structural degradation process that occurs when an applied mechanical force exceeds the shear strength of a soil, resulting in the destruction of aggregates, collapse of interstitial pores, and a higher-density packing of particles. Various construction and postconstruction activities can damage soil structure to cause closer particle packing, leading to negative secondary edaphic consequences to infiltration, drainage, plant-available moisture, aeration, and available rooting area.

An urban tree census conducted recently in Hong Kong provided hints that physical soil limitations are important determinants of tree performance. A lack of relevant local research hinders the understanding and solution of the common problem. The present study addresses urban soil compaction as one of the crucial physical limitations of the substrate that commonly plague the planting and survival of urban trees in the heavily built-up areas of Hong Kong. Soils in different types of roadside and park habitats were studied in the field and analyzed in the laboratory to assess the status and extent of the structural degradation problem, the relationship between compaction and other soil attributes, and associated soil-management measures to alleviate and prevent the occurrence of this constraint.

Study Areas and Methods

Soil sampling focused on actual tree planting sites to include a wide range of habitats at roadsides and in public parks, all situated in the core urban areas of Hong Kong around the harbor. A total of 100 soil samples was obtained from 40 soil pits approximately 1 m³ (33 ft³) large. Soil conditions on the four vertical cut faces of the pits were evaluated in the field with reference to profile morphology and selected measurable attributes using standard soil survey field techniques (12). Soil horizons or layers were identified and demarcated, and for each main soil layer thicker than 30 cm (11.8 in.), two types of soil samples were taken. Undisturbed samples were extracted with the core method by driving carefully with a rubber-headed mallet a stainless steel cylinder measuring 10 cm (3.9 in.) in diameter and 15 cm (5.9 in.) in length into the four sides of the soil pit. Disturbed samples were collected by excavating soils on the four vertical pit walls and mixing them together to form a composite sample for a given layer.

Samples were air dried and analyzed in the laboratory using standard methods on the following properties:

- air-dried and moist soil color according to Munsell Color Notation (9)
- the weight of the stone fraction (> 2 mm [0.08 in.] diameter) by sieving
- particle-size distribution in the clay, silt, and sand fractions using the hydrometer method (6), and textural classification using USDA particle-size class limits
- soil structure with reference to shape, size, and degree of development of the peds (aggregates)
- soil aggregate stability using the wet-sieving technique based on 1 to 2 mm (0.04 to 0.08 in.) diameter aggregates (10)
- soil consistency in terms of ped strength, maximum stickiness, and maximum plasticity
- soil bulk density using the clod method, with clods greater than 2 cm (0.8 in.) diameter obtained from cylinders described above (1), and with volume measurement of clods coated by Saran resin (3)
- total porosity by calculation based on bulk and particle density results (1); an evaluation of pore-size distribution of selected aggregate samples was attempted using mercury intrusion porosimetry (5)
- soil organic carbon using the wet combustion method according to Walkley-Black (11)
- total nitrogen contents using the Kjeldahl method (4)

Morphological and Physical Characteristics

All sites have free drainage with no evidence of waterlogging. Soil colors are dominated by the yellow and red groups indicative of an oxidative environment. Most soils are composed of highly disturbed fill materials with clear signs of structural damage and lack of aggregation. Natural soil horizons can hardly be found, and most soil layers are the result of haphazard earth dumping and spreading. The O and A topsoil horizons are absent in roadside sites and are feebly represented in park samples. Lithologic discontinuities are commonly present, in the form of multiple layers well defined by differences in composition, texture, structure, and color. Profile morphology indicates that all the soil sites, including those in parks, have been drastically disturbed by construction activities. The high-intensity and high-density mode of urban development in Hong Kong has left a pervasive imprint on urban soils. Some sites could have been subjected to many cycles of intensive activities including grade change, truncation, burial, mixing, contamination, and compaction.

Results of laboratory analysis have been summarized statistically in Table 1. Stone contents are excessive in most samples, reaching a mean of 39.8% and a maximum 81.8%. Some stones are broken pieces of construction rubbles. Various types of artifacts were frequently encountered in the field and in the course of sample preparation in the laboratory. The soils are largely a random mixture of *in situ* as well as transported natural soils, weathered materials locally known as decomposed granite, construction debris, and miscellaneous wastes. The soil textures are overwhelmingly dominated by sand-sized particles, mainly in the coarsest categories of sand, loamy sand, and sandy loam—with loamy sand being the dominant class (Figure 1). On average the samples have sand contents attaining as much as 81%, with silt and clay as minority components for most cases.

Peds (aggregates) tend to be limited in size (few exceed 3 cm [1.2 in.] diameter), poorly formed, and weak in strength. Granular and weak, blocky structural types are commonly found. High-grade structural development is absent. Aggregate stability results cluster around 36% to 54%, implying that over half of the aggregates could be easily disintegrated by mechanical forces. Soil consistency tends to be nonsticky to slightly sticky, and nonplastic to slightly plastic, reflecting the lack of the active colloidal clay minerals and organic matter. The very low contents of total carbon and total nitrogen verify the paucity of organic constituents. Overall, soil structural development and maintenance are much hampered by the lack of aggregating agents. The fragile soil organization is prone to damage by external forces. The inherently unstable soil structural units could easily break down, resulting in pore collapse and

Table 1. Summary of selected soil physical properties related to compaction and tree growth in urban Hong Kong (n =100).

Soil attribute	Unit and class limit	Mean	Minimum	Maximum	Range	Std. Dev.	Variance
Bulk density	Mg/m³	1.67	1.14	2.63	1.49	0.25	0.06
Stone content	% (w/w) > 2.0 mm	39.76	5.9	81.8	75.9	14.37	206.62
Sand content	% (w/w) 0.05–2.0 mm	80.97	68.3	96.2	27.9	4.88	23.82
Silt content	% (w/w) 0.002–0.05 mm	11.91	2.6	23.2	20.7	3.12	9.71
Clay content	% (w/w) < 0.002 mm	7.12	0.1	20.4	20.4	3.79	14.36
Sand + silt	% (w/w)	92.88	79.6	100.0	20.4	3.79	14.36
Silt + clay	% (w/w)	19.03	3.8	31.7	27.9	4.88	23.82
Textural class	USDA classification[w]	2.09	1	4	3	0.55	0.30
Aggregate stability	% (w/w)	56.33	30.3	96.0	65.8	18.85	355.51
Maximum stickiness	USDA classification[x]	1.55	1	3	2	0.62	0.39
Maximum plasticity	USDA classification[y]	1.50	1	4	3	0.90	0.81
Ped strength	Hodgson (1974) scheme[z]	2.39	1	5	4	0.98	0.96
Sampling depth	cm	60.65	2	100	98	25.56	653.53
Total carbon	% (w/w)	0.79	0.08	7.36	7.28	1.07	1.14
Total nitrogen	% (w/w)	0.04	0.01	0.47	0.46	0.07	0.00

[w]1 = sand; 2 = loamy sand; 3 = sandy loam; 4 = sandy clay loam.
[x]1 = nonsticky; 2 = slightly sticky; 3 = moderately sticky; 4 = very sticky.
[y]1 = nonplastic; 2 = slightly plastic; 3 = moderately plastic; 4 = very plastic.
[z]1 = loose; 2 = weak; 3 = firm; 4 = strong; 5 = rigid.

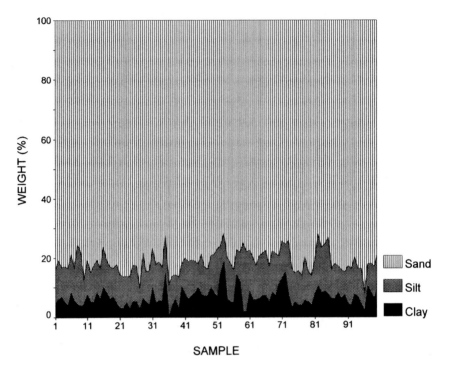

Figure 1. The particle-size distributions of soil samples in urban Hong Kong are dominated by the sand fraction, which takes up more than 70% by weight in most cases, with silt and clay fractions as minor components (n = 100).

rearrangement into a tighter fabric. The degradation of soil structure engenders an unfavorable physical condition, which is one of the most important limitations to urban tree performance.

Bulk Density and Porosity

Bulk densities range from a minimum of 1.14 to a maximum of 2.63, with the mean at 1.67 Mg/m³ (Table 1 and Figure 2). The spread is wider than those reported in the literature for urban soils, which registered a minimum of 1.25 (similar to natural soils) and a maximum of 2.18 Mg/m³, which indicates severe compaction. The present results suggest that local soils are heterogeneous in composition and have been subject to a heterogeneous compaction regime. Roadside sites have inherited soils precompacted to meet engineering specifications to provide a stable load-bearing base, sub-base, and subgrade immediately below a wearing surface (the concrete paving). A Proctor Optimum Density of 85% compaction is specified locally. Road engineering requirements have dictated sidewalk soil-packing density, with no compromising allowance for tree roots. Opening of tree pits could only loosen a restricted volume of soil, often less than 1 m³ (33 ft³), delimited by the walls of compacted site soils. For a newly planted tree, root growth is likely to be confined in the backfill upon reaching the densely packed site soil—a dire situation analogous to the potbound phenomenon.

Bulk density exceeding 1.6 Mg/m^3 is commonly regarded as restrictive to root growth. Some studies, however, found that roots were restricted at the lower density of 1.4 Mg/m^3, whereas others suggested that roots could penetrate through lines of weakness in soils with a bulk density up to 1.68 Mg/m^3. In the present study, some 40% of the samples registered readings above the 1.6 Mg/m^3 threshold. The closure of macropores (air capacity [AC] pores at > 60 μm diameter) due to geometric reorganization of the solid components leaves inadequate physical room for root growth. Closer packing of soil also increases the shear strength of the soil due to particle interlocking and enhanced electrostatic attraction, making it more difficult for roots to elongate by axial pressure or to expand (secondary thickening) by radial pressure. The hydrostatic pressure exerted axially by a growing root tip has been measured to be 1.2 MPa, and radially it is at a much lower level of 0.5 MPa. The high bulk-density values commonly encountered in the present study are restrictive to root development and are believed to be an important cause of widespread poor performance in urban trees.

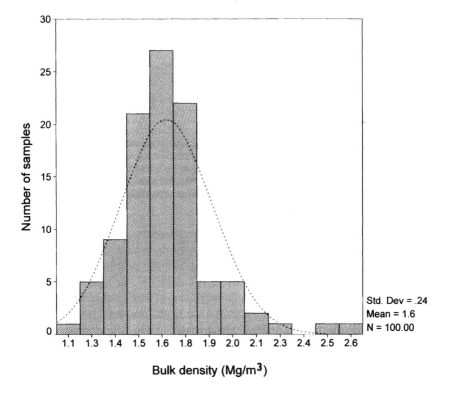

Figure 2. The frequency distribution of bulk-density values of 100 samples of urban soils in Hong Kong collected from roadside tree pits and in urban parks.

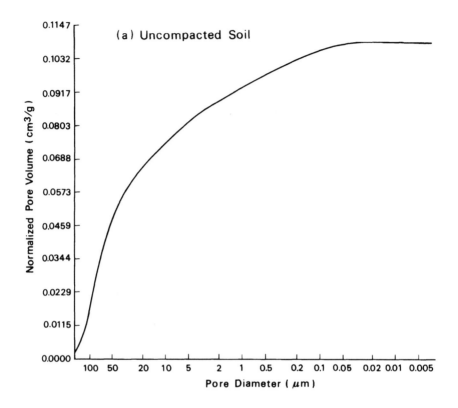

Figure 3. The pore-size distributions of a relatively uncompacted subsoil sample at bulk density 1.42 Mg/m³ (above left) compared to a compacted topsoil sample at 1.82 Mg/m³ (above right). Both samples have a sandy loam texture. Note that the compacted soil shows significant reduction of pore volume in the air capacity (AC > 60 μm diameter) and available water (AW 0.2 to 60 μm diameter), but an increase in the unavailable moisture (UM < 0.2 μm diameter).

Changes in total porosity in response to compaction implies the collapse of macropores, some of which are converted into mesopores (available water [AW] pores at 0.2 to 60 μm diameter) and micropores (unavailable moisture [UM] pores at < 0.2 μm diameter). At the critical bulk density of 1.6 Mg/m³, the total porosity stands at 39.6% by volume—somewhat below the 40% level generally regarded as the minimum below which root growth can suffer. At 1.8 Mg/m³, the total porosity drops to 32%, and at 2 Mg/m³ to merely 24.5%. At such a high compaction level, the decline in total porosity is likely to be accompanied by a drastic reduction in macropores, thus compounding the problem of rooting-room confinement.

The pore-size distribution results obtained by mercury intrusion porosimetry of a relatively uncompacted subsoil sample with a bulk density of 1.47 Mg/m³ and a compacted topsoil sample at 1.82 Mg/m³, both of sandy loam texture, are depicted in Figure 3. The instrument is capable of detecting pores in the range of 0.002 to 450 μm

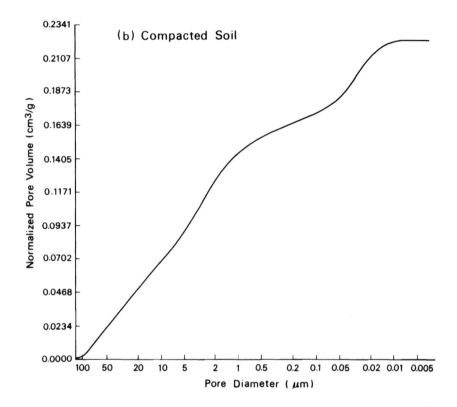

diameter, covering the lower portion of AC, the entire AW, and the upper portion of UM pores. In comparison, the compacted topsoil has a much smaller proportion of pores in the AC and AW range, and a large concentration of pores in the UM range. The results confirm the tendency in compaction for the large pores to collapse into small ones, resulting in decreased storage capacity for available water (AW pores) and suppression of infiltration, drainage, and aeration capabilities (AC pores). The pore-size distribution in the compacted soils has undergone a significant shift toward the less useful residual voids. With AC pores reduced to a less than 10% volume threshold, pore continuity is likely to restrict gas exchanges between the soil and the atmosphere. Furthermore, the tortuosity of pore pathways is increased at elevated bulk density to restrain air permeability and gas diffusion.

Roadside soils are usually precompacted before tree insertion. Because most road-side trees in Hong Kong are grown in tree pits rather than tree strips or tree lawns, and because most pits are protected by grilles, the possibility of additional postplanting compaction due to pedestrian traffic is limited. Soils in urban parks, however, have a different stress regime. They were partly compacted during the park construction phase during which many disturbances could be imposed by earth-moving, filling, stockpiling, and building activities. The severe shortage of urban parks in Hong Kong means those parks are heavily patronized and experience congestion during peak usage hours. After the opening of the parks, the inexorable impacts of human foot traffic continues to contribute to compaction. This postplanting damaging force explains the common occurrence of a surface crustlike compacted layer in the degraded parts of urban parks. In comparison with confined roadside sites, trees in urban parks have a much larger soil volume to explore. The common occurrence of trampling degradation in parks, however, could impose an alternative limiting factor in the form of a surface cap.

Variabilities in the magnitude of compaction occurred both between and within sites. For most soil pits, bulk densities are higher in the upper layers and decrease somewhat with depth. With more roots (especially the finer absorbing ones growing in the upper soil layer), surface-layer compaction could be especially detrimental. Dense particle packing in the surface soil also reduces infiltration rate, hence limiting the replenishment of soil moisture from rain or irrigation water. Similarly, aeration is restricted by the lack of suitably wide and continuous porosity pathways in the AC size class. Even though the subsoil layers are usually less compacted and not so harmful to roots, the dense surface layers form a sealing barrier imposing indirect deleterious impacts on the underlying soils.

Compaction and Soil Texture

Variations in the degree of compaction in the soil samples are associated with some physical soil attributes (Table 2). The properties related to particle size and texture are significantly correlated with bulk density (P < 0.001), although the correlation coefficients at 0.318 to 0.395 are not unduly strong. Sand content is inversely correlated with bulk density (Figure 4), indicating the disruptive effects of coarse particles on packing of soil. With a high sand content, compaction could gradually bring coarse particles closer together until they form a coarse matrix with sand grains in physical contact. Once this critical stage has been reached, the contiguous sand grains resist further geometric rearrangement into a denser packing configuration. Thus, the compaction process in coarse-textured soils is self-limiting, subject to a negative feedback control.

The compactability of sandy soils is therefore practically arrested once physical contiguity of the grains has been established. The interstitial voids within the coarse matrix, however, could be filled by fine particles (the fines). Clay as well as silt-sized particles could be trapped in the voids. For a given coarse matrix, an increase in the fines occluded within the voids could result in a higher bulk density. This hypothesis is partly verified by the positive correlation ($R = 0.325$, $P < 0.001$) between bulk density and clay content (Table 2). The role played by silt is somewhat ambivalent. Correlation between bulk density and silt is weak and insignificant. Correlations when silt is added to sand and clay, respectively, to form two new variables are statistically significant, with sand + silt at $R = -0.325$ and silt + clay at $R = 0.318$. Such results suggest that silt as a intermediate-sized particle class played the role of both coarse and fine particles in the packing of soil. Silt could work in tandem with sand to constitute the coarse matrix, or else together with clay to fill the interstices of the coarse matrix.

Table 2. Correlation coefficients between selected pairs of soil properties in relation to compaction in urban Hong Kong (n = 100).

Selected soil attribute	Bulk density	Selected soil attribute	Bulk density
Stone content	0.020	Aggregate stability	−0.009
Sand content	−0.318***	Maximum stickiness	0.133
Silt content	0.081	Maximum plasticity	0.354***
Clay content	0.325***	Ped strength	0.673***
Sand + silt	−0.325***	Sampling depth	−0.209*
Silt + clay	0.318***	Total carbon	−0.053
Textural class	0.395***	Total nitrogen	0.064

*$P < 0.05$.
**$P < 0.01$.
***$P < 0.001$.

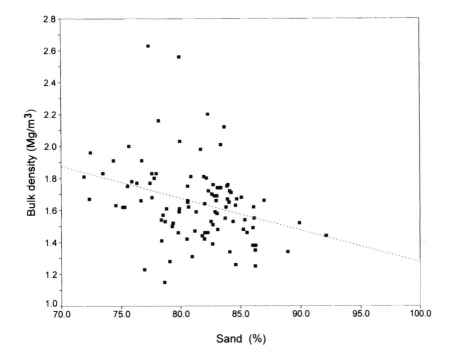

Figure 4. Statistical relationship between soil bulk density and the weight contents of sand ($R = -0.318$; $R^2 = 10.11\%$; n =100; $P < 0.001$).

The exceptionally high sand contents of local urban soils, reaching an average of 81%, provide ample materials of the right size to form a coarse matrix. A more equitable distribution of sand, silt, and clay particles could not have provided such a particle organizational framework. The soils thus have an inherent capability to resist excessively dense packing. The low contents of silt and especially clay imply an inadequate quantity of fines to fill the interstitial voids of the coarse matrix, thus keeping the soil somewhat open and porous; therefore, the bulk densities are not inordinately low. This could explain why 60% of the samples have bulk densities at or lower than the critical limit of 1.6 Mg/m³, despite the common occurrence of engineering and other compaction forces on urban soils.

The same phenomenon could maintain a certain quantity of AC and AW pores in the compacted soils, allowing air and water to penetrate and tree roots to grow without undue difficulty. The continuity of pores can be sustained to a certain extent despite the imposition of compaction stresses. In a sandy soil, the lower cohesive force between particles also renders them more amenable to displacement by growing roots. Thus, for the same bulk density, the coarse-textured soils pose less of a hindrance to root development than the fine ones. Whereas the domination by sand particles brought unfavorable properties, particularly with reference to inadequate storage of available water and proneness to drought, it bestows to a certain extent a desirable control against the deleterious impacts of compaction. The inadvertent use of highly sandy soils at urban tree sites in Hong Kong has brought an expected benefit that mitigates against pervasive compaction forces. The presence of too many stones, forming rather insurmountable obstacles to root growth, has partly negated the benefits of the sandy matrix.

Soil Management Implications and Conclusions

Much of the soil management effort in urban Hong Kong has been directed towards the amelioration of chemical problems, with scanty attention paid to physical ones. This study illustrates the common occurrence of a neglected attribute in the tree-management equation. The imbalance in the attitude and knowledge base of urban foresters and arborists needs to be rectified so as to minimize the major landscape-below-ground restrictions and to optimize tree performance in city habitats. Urban soils in different habitats have to be studied to build up the scientific basis for proper management. Besides interpreting the causes and consequences of soil compaction on tree growth, measures to prevent and ameliorate the problems should be sought.

To ameliorate the compacted soils before inserting trees, various mechanical devices and approaches could be adopted to loosen the soil, such as conventional drilling, vertical mulching, deep plowing, and subsoiling, or the more innovative pneumatic and other techniques. For existing trees, the application of such disruptive techniques could damage the roots; localized soil replacement in the rooting zone could be considered as an alternative. For instance, the hydraulic technique could be employed to wash away the compacted soils and replace them with a suitable soil mix (14) containing appropriate organic amendments. At drastically disturbed sites that need to support loads, it is desirable to use a prescribed soil mix (7, 8) preferably in an expanded tree pit, soil corridor, and vaulting configurations. A soil specification for urban trees for different habitats should be developed using locally available soil materials.

The prevention of compaction should be adopted as a routine measure in urban tree programs. A survey of soils in urban areas and a suitable urban-soil classification scheme (2, 13) can furnish synoptic and spatial information to preserve good-quality soils and accordingly design urban soil-management plans. The evaluation of site and backfill soil using standard field and laboratory methods should be included as an integral part of tree projects. The maintenance of good soil structure in construction sites could be more assiduously implemented with appropriate guides and training for the construction crew. Urban tree sites could be designed with specific attention paid to the soil needs of trees rather than as an adjunct to domineering engineering requirements.

Urban soils in Hong Kong suffer from more acute and pervasive soil problems in comparison with other inner-city areas. The small number of available planting sites in relation to the large human population warrants a more stringent site-preparation standard. The hitherto cursory attitude in tree programs toward the subterranean realm should be drastically modified by involving the parties concerned in the development process—including developers, planners, architects, landscape architects, engineers, tree managers, and citizen groups—with a view to forming a partnership to hammer out a working procedure, to move out of the ruts, and to incorporate the fruits of arboricultural research into site design and soil specifications.

Acknowledgments

The author would like to acknowledge the research grant support provided by the Environment and Conservation Fund and the Woo Wheelock Green Fund for the project entitled Better Environment for Better Trees in Urban Hong Kong.

Literature Cited

1. Blake, G.R., and K.H. Hartge. 1986. Bulk density, pp 363–375. **In** Klute, A. (Ed.). Methods of Soil Analysis, Part 1: Physical and Mineralogical Methods (2nd ed.). American Society of Agronomy, Madison, WI.

2. Blume, H.-P. 1989. *Classification of soils in urban agglomerations.* Catena 16:269–275.

3. Bradsher, B.R., D.P. Franzmeier, V. Valassis, and S.E. Davidson. 1966. *Use of Saran resin to coat natural soil clods for bulk-density and water-retention measurements.* Soil Sci. 101:108.

4. Bremner, J.M., and C.S. Mulvaney. 1982. Nitrogen-total, pp 595–626. **In** Page, A.L., R.H. Miller, and D.R. Keeney (Eds.). Methods of Soil Analysis, Part 2: Chemical and Microbiological Properties (2nd ed.). American Society of Agronomy, Madison, WI.

5. Danielson, R.E., and P.L. Sutherland. 1986. Porosity, pp 443–461. **In** Klute, A. (Ed.). Methods of Soil Analysis, Part 1: Physical and Mineralogical Methods (2nd ed.). American Society of Agronomy, Madison, WI.

6. Gee, G.W., and J.W. Bauder. 1986. Particle-size analysis, pp 383–411. **In** Klute, A. (Ed.). Methods of Soil Analysis, Part 1: Physical and Mineralogical Methods (2nd ed.). American Society of Agronomy, Madison, WI.

7. Grabosky, J., and N. Bassuk. 1995. *A new urban tree soil to safely increase rooting volumes under sidewalks.* J. Arboric. 21:187–201.

8. Grabosky, J., and N. Bassuk. 1996. *Testing of structural urban tree soil materials for use under pavement to increase street tree rooting volumes.* J. Arboric. 22:255–263.

9. Kawai, K. 1970. Revised Standard Soil Color Charts. Research Council for Agriculture, Forestry and Fisheries, Tokyo, Japan.

10. Kemper, W.D., and R.C. Rosenau. 1986. Aggregate stability and size distribution, pp 425–442. **In** Klute, A. (Ed.). Methods of Soil Analysis, Part 1: Physical and Mineralogical Methods (2nd ed.). American Society of Agronomy, Madison, WI.

11. Nelson, D.W., and L.E. Sommers. 1982. Total carbon, organic carbon, and organic matter, pp 539–579. **In** Page, A.L., R.H. Miller, and D.R. Keeney (Eds.). Methods of Soil Analysis, Part 2: Chemical and Microbiological Properties (2nd ed.). American Society of Agronomy, Madison, WI.

12. Soil Survey Division Staff. 1993. Soil Survey Manual. Handbook No. 18. United States Department of Agriculture, Washington, DC. 427 pp.

13. Stroganova, M.N., and M.G. Agarkova. 1993. *Urban soils: Experimental study and classification (exemplified by the soils of southwestern Moscow).* Euras. Soil Sci. 25:59–69.

14. Watson, G.W., P. Kelsey, and K. Woodtli. 1996. *Replacing soil in the root zone of mature trees for better growth.* J. Arboric. 22:167–173.

PART IV

PLANTING

Tree Root Improvements by the Nursery Industry

Bonnie Lee Appleton

For successfully transplanting to and establishment in the landscape it is essential that trees have a well developed root system. Many nursery practices, including field harvesting that leaves the bulk of a tree's roots behind in the nursery soil, and container production that often results in contorted and circling roots, seem counterproductive to successful establishment. New nursery production systems, including pot-in-pot, improved in-ground root control bags, and copper treatment of containers and fabric bags, as well as new production products such as herbicide impregnated bags, the in-ground Cellugro unit, and the double container AGS (Above Ground System), are improving the quality and quantity of roots on nursery grown trees. In addition, new holding techniques currently being tested for field dug (B&B) stock, such as stretch and shrink wrapping and inoculation with mycorrhizae, may help to prevent root system degradation during the transition time from the nursery to the landscape.

Field Production and Holding Methods

Whether grown in the field or in containers, trees coming from commercial nurseries may have production-related root problems that can interfere with successful landscape establishment. In addition, decline in the quality of root systems may occur if the trees must be held for several months after field harvest before being planted. Several new nursery production and holding methods have been developed to help enhance tree root systems and prevent post-harvest decline.

Cultural Methods

When field-grown trees are harvested, the greater portion of their roots (as high as 98%) are left behind at the production nursery (19). Cultural methods—including installing drip irrigation close to the tree stem (10) and root pruning one or more times prior to harvest (9, 12)—are intended to concentrate as many roots as possible within the harvest rootball.

In-Ground Containers

Traditionally, trees could not be grown in the ground in single plastic containers due to drainage problems. A single-container system that permitted drainage has not

---

Bonnie Lee Appleton, Landscape and Nursery Specialist, Virginia Cooperative Extension, Hampton Roads Agricultural Research and Extension Center, 1444 Diamond Springs Road, Virginia Beach, VA 23455-3315.

been widely adapted (2), but the use of fabric containers, a multiplant unit, and a double-container system (pot-in-pot) are becoming more widely used for in-ground field production.

In-Ground Fabric Containers. In-ground fabric containers (grow bags) are made from porous synthetic fabrics (usually polypropylene). These fabrics permit exchange of moisture between in-container soil and the surrounding soil while preventing some or all of the tree's roots from growing outside the container. The earliest versions of the fabric containers were often difficult to remove at transplant due to penetration of large roots or root entanglement in the fabric's fibers. Fabric containers are now easier to remove due to fabric improvements (Root Control® Bag) or the use of fabrics with small holes (Knit Fabric Container), copper impregnation (Tex-R® Agroliner), or a herbicide delivery system (GeoCell) (1, 3, 5, 8). Due to root restriction within the fabric container, drip irrigation is essential with fabric containers. The fabric containers are often removed prior to sale and the rootballs containerized to ensure that roots will not be restricted by nonremoval of the fabric container when trees are transplanted.

Multiplant Unit. The Cellugro® System is a multiplant in-ground system for production of liners and small trees (Figure 1). The standard unit, measuring 8 × 20 ft (2.4 × 6.1 m), holds 561 six-quart-sized (5.7 L) plants in a polyliner/drainboard/production cell unit. The unit is installed either into the ground (approximately 8 in. [20 cm] deep) or set above ground with soil bermed around it. Not only are root temperatures buffered, but water consumption is dramatically reduced compared to above-ground containers (3, 5, 6, 7, 11). Very little root circling or deformation has been observed with this system due to the oblong shape of the individual production cells and the air root pruning that occurs due to the fabric-covered drainboard under the cells (Figure 2).

Double-Container System. The pot-in-pot (P&P) system uses two containers—a production container nested inside the holder (sleeve or stock) container—both sunk into the ground (1, 3, 8, 18). Above-ground production temperature extremes are eliminated, as are such problems as breakage and loss of top-dressed fertilizers and herbicides associated with container blowover. Tree calipering occurs considerably faster with P&P than with above-ground container production. Roots escaping from the inner (production) container have been one of the major production problems to overcome (16, 17).

Holding Methods

When trees are dug for conventional balled-and-burlapped (B&B) production, they frequently are held for several months before planting because of rewholesaling, construction-related installation delays, growers preferring not to summer dig (trees are therefore dug in spring), and landscapers buying in quantity to get lower prices. While trees are held under such circumstances, their roots may dry out, leaves may scorch, balls may flatten (pancake) or harden, and weeds may grow on the ball and compete with the tree roots for limited moisture.

Most nurseries or landscapers that hold trees do so by placing them in a holding area with some form of irrigation, mulch (heeling-in with wood chips or sawdust), or

Figure 1. Cellugro® System being used for tree seedling production.

Figure 2. Loblolly pine grown in the Cellugro® System (left) and in a conventional vertical ribbed container (right).

containerization (potted up). During holding, if the rootballs are wrapped with natural or jute burlap, the burlap may degrade and/or roots may grow out through the burlap and into the mulch or potting medium. This rooting out can cause problems when the trees need to be moved and planted, yet most growers prefer not to use synthetic wrapping materials to combat this problem to ensure that an artificial barrier to root growth doesn't exist when trees are transplanted (14). A new alternative is copper-treated burlap to prevent rooting out. (15).

Several new holding options are available, with additional possibilities being tested (4). Rootballs can be put into fabric sleeves—one for above-ground holding where air root pruning occurs (The Tapered Bag), and one with copper for above- or in-ground holding (Tex-R® Agroliner). In addition, rootballs can be wrapped with plastic, either a stretch form (Braun Horticulture) or a shrink wrap form (Cadillac Products) (Figure 3). Combined with drip irrigation, the use of white shrink wrap moderated rootball temperatures, prevented weed growth, and eliminated most rooting out, and appears to be a good new rootball-holding alternative (6).

Container Production
Root Circling Prevention

With container production of trees comes the problems of root deformation caused by roots circling against container walls (2) and root death due to heating of dark containers (13).

Engineered Containers. To help reduce or eliminate the problem of circling roots that often develop in smooth- or slick-walled plastic containers, a variety of containers were tried that were designed to deflect or redirect roots via molded container-wall baffles (1). Most of these containers were very costly to produce, and were therefore not economically feasible for the nursery industry to use. A better approach has been to use containers with holes in the container walls, in which root tips are killed and circling stopped when the tips encounter air (air root pruning) (Rootmaker) (1). If conventional containers must be used, those with vertical ribs help reduce circling roots, compared to those with horizontal ribs that encourage circling root formation. Also good for stopping circling root formation are soft-walled polybag containers with gusseted bottoms (Menne Polybags).

Copper-Coated Containers and Copper Inserts. A copper-containing product has been developed (Spinout®) that can be applied to smooth container walls to reduce or eliminate root circling (1, 3). The copper acts as a growth regulator, stunting the root tips rather than redirecting or killing them. The product is effective for one growing season in the container, and normal root growth resumes when the container is removed and the tree transplanted into the landscape. Containers are now being pretreated with copper by one of the container manufacturers (Lerio).

Also available are the Tex-R® Agroliners which, instead of being used for in-ground field tree production as mentioned above, can be used to line standard containers to provide copper to prevent root circling (5, 6) (Figure 4).

Low-Profile Container/The Accelerator®. Low profile containers are generally bottomless containers that sit on plastic or other synthetic fabric. They are wider and

Figure 4. Tex-R® Agroliner (copper-impregnated fabric bag) being used to line a conventional container to retard root circling.

Figure 3. Applying white shrink wrap to a 28-in. Norway maple rootball for holding.

shallower than conventional containers to encourage development of shallow, broad root systems that more closely mirror natural tree root systems. Root circling is prevented either by air root pruning at the container wall/bed covering interface, or, with the commercially available The Accelerator®, by holes in and corrugations of the aluminum container walls (1, 3, 8).

Heat Kill Prevention

AGS. The Above Ground System (AGS) is a double-container system for use above ground. A production container nests in a double-walled holder container that serves to insulate the tree's roots and buffer hot and cold temperature extremes. The AGS can have ballast added to prevent blowover, and is easier to harvest than the P&P inground, double-container system (3).

Literature Cited

1. Appleton, B.L. 1993. *Nursery production alternatives for reduction or elimination of circling tree roots.* J. Arboric. 19(6):383–388.
2. Appleton, B.L. 1994. Elimination of circling tree roots during nursery production, pp 93–97. In Watson, G.W., and D. Neely (Eds.). The Landscape Below Ground: Proceedings of an International Workshop on Tree Root Development in Urban Soils. International Society of Arboriculture, Champaign, IL.
3. Appleton, B.L. 1995. *Nursery production methods for improving tree roots—An update.* J. Arboric. 21(6):265–270.
4. Appleton, B.L. 1996. *Examine ways to wrap root balls.* NMPro 12(3):52–54.
5. Appleton, B.L. 1997. *What's new in growing, harvesting, transplanting.* NMPro 13(1):67–68.
6. Appleton, B.L. 1998. *Nursery resolutions: Apply these research results.* NMPro 14(1):61–63.
7. Appleton, B., and S. French. 1996. *The Cellugro System™—A new nursery production method.* Proc. SNA Res. Conf. 41:107–110.
8. Cuny, H. 1996. *Alternative production.* NMPro. 12(12):34–36.
9. Davidson, H., R. Mecklenburg, and C. Peterson. 1988. Nursery crop production. In Nursery Management: Administration and Culture. Prentice Hall, Englewood Cliffs, NJ.
10. Fuller, D.L., and W.A. Meadows. 1987. *Root and top growth response of five woody ornamental species to fabric Field-Grow™ containers, bed height, and trickle irrigation.* Proc. SNA Res. Conf. 32:148–151.
11. Gill, S., R. Balge, and D. Ross. 1997. *A new closed-loop system.* Amer. Nurseryman 186(7):68–70, 72, 74, 76, 78–79.
12. Gilman, E. F., T. H. Yeager, R. Newton, and S. Davis. 1988. *Response of field-grown trees to root pruning.* Proc. SNA Res. Conf. 33:104–105.
13. Hight, A., and T.E. Bilderback. 1994. *Substrate temperatures in above- and below-ground containers in a pot-in-pot system.* Proc. SNA Res. Conf. 39:113–115.

14. Kuhns, M.R. 1997. *Penetration of treated and untreated burlap by roots of balled-and burlapped Norway maples.* J. Arboric. 23(1):1–6.
15. Maynard, B.K., and W.A. Johnson. 1997. *Controlling rooting-out of B&B nursery stock during storage.* J. Environ. Hort. 15(2):111–114.
16. Newman, S.E., and J.R. Quarrels. 1994. *Chemical root pruning of container-grown trees using trifluralin and copper impregnated fabric.* Proc. SNA Res. Conf. 39:75–76.
17. Ruter, J.M. 1994. *Evaluation of control strategies for reducing rooting-out problems in pot-in-pot production systems.* J. Environ. Hort. 12(1):51–54
18. Ruter, J.M. 1997. *The practicality of pot-in-pot.* Amer. Nurseryman 185(1):32–37.
19. Watson, G.W., and E.B. Himelick. 1982. *Root distribution of nursery trees and its relationship to transplanting success.* J. Arboric. 8:225–228.

Product Sources

Containers

AGS
Nursery Supplies, Inc.
534 W. Struck Avee
Chambersburg, PA 17201
(800) 523-8972

Cellugro® System
ACF Environmental
1801-A Willis Rd.
Richmond, VA 23237
(800) 448-3636

GeoCell
EaCon Industries, Inc.
7853 South Leewynn Ct.
Sarasota, FL 34240
(914) 379-7978

Knit Fabric Container
Lacebark, Inc.
P.O. Box 2383
Stillwater, OK 74076
(405) 377-3539

Menne Polybags
Menne Nursery Corp.
3100 Niagara Falls Blvd.
Amherst, NY 14228-1696
(716) 693-4444

Pot-in-Pot System
Lerio Corp.
P.O. Box 2084
Mobile, AL 36652
(800) 457-8112

or

Nursery Supplies, Inc.
534 W. Struck Avee
Chambersburg, PA 17201
(800) 523-8972

Root Control® Bags
Root Control, Inc.
7505 N. Broadway
Oklahoma City, OK 73116
(405) 848-2302

Rootmaker
Lacebark, Inc.
P.O. Box 2383
Stillwater, OK 74076
(405) 377-3539

Tex-R® Agroliner
Texel USA Inc.
P.O. Box 207
Henderson, NC 27536
(888) TEXEL-4U (toll-free)

(Product Sources continued next page)

Containers (continued)

The Accelerator®
Hold Em, Inc.
1283 Ranchette Road
West Palm Beach, FL 33415
(561) 683-7608

Copper, Holding Sleeves, and Wraps

Root Wrap
Braun Horticulture Inc.
P.O. Box 260, Bridge Station
Niagara Falls, NY 14305
(716) 282-6101

Shrink Wrap
Cadillac Products Inc.
5800 Crooks Road
Troy, MI 48098-2830
(248) 879-5000

SpinOut®
Griffin Corp.
P.O. Box 1847
Valdosta, GA 31603-1847
(800) 237-1854

The Tapered Bag
Root Control, Inc.
7505 N. Broadway
Oklahoma City, OK 73116
(405) 848-2302

Urban Tree Soil and Tree-Pit Design

Els Couenberg

Tree soils are intended to enlarge rooting space underneath pavements. However, they are effective only if the tree pits in which they are used are properly designed. The proper design of a tree pit is explained through use of two examples, one in Ripley, Derbyshire, UK, and one in Amsterdam, the Netherlands. Calculations include water balance, expected tree growth, oxygen supply, influence of pavement, and stability. Finally, a checklist for designing pits with tree soil is given.

At the end of the 1970s, urban horticulturists of Amsterdam, together with the Agricultural University, engineered Amsterdam Tree Soil, an artificial soil mix designed to extend the tree pit underneath sidewalks and other pavements that bear a relatively light load (3). Later, other tree soils were developed (7).

Tree soils are not wonder mixes. They are a compromise between the demands of the tree (a place to grow, nutrients, and oxygen), and the demands of the civil engineer (a load-bearing device). They have limited water storage, a limited bearing capacity, and limited possibilities for oxygen transport. Amsterdam Tree Soil, for example, was designed to have a relatively low penetration resistance, which has compromised the bearing capacity. As a result, Amsterdam Tree Soil cannot be used under roads and can only be used under parking areas in certain conditions.

The oxygen and water balance of tree soil is highly dependent on the underground environment. The accessibility of groundwater and the type of pavement make a huge difference in the amount of water and oxygen available to the tree roots. Thus, the establishment of trees with Amsterdam Tree Soil will only be successful if the tree pit, including its cover, is carefully designed.

The four main parameters that are important when designing a tree pit are oxygen in the rootball, water, room to grow (low penetration resistance), and stability. Generally, the amount of nutrients is generally not a problem. If required, these can be added to the soil later. In this paper, two examples of tree-pit design are given. The first example concerns the central market square of Ripley, Derbyshire, UK. The second example is a row of trees in front of Central Station in Amsterdam, the Netherlands.

Els Couenberg, Department of Engineering and Physics, Agricultural University of Wageningen, Wageningen, the Netherlands.

Tree-Pit Design in Ripley, UK

Situation

In Ripley, the central market square was redesigned. Originally, it was completely covered with asphalt and was used as a marketplace on weekdays. It was covered with stalls and accessed by small trucks. During the weekends, the square was used as a car park. Once or twice a year, a fair was held on the square, which meant that heavy trucks and equipment were placed on it.

This square usage was seen as practical but outdated. A new landscape plan was designed, in which the edges of the square were planted with trees and the whole square was covered with concrete block pavers (Figure 1*). The trees to be used in the parking area were *Platanus acerifolia*, and the trees in the pedestrian area were to be linden. Because of the high number of previous failures with tree plantings in such places, and because of the good results reported with Amsterdam Tree Soil, it was decided to prepare tree pits using this soil.

Water. The first parameter to consider when designing a tree pit is water. In Figure 2a, the paths are shown along which water gets in and out of a tree pit. There are five ways of making water available for a tree: 1) uptake from groundwater, 2) uptake from water stored in the soil around the roots, 3) uptake from precipitation infiltrating through the pavement into the pit, 4) water seeping in from the soil on the side, sometimes by infiltration through adjacent pavement, and 5) water added through irrigation.There is also water loss through leakage out of the pit because of gravitational forces (1).

Water Requirement. The best way to estimate the water requirement is to consider a fully mature tree. A tree in a row in this climatic zone is supposed to need 600 L water per m² of crown projection per year (1, 2). A mature planetree can have a crown diameter of up to 10 m (33 ft), which gives a crown projection of 79 m² (850 ft²). The maximum amount of water required is thus about $79 \times 600 \text{ L} = 47,400 \text{ L}$ (12,514 gal) per year.

Uptake from Groundwater. The soil underneath the market square was a sandy limestone, which was freely draining. The groundwater table was 3 to 4 m (10 to 13 ft) below the surface, which meant that no groundwater was available for the trees. Because no groundwater is available, all required water should be provided by stored water and precipitation. Table 1 provides information about capillary rise of groundwater for other situations.

Water Storage in Amsterdam Tree Soil. Each type of soil can store a certain amount of water against gravity. Amsterdam Tree Soil can store about 150 L/m³ of water that is available for a tree (Table 2). This storage is filled up during winter time, when in the local climate, precipitation exceeds evaporation. If stored water in Amsterdam Tree Soil alone is to provide the total amount of water for the tree, then 47,400/150 = 316 m³ (413 yd³) tree soil is needed per tree. With a maximal depth of 1 m (3.3 ft) (see oxygen requirements), this would mean a tree-pit surface of 316 m² (378 yd²) per tree. Such a gigantic pit is not usually possible.

---

*All figures are located at the end of this chapter.

Precipitation. Precipitation during the growing season in our countries is approximately 350 L/m² (1, 2). The amount of precipitation that infiltrates into the tree pit depends on the kind of pavement (Table 3). When the tree pit is covered with asphalt or concrete, which do not allow water to enter, the tree grille is the only place where precipitation can reach the actual pit. The amount of water that reaches the tree is then computed by multiplying the surface of the grille by the amount of precipitation. In Ripley, the market square was to be paved with relatively small and thick concrete block pavers. These pavers have irregular and relatively wide joints, which meant that the percentage of infiltration was about 95%. The infiltration therefore amounts to 335 L/m² per year. Except for the first year (to help the trees establish), the trees were not to be irrigated.

Total Amount of Water. If one assumes a depth of the tree pit of 700 mm (27.5 in.), then 1 m³ (35.3 ft³) of tree soil covers 1.4 m² (49.4 ft²) surface area. The total amount of water available per m³ for this soil will be 150 L storage + 1.4 × 335 L precipitation = 619 L/m³. Fulfilling the water requirement of a mature tree therefore would require a pit volume of 76 m³ (99.4 ft³). With a depth of 700 mm, this corresponds with a pit surface of 1.4 × 76 = 104.6 m² (125 yd²). Due to the presence of the road on one side

Table 1. Distance in mm that water can rise in a soil by capillary forces and thus be available for tree roots. Adapted from (1).

Soil type	Height (mm)
Sand	400
Sandy clay loam	1300
Loamy clay	900
Loamy sand	1600
Heavy clay	400
Peat	400

Table 2. Amount of water in L/m³ soil when the soil is at field capacity. Adapted from (1).

Soil type	Available water L/m³
Paving sand	70
Heavy clay	110
Amsterdam Tree Soil	150
Sand + 8% organic matter	200
Loam	230
Loam with organic matter	280
Frozen peat (60% organic matter)	400

Table 3. Percentage of precipitation that will infiltrate through different pavements (600 × 600 × 70 = length × width × height ZOAB = highly porous asphalt [32% pores].) Adapted from (1).

Pavement	% joints	% infiltration
Asphalt	0	0
Tiles 600 × 600 × 70	0.5	61
Tiles 300 × 300 × 50	1.1	79
Tiles 200 × 100 × 100	4.0	94
Tiles 200 × 50 × 100	7.7	95
Ventilation tiles (300 × 300 × 50)	5.6	95
Grasscrete	30	95
Porous tiles (new)	n/a	100
Porous tiles (after 3 years)	n/a	37
Open soil	n/a	100
ZOAB new	n/a	100
ZOAB (after 12 years)	n/a	100

and a sewer on the other, the maximum possible width of the trench was 4.3 m (14 ft). This means that the distance between the trees should be 25 m (82 ft). However, there was not that much space. In most cases, only 10 m (33 ft) was available between trees; in some cases, only 4 m (13 ft). These distances, respectively, have a surface of 43 m^2 (51.4 yd^2) or 17.2 m^2 (20.6 yd^2). The amount of available water for the larger pits is therefore 19,000 L (5,016 gal), and for the smaller pits only 7,500 L (1,980 gal). This does not mean that *Platanus* trees should not be planted in these pits. However, the maximum crown diameter will be only 6 m (20 ft) for the large pits and 4 m (13 ft) for the small pits. Such sizes were considered acceptable. Figure 2b shows the water supplies and drainage that play a role in Ripley.

I have repeated the same calculations using standard tree pits for small trees, with a surface of 1 m^2 (10.8 ft^2) and a depth of 1 m. The soils used for these pits, however, often contain more organic matter and loam, so a storage capacity of 280 L/m^3 is assumed. The pit is open, or covered with a tree grille, so that the precipitation infiltration is 350 L (92.4 gal) during the growing season. The amount of available water (excluding groundwater) is therefore 630 L (166 gal). This amount is adequate only for a tree with a crown projection of 1.05 m^2 (11 ft^2), which corresponds to a diameter of 1 m. No wonder that these trees do not grow! However, if groundwater is directly available or the tree is irrigated on a regular basis, the water requirement will be fulfilled by these supplies. Big trees, however, need more room than 1 m^2. Stability and oxygen availability become the other limiting factors.

If a tree pit is planned in a poorly drained soil, the pit will start to function as a drain for the adjacent soil. Water will accumulate in the tree pit and will form a false groundwater table (Figure 3). It is important to estimate accurately how much water might accumulate during one year under heavy rainfall. A little water accumulating in a tree pit might be useful, but too much will drown the tree. The danger is more immediate in winter, when there is less evaporation.

Oxygen

Tree roots need oxygen to live. Calculating the oxygen requirements is more difficult than calculating requirements for water, but a simplification will do. Possible ways of oxygen entrance into the soil are shown in Figure 4a. Asphalt and concrete are impervious to oxygen. Whatever the calculation method, a tree grille or hole of 1 m^2 or larger will lead to insufficient oxygen for the roots (Table 4). In Ripley, the only way for oxygen to infiltrate the soil was through grille and pavement on top of the tree pits (Figure 4b). The pavement used in Ripley consists of pavers with irregular joints that were wide in the middle and narrow at the end. For the computation, the pavers were assumed to behave similar as the tiles "200 × 100 × 100B" with the joints filled with sand. These have a potential oxygen transport of 7.32×10^{-6} mg/(cm$^2 \cdot$ sec). Tree roots need oxygen transported at a rate of 2.8 to 5.6×10^{-6} mg/(cm$^2 \cdot$ sec) (1). The soil also requires oxygen: Stable tree soil requires about 0.24×10^{-6} mg/(cm$^2 \cdot$ sec) (1). This means that these pavers, with sand as filler, allow for enough oxygen. However, mortar or other impervious materials should not be used as filler.

Table 4. Resistance of different pavements to oxygen infiltration and transport of O_2 in 10^{-6} mg/cm²/sec if air under tiles has 10% of O_2 (600 × 600 × 70 = length × width × height ZOAB = highly porous asphalt [32% pores]; resistance = time air gets through in sec/cm.) Adapted from (1).

Pavement	% joints	Resistance sec/cm	Transport 20–10%
Asphalt	0	>1,000,000	< 0.1
Tiles 600 × 600 × 70	0.5	140,000	1.03
Tiles 300 × 300 × 50	1.1	45,000	3.16
Tiles 200 × 100 × 100A	1.5	67,000	2.15
Tiles 200 × 100 × 100B	5.1	20,000	7.32
Tiles 200 × 50 × 100	7.7	13,000	11.06
Ventilation tiles (300 × 300 × 50)	5.6	9,000	16.08
Grasscrete	30	11,000	12.92
Porous tiles	n/a	10,000	14.4 (wet)
ZOAB after 6 year extensive use	n/a	700	205.2
Sandy clay loam	n/a	16,000	9.08
Tree soil, relatively dry	n/a	2,500	57.44

As a general rule, from about 1,000 mm (39 in.) below ground level there is not sufficient oxygen for roots. Therefore, the bottom of tree soils should not be deeper than that (1).

Stability

Toppling. In a city, toppling of big trees from strong wind is a important risk factor. To ensure adequate stability, the rootball should be big. But how big? Studies of toppled trees in forests show a relationship between trunk radius and rootball radius (6) (Figure 5). Even though the study was performed in the woods, we consider the results applicable for the urban environment. In cities there is more wind, but this effect is counteracted by the increased stability of the ground. The pavement and the higher soil compaction keep the roots fairly well in place. Figure 5 shows that a tree with a diameter of 10 cm (4 in.) should have a rootball 10 times its trunk diameter to be fully stable, which in this case would mean a rootball of 1 m (3.3 ft). If the diameter of the tree is 40 cm (16 in.) , 8 times that size is sufficient—a 3.2-m (10.5-ft.) rootball is needed. If a tree trunk is bigger than 1 m, then 6 m (20 ft) is an adequate rootball size. In the case of Ripley, a 4.3-m (14-ft) wide trench will provide stability for at least a 50-cm (20-ft) wide trunk, which is a respectable tree. Because the water conditions will limit the growth before such a trunk width is reached, it is unlikely that the trees will become unstable.

Settling of the Pavement. The Ripley design included a pedestrian zone and a parking zone (Figure 1). The pedestrian area was not driven on by cars. Half of it was on a platform. Tree soil, if compacted according to standards (a penetration resistance of 2 MPa) has proven to have a settlement of less than 25 mm (0.1 in.) in such cases, which is considered acceptable. The parking zone, however, should be able to handle a much higher load. This was solved by two means. First, thick pavers were used. The thicker the pavers, the higher the bearing capacity. (Data for the bearing capacity of pavements should be acquired from the local road engineering department.) Second, between the pavers and Amsterdam Tree Soil, a bedding of compacted sand (200 mm

[8 in.] thick) was used. The tree soil itself was first compacted until a penetration resistance of 2 MPa was measured with a penetrometer. The 200-mm-depth sand on top was next fully compacted with a flatbed vibrating machine weighing 100 kg (220.5 lb), providing a relatively superficial compaction. This machine was also used for a final compaction after the tiles were put into place. The actual penetration resistance in the tree soil became 2.5 MPa, which is somewhat high. Because the tree species used was *Platanus*, however, this resistance level was not such a problem. The final design of the tree pit is fairly straightforward (Figure 6). The trees were planted in the spring of 1994 and are reported to be growing very well.

Amsterdam Central Station

A somewhat more complicated tree-pit design was used in this case. However, most of the calculations are left out because they are similar to the previous example. The difficulties in this design (Figure 7) were as follows: The trees (elm), were to be planted in a row in a small area between a bus terminal and a quay. Because of bearing capacity, the bus terminal was totally covered with concrete 400 mm (16 in.) thick. Also the quays used in Amsterdam consist of a all-concrete structure, which had a lot of implications.

Water

Under the circumstances, no groundwater was available for the trees. The width of the trench was 3 m (10 ft); the distance between the trees about 6 m (20 ft). This situation provides about 2,200 L (581 gal) water storage capacity, which is too little to support mature trees. To amend this, groundwater had to be made available to the trees. This was achieved by two means. First, a drainage pipe was installed through both the concrete bottom of the quay and the quay wall, so open water could freely flow into the sand underneath the tree pit. Second, a connection was made between the tree pit and groundwater by the construction of ground pillars. These were filled with a loamy sand, which has a capillary rise of 1300 mm (51 in.) above groundwater (Table 1). In this case, a rise of only 1,000 (39 in.) mm was needed, so that groundwater was always available for the trees.

Oxygen

The pavement on top of the tree pit consisted of standard tiles of 300 × 300 × 50 mm^3 [conversion needed here??]. The oxygen diffusion rate of these tiles is 7 times lower than the pavers used in Ripley (Table 4). Oxygen influx from the side was not possible because of the concrete pavement, so the total amount of available oxygen was insufficient. Therefore, an aeration system was installed, consisting of a 100-mm (4-in.) thick perforated tube (30% perforation). Such an aeration system functions only when air is constantly flowing through the tubes. Therefore, it has to have two outlets. Here, one outlet was made in the tree pit and one in the quay wall through the concrete (Figure 8).

Stability

A 3-m-wide pit is sufficient for a tree with a trunk of 40 cm in diameter (Figure 5) (6). On this site the trees might become bigger because of the sufficient availability of water. Mattheck's work was not known when this design was made (the trees were planted in 1985). The implication is that these trees will have to be monitored carefully after they have reached this 40-cm diameter. It would have been better to use a larger tree pit. Bearing capacity was ensured by compacting the soil until a penetration resistance of 2 MPa was reached—about 80% Proctor density—and covering the soil with paving sand and tiles.

The elm trees were planted in March 1985 and are growing well.

Recommendations

Tree soils should not be used at random but always with a tree-pit design carefully fitted to the situation. When designing the tree pit, use the following procedure.

1. First make a site visit and determine the surroundings. How much room below surface (in m^2) can you maximally claim, considering utilities and roads?
2. If open tree pits are possible, oxygen supply and bearing capacity are not issues. Concentrate on water requirements.
3. Is a sufficient amount of groundwater available? If so water is not an issue. Calculate the amount of available water. How big can the tree pit maximally be? How much water will it store?
4. Next consider the pavement, and estimate the oxygen and water infiltration. If it is insufficient, the situation might be improved by choosing another type of pavement. Otherwise, consider installing an aeration system with openings to the outer air at two sides.
5. If too little water is infiltrating, install an irrigation system or select trees that need less water. If there is too much water, install a drainage system (see, for example, *Landscape Below Ground* 1994, cited as [3]).
6. Finally, consider the stability: Is the tree pit wide enough to provide stability for a mature tree? Are heavy vehicles driven across the area? If so, a thicker pavement is needed, along with careful installation specifications. Use a tree soil that can bear heavy vehicles.

Acknowledgments

Much of the technical information (apart from the designs) in this paper is derived from references 1, 2, and 6.

Literature Cited

1. Atsma, J., and Y. in 't Velt. 1992. Stadsbomen Vademecum. Part 2: Groeiplaats en Aanplant. Ministry of Agriculture, Nature Management and Fishery, the Netherlands. 527 pp. (In Dutch).

2. Bakker, J.W. 1992. Techniques to promote plant growth applied to urban sites, pp 223–228. **In** Verplancke, H.J.W., et al (Eds.) Water-Saving Techniques for Plant Growth. Kluwer Academic Publishers, Dordrecht, the Netherlands.

3. Couenberg, E.A.M. 1994. Amsterdam tree soil, pp 23–30. **In** Watson, G.W., and D. Neely (Eds.). The Landscape Below Ground: Proceedings of an International Workshop on Tree Root Development in Urban Soils. International Society of Arboriculture, Champaign, IL.

4. Grabosky, J., and N. Bassuk. 1995. *A new urban tree soil to safely increase rooting volumes under sidewalks.* J. Arboric. 21(4):187–200.

5. Lindsey, P., and N. Bassuk. 1991. *Specifying soil volumes to meet the water needs of mature urban street trees and trees in containers.* J. Arboric. 17(6):141–149.

6. Mattheck, C., and H. Breloer. 1995. Handboek Boomveiligheid. Pius Floris Productions. 254 pp. Translation from Handbuch der Schadenskunde von Baumen: Der Baumbruch in Mechanik und Rechtsprechung. Freiburg im Breisgau: Rombach. 1994.

7. Ros, E., and A.J. Koolen. 1991. Stadsbomen en bodemverdichting. Groen 12(9):40–43.

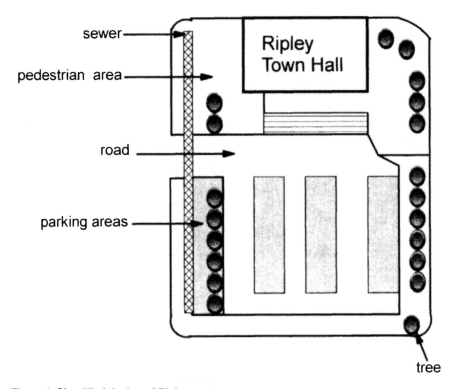

Figure 1. Simplified design of Ripley market square.

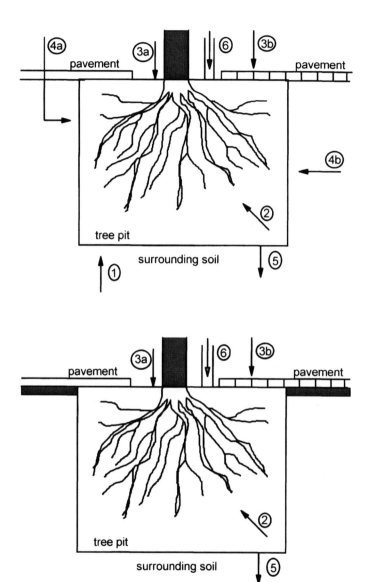

Figure 2. (a, top) Water balance of a tree pit (excluding evaporation). Sources: 1—groundwater; 2 storage of water in the soil; 3a—water infiltrating through open soil; 3b—water infiltrating through pavement; 4a—water seeping in from adjacent soil, infiltrating through pavement; 4b—water seeping in from adjacent soil; 5—drainage, natural or artificial; 6—irrigation. Adapted from (1). (b, bottom) Sources and losses of water in the tree pit in Ripley. Due to concrete underneath the adjacent pavement (gray area) and the depth of the groundwater, sources 1 and 4 (Figure 2a). are virtually nonexistent for the tree. Irrigation was only planned for the first season.

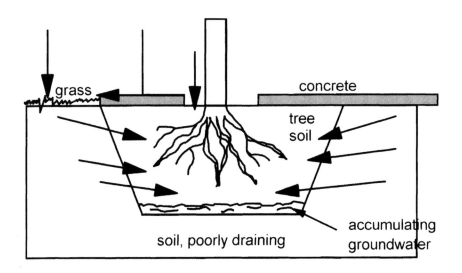

Figure 3. Water accumulation in a tree pit. Arrows indicate sources of water. Water will not drain downwards through the soil. A false groundwater table will occur.

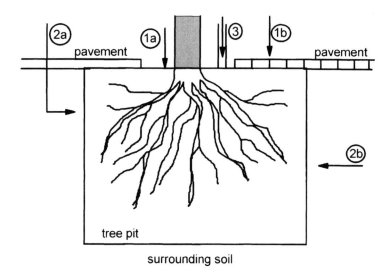

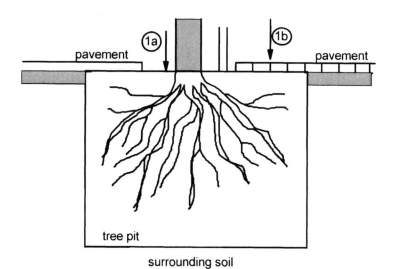

Figure 4. (a, top) Possible sources of oxygen for soil in a tree pit. 1a—through the open soil above the tree; 1b—through pervious pavement; 2a—from adjacent soil, through pervious pavement; 2b—from adjacent soil; 3—through aeration systems. Adapted from (1). (bottom, b) Possible ways of oxygen supply into the tree pit in Ripley. Because of the concrete layer underneath the adjacent pavement (gray area), supply of oxygen from the adjacent soil was not possible.

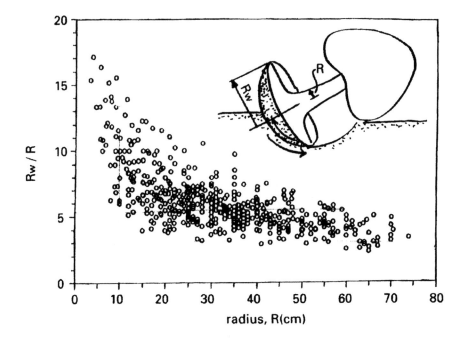

Figure 5. Relationship between radius of a tree trunk and size of the rootball when toppling over. R = radius of the tree trunk. Rw is radius of the rootball. From (6).

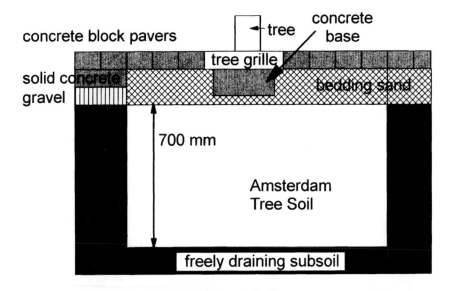

Figure 6. Final design of the tree pit/trench in Ripley.

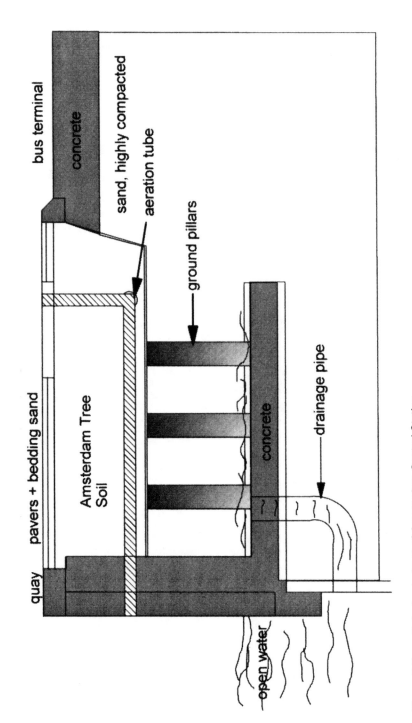

Figure 7. Tree-pit design in front of Amsterdam Central Station.

Figure 8. Tree pit and aeration system used in front of Amsterdam Central Station. The tube is the aeration system. The applied soil is Amsterdam Tree Soil.

Structural Soil Investigations at Cornell University

Jason Grabosky, Nina Bassuk,* Lynne Irwin, and Harold van Es

Over the past several years, Cornell's Urban Horticulture Institute, among others, has been developing alternative layered pavement systems to integrate pavement stability and horticultural requirements for street trees surrounded by pavement. The most recent approach has focused on gap-graded skeletal soil materials (SSMs). Initial testing formulations of SSMs were successful in establishing seedlings and demonstrating the efficacy of a hydrogel in preventing aggregate separation. A second study demonstrated the potential for English oak to quickly establish in fully compacted materials with bearing strengths exceeding minimum criteria for pedestrian and parking sub-base materials. Several observations were made from these studies. Adding fine-grained material quickly impacts the formation of the stone skeleton and its strength. Excessive soil can result in structural and horticultural failure. A zone of overlap exists between horticultural and structural requirements. The maximum amount of soil is likely to be dictated be engineering demands and the minimum soil by horticultural demands. Larger paved installations were deemed necessary for observing plant response over time.

Street trees surrounded by pavement have historically displayed a short average lifespan. We believe one of the most ubiquitous limitations faced by the typical street tree—and hence the greatest challenge to tree establishment—is the volume of root-penetrable soil available to support sustainable healthy tree growth. The current standardized tree pit designs (16 to 24 ft^2 [1.5 to 2.2 m^2] openings of 36 in. [91.4 cm] maximum depth) do not provide enough soil volume for even the most conservative of estimates for sustainable tree growth and health. While the situation may be improving with new construction design methods, trees that do survive in conventional pavement designs often become problematic by heaving curbs and sidewalks. It is the older established trees that often cause pavement failure when roots grow directly below the pavement in the interface between the wearing surface and the base material. Displacement of pavement becomes a tripping hazard; as a result, legal liability compounds expenses associated with structural repairs. Pavement repairs often have detrimental impacts on the trees with significant damage and removal of major roots, resulting in tree decline and death.

Jason Grabosky and *Nina Bassuk (presenter), Department of Floriculture and Ornamental Horticulture;
Lynne Irwin, Department of Agricultural and Biological Engineering;
Harold van Es, Department of Soil Crop and Atmospheric Sciences;
Cornell University, Ithaca, NY 14853

The problem does not necessarily lie with the plant installation but with the design of the system in which the tree and the pavement—two elements with conflicting requirements—are expected to coexist. The tree needs a porous soil that can be freely explored by its roots, while the pavement requires a dense, load-bearing base that will not allow the pavement to subside or fail. Moreover, the green industry has largely neglected to communicate to design and engineering professionals a reasonable understanding of what is required for healthy tree growth in safe pavement design. A concerted effort to work with designers and engineers to develop innovative details and site-specific creative solutions to pavement and tree installation is essential. One potential tool for urban tree establishment and management is a new design for the entire pavement profile to meet traffic loading on pavement while encouraging deep root growth away from the pavement wearing surface.

In 1993, Cornell's Urban Horticulture Institute (UHI) initiated its current approach to resolving the opposing needs of trees and pavement. The approach was influenced by Spomer's critical sand component work in amended landscape soils (7), Patterson's work with expanded shales in highly trafficked turf applications (6), the PGA golf-green specifications for rooting zones (8), and UHI's prior experience with similar material from earlier trails. The system we have developed is essentially a gap-graded stone-soil mixture that depends on the stone fraction establishing a load-bearing lattice or skeleton. In the desired mixture the soil is "suspended" within the stone lattice voids during mixing, placement, and compaction.

Stone-Soil Mixes

In identifying an appropriate stone-to-soil mixing ratio, we attempt to maximize the soil fraction without unduly compromising the formation of the load-bearing stone skeleton. The soil is meant only to partially fill the voids in the stone skeleton to allow rapid aeration potentials, retain some moisture reserve for transpirational demand, and allow some expansion room for roots to grow (Figure 1). The new approach focused on two immediate goals. The first was to address the problem of aggregate separation, seen as a major problem in early mixing attempts in field trials. The second goal was to identify a family of stone-soil mixtures and establish the existence of a "zone of overlap" in acceptable mix design for plant establishment and engineering behavior prior to field testing.

The first goal was to prevent separation of the fine soils from the stone that occurred during the mixing, and prevent the migration of soil through the stone matrix during placement, compaction, and watering. This was easily met with the addition of a small amount of tackifier in the system to stabilize the mixture. We used a cross-linked, potassium salt, polyacrylamide hydrogel as the tacking agent. The addition of hydrogel was observed to simplify mixing, prevent the separation of soil and stone, and prevent washing of soil without influencing plant response in the first planted study (4, 5). The specific hydrogel used in the study (Gelscape®, Amereq Corp., New City, New York) provided the additional benefit of increasing the plant-available water in the bulk system. The use of a tackifier allowed us to introduce very small amounts of soil into the stone matrix in a uniform manner.

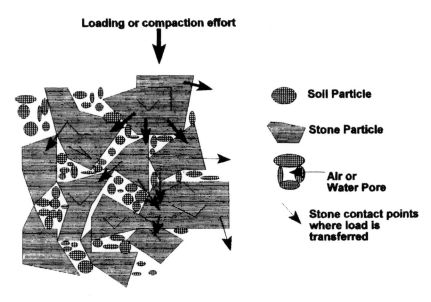

Loading or compaction effort

Soil Particle

Stone Particle

Air or
Water Pore

Stone contact points
where load is
transferred

Figure 1. The stone matrix bears loading while the soil partially fill the matrix voids.

The second objective was more complex. Use of readily available materials and technology, low cost, and ease of manufacture governed the project approach. The material is designed to work as a high-strength, well drained sub-base within the existing layered design familiar to pavement engineers. In a standard design, there is a surface pavement material, such as concrete, and a highly compacted base material over-arching the rooting zone (Figure 2). Below that would be the compacted sub-base rooting material that is placed over the compacted preexisting subgrade material. Full compaction of the rooting zone is required to meet the need for strength to support overlying materials. Working within this layered design allows for the use of the base material as a root exclusion zone to act as a buffer, distributing the potential root expansion pressures over a larger area on the bottom side of the wearing surface. If the structural soil mixture is strong enough, it could be used as a base material with a minimal buffer if it could be demonstrated that the roots were not predisposed to running near the surface (pavement heaving).

Defining measurable parameters to evaluate the structural soils under consideration has been driven by engineering behavior. We have chosen a compaction effort level of 592.7 kJ/m^3 (12,375 ft $\cdot$ lbf/ft^3), which translates to a standard Proctor compaction test (1). From this standardized test, the best moisture content for compaction and an expected density to specify in field installation can be identified. From this information, materials can be tested for bearing capacity relative to a material of empirically known strength in penetration/deflection resistance, known as a California Bearing Ratio (CBR) (2). A CBR of 50 at peak density is now the minimum criterion we suggest for potential mixtures.

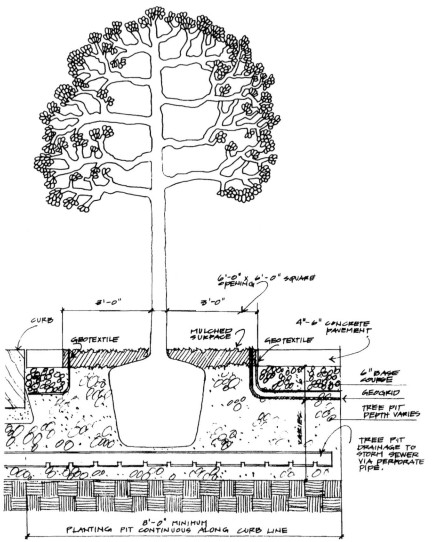

Figure 2. Elevation plan of a proposed structural soil pavement profile using the sub-base as the rooting zone.

Optimizing Soil Content

We have confirmed that the formation of the stone skeleton is changed with the addition of any fine material (soil). This is caused by the physical presence of additional soil particles between the stones as they come together and the presence of moisture and clays impacting the frictional "lock-in" of the stones into a load-bearing matrix. Figure 3 demonstrates this effect by tracking the decrease in fractional density of the stone (at peak AASHTO T-99 density) as increasing amounts of soil are added to the mixture. As the density of the stone matrix is decreased, the porosity of the lattice is increased and mixture strength is decreased. This effect is shown in Figure 4 as the strength (California Bearing Ratio) increases with the stone fractional density in compacted structural soil test specimens. Because the stone lattice is changed as soil is added, a straightforward calculation of the optimal soil content for any given stone source is not yet available.

Optimizing the soil content definitely cannot be calculated from a presumed stone density and porosity from its unit weight in a stockpile. We can, however, suggest very conservative estimates of soil that could be added, test the resulting mixtures, and amend the mixture accordingly. These estimates can range from 13% to 22% soil by weight. Variables influencing the first estimation for mixing ratios include the size distribution and angularity of the stone and the soil properties. Overestimation of the desired soil content can lead to the soil dominating the behavior of the mix rendering the system useless for trees *and* pavement.

The second planted study tested a family of structural soil materials matched with materials known to be structurally sound and expanded the soil component to a point of engineering failure (especially in light of the increased minimum acceptable strength). We found the plant response to encompass a wider range of mixtures than the engineering strength requirements allowed (3). The roots were also observed to deform and wrap around the stones in the profile rather than displace them upward.

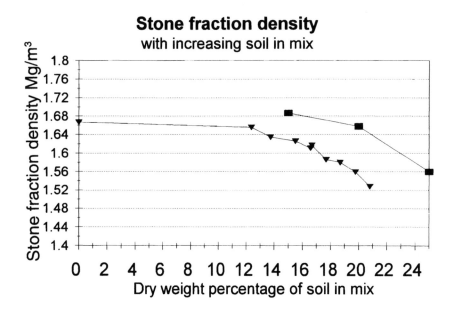

Figure 3. Addition of soil into the system changes the formation of the stone matrix.

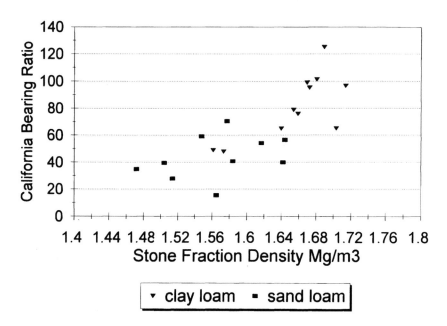

Figure 4. The formation of the stone matrix influences the bearing strength of the mixture.

Based on these encouraging results on short-term tests, larger installations for long-term monitoring were considered.

For more controlled testing, a field study monitoring the rooting zone environment, evaluating above-ground plant responses, and observing root distribution was initiated. The preliminary results from this study are presented in the following article, Pilot Field Study of Structural Soil Materials in Pavement Profiles. Completion of the root excavation work and final analysis will continue during 1998. Current testing of these systems includes plant-available moisture measurement, preliminary testing of organic component limits in design, pore size distribution, and hydraulic conductivity measurement. Several other avenues for testing have presented themselves for future investigations.

Literature Cited

1. American Association of State Highway Transportation Officials. 1995. T 99-9: The moisture-density relations of soil using a (2.5 kg) 5.5 lb rammer and a (.305 m) 12 in. drop, pp 123–128. In Standard Specifications for Transportation Materials and Methods of Sampling and Testing (17th ed). Part II: Tests. AASHTO, Washington, DC.

2. American Association of State Highway Transportation Officials. 1995. T 193-93: The California Bearing Ratio, pp. 367–372. In Standard Specifications for Transportation Materials and Methods of Sampling and Testing (17th ed). Part II: Tests. AASHTO, Washington, DC.

3 Grabosky, J. , N. Bassuk, and H. van Es. 1996. *Further testing of rigid urban tree soil materials for use under pavement to increase street tree rooting volumes.* J. Arboric. 22(6):255–263.

4. Grabosky, J.C. 1996. Developing a structural soil material with high bearing strength and increased rooting volumes for street trees under sidewalks. M.S. Thesis, Cornell University. 152 pp.

5. Grabosky, J., and N. Bassuk. 1995. *A new urban tree soil to safely increase rooting volumes under sidewalks.* J. Arboric. 21(4):187–201.

6. Patterson, J.C., J.J. Murray, and J.R. Short. 1980. The Impact of Urban Soils on Vegetation. Proceedings of the Third Conference of the Metropolitan Tree Improvement Alliance (METRIA).

7. Spomer, L.A. 1983. *Physical amendment of landscape soils.* J. Environ. Hort. 1(3):77–80.

8. United States Professional Golf Association. USGA Green Section Record. March/April 1993.

Pilot Field Study of Structural Soil Materials in Pavement Profiles

Jason Grabosky,* Nina Bassuk, Lynne Irwin, and Harold van Es

A rhizotron pilot study was conducted to evaluate plant responses in a standard sidewalk installation in comparison to a test profile of skeletal soil material (SSM) and a field control. Chlorosis was detected in the standard sidewalk trees, whereas the SSM profile was comparable to the agricultural control. Roots were observed at the rhizotron wall in 1996. Root counts and distribution by depth suggested an increase in roots for *Acer campestre* and *Tilia cordata*, with roots in the SSM profile occurring predominately in the lower regions of the pavement profile. Trees in the standard sidewalk profile were relegated to the shallow base course layer typical in northeastern sidewalk construction. Roots of *Malus* 'Adirondack' followed the same pattern of rooting depth, but there were more roots observed in the standard sidewalk profile. Several parameters were investigated to account for the preferential root growth deeper into the SSM profile. After ascertaining the consistency with depth of moisture, density, and oxygen levels in the SSM profiles, it is suggested that temperature fluctuations may be a contributing factor for the root distribution phenomenon.

The Urban Horticulture Institute at Cornell University (UHI) has been designing and testing sub-base materials that can be compacted with typical construction equipment, meet normal engineering expectations for materials under pavement, and encourage root growth.

So-called "structural soil materials" under consideration are extremely gap-graded materials lacking medium and large sands. The mixes tested thus far consist of a narrowly graded stone fraction (1.5 to 0.5 in. [3.8 to 1.3 cm]), a clay loam soil, and a small amount of hydrogel. The system works by producing a rigid stone matrix, to bear loading, and partially filling the stone matrix voids with soil. The hydrogel is added as a stabilizing agent, holding the soil in place during the mixing, placement, and compaction phases of construction.

Structural soil materials have performed to our satisfaction in planted studies lasting one and two growing seasons and in laboratory testing for bearing strength (5, 6). Verifying the benefit of using such materials outside of the lab is limited by the finan-

*Jason Grabosky (presenter) and Nina Bassuk, Department of Floriculture and Ornamental Horticulture;
Lynne Irwin, Department of Agricultural and Biological Engineering;
Harold van Es, Department of Soil Crop and Atmospheric Sciences;
Cornell University, Ithaca, NY 14853

cial and logistical difficulties of planting in pavement situations and the destructive harvesting and analysis of the tree root system. While above-ground measurements can provide useful information, more information is needed on the condition of the rhizosphere and of root growth patterns below the pavement. The experimental pilot study described here attempted to provide rhizosphere and root growth data by constructing sidewalks around trees in an instrumented root-viewing chamber (rhizotron). The study translated mixing our test materials to a commercial scale and allowed observation of plant responses and material behavior in a controlled experiment that approximated a working sidewalk.

Materials and Methods

Two pre-existing rhizotrons located in Ithaca, New York (8), were used in this study. Each chamber was 4 ft (1.2 m) wide, 24 ft (7.3 m) long, and 3 ft (0.9 m) deep, fitted with 0.25-in. (6.35-mm) Lexan® windows along their length, with a viewing area from the bottom of the pavement wearing surface to a depth of 2 ft (0.6 m). Two additional viewing windows were installed on one end of the chamber to bring two additional trees into the study (Figure 1*). Two pavement profiles were used. Each profile ran the length of the rhizotron on opposing sides, so a side-by-side comparison was available for on-site demonstrations (Figure 2). Each profile was installed into an excavated trench equaling the dimensions of the chamber pit. In this study, the excavation was made to a common depth of 2 ft. The trench bottom was compacted to 1.5 Mg/m³, 97% of its AASHTO T-99 peak density (2).

The first pavement profile simulated a typical sidewalk installation in central New York State, in which there is minimal excavation and then compaction of the existent material, upon which a base material is added, followed by the wearing surface (Figure 2). The subgrade was rebuilt and compacted to 1.7 Mg/m³, 98% AASHTO T-99, in 6-in. (15-cm) lifts to a plane approximately 8 in. (20 cm) from the top of the viewing chamber window. A base material of well-graded gravel was then placed and compacted to 2.1 Mg/m³ in two lifts. The wearing surface for both profiles consisted of 6,000 psi concrete 4 in. (10 cm) in depth. All materials were compacted with a Wacker B5 45Y ram tamper (Wacker Corp. Menomonee, Wisconsin). Bulk density was monitored during installation and demolition by the sand cone replacement method, undisturbed soil coring, and the balloon volume replacement method (soil test equipment).

The test profile was a 2-ft (0.6-m) structural soil material base compacted in 6-in. (15-cm) lifts to 1.8 Mg/m³, an estimated 95% AASHTO T-99 (Figure 2). The structural soil resembled materials being tested in the laboratory at the time, which displayed a high bearing strength (5). The structural soil material consisted of 80% by weight NYSDOT §702-02 #2 gravel, 20% clay loam, and 0.025% of a polyacrylamide stabilizing hydrogel (Gelscape, Amereq Corp. New City, New York) (9). The material was mixed in a 7 yd³ (5.4 m³) concrete mixer mounted on a stationary frame with an external power unit. The material was stockpiled on site and covered with

---

*All figures are located at the end of this chapter.

tarps until installation. Density was monitored during installation and destruction by the sand cone replacement method.

Agricultural controls were installed around the perimeter of the test area without viewing chambers (Figure 1). The control soil was not compacted because it was meant to simulate a nonconfined field-growing condition in the existing Niagara silt loam. As such, the controls were covered with 4 in. (10 cm) of hardwood mulch. The control consisted of pre-existing soil excavated to loosen the soil volume and to eliminate any plow pans in the profile, then replaced. Three trenches for three trees were positioned around the paved treatments. All soils used in the project were excavated within 660 ft (200 m) of the test site.

Bare root *Tilia cordata* 'Olympic' (6 ft [1.8 m]), *Acer campestre* (7 ft [2.1 m]), and *Malus* spp. 'Adirondack' (4 ft [1.2 m]) were established for five months on the Cornell campus in #10 nursery containers filled with the same clay loam used at the interstitial material in the structural soil material and existent on the rhizotron site. Due to the expense of installing the system and the lack of any prior use of the structural soil system, the plants were selected so as to observe responses over a range of species. This allowed for three plant replicates per treatment in this pilot study. Due to the limited number of replicates, the plants were assigned locations in the test profiles and control to spatially distribute them uniformly. Each tree was allotted a $4 \times 6 \times 2$ ft ($1.2 \times 1.8 \times 0.6$ m) volume of the profile. Trees were planted into holes held open in the pavement profile by gravel-filled containers of equal size. This allowed a planting space to be opened without destroying the compactive effort applied to the surrounding profile. A 25-cm (9.8-in.) diameter opening in the concrete was left around each tree. The trees were installed into the test profiles on June 20, 1995, and irrigated each day for one week. No additional irrigation was used after that time. The pavement was installed on July 1, 1995.

Rhizosphere oxygen content was monitored at five levels. The first depth was at 3.2 in. (8 cm), with increments every 5 in. (12.5) cm down to 28 in. (71.5 cm). The collection ports were patterned after those used by Yelenosky, constructed of 4-in. (10-cm) lengths of 0.75-in. (1.9-cm) i.d. PVC tubing connected to the surface with 0.25 in. (0.64 cm) i.d. Nalgene tubing capped by a rubber septum (10). Clusters of tubes were placed 36 in. (90 cm) from the viewing window at 6-ft (1.8-m) intervals beginning 12 in. (30.5 cm) from the south end of the pavement pad. Samples were collected by removing 20 mL of air from the system with a syringe and drawing a 20-mL sample. Many of the samples collected in the subgrade were drawn as water, in which case a 0.00 value was entered into the data set, assuming anaerobic conditions in sections where pore-water pressure filled the voids in the sampling port. Samples were analyzed in a Servomix 574 Oxygen Analyzer (Servomix, Norwood, Massachusetts). Samples were drawn weekly from the paved profiles from June 11, 1996, though July 23,1996.

Temperature was monitored with copper constantan thermocouples (Omega type T) at depths of 6, 12, and 24 in. (15.25, 30.5, and 61 cm). Clusters were placed 24 in. from the viewing window at intervals of 6 ft (1.8 m) from the south edge of the pavement pad. Weekly measurements were made in 1996 for treatment and blocking effects. Hourly data were collected July 30 and 31, 1997, to track diurnal temperature fluctuations. This was compared to the Northeast Regional Climate Center field station data collected 1 mile (1.6 km) from the site.

Root distribution data were collected off of the viewing windows within one week of first root contact (August 5, 1996). The data were collected a second time on October 4, 1996.

Each tree was assigned a rooting window length of 6 ft (1.8 m), centered on the tree trunk. A wire mesh grid 2 × 4 in. (5 × 10 cm) was affixed to the window. Root intersections with the wire were counted at five depth increments and recorded, resulting in a relative root distribution.

Relative moisture content and bulk density were monitored with high-speed neutron and gamma radiation via a CPN 501 DR Hydroprobe moisture depth gauge. Access tubes were placed 24 in. (61 cm) from the viewing window at intervals of 6 ft (1.8 m) from the north edge of the pavement pads. Data collection was based on 32-second readings with the neutron/gamma source positioned 12 and 20 in. (30.5 and 50.8 cm) from the pavement surface. Calibration was conducted by destructive sampling and repetitive 256-second testing against sand cone and balloon methods during the duration and harvest of the field study, as well as testing within samples of known density and moisture. The final calibrations are not fully completed at this writing, but the raw particle-count data were used to demonstrate consistency within treatments between pavement sections.

Relative chlorophyll content was measured August 18, 1996, with a SPAD meter (Minolta SPAD 502) to verifiy visual signs of chlorosis in the trees in the standard pavement profile. SPAD meters have been successfully used to measure leaf transmittance as a field diagnostic tool to gauge chorophyll content and/or nutrient status in leaf tissue (1, 4). Ten leaves, the first of the current year's shoot extension on ten separate shoots, were measured three times and averaged for ten measurements per tree. 1997 data from repetitive harvests coincided with matched leaf tissue analysis but are not fully available as of this writing.

Statistical analysis was conducted by dropping the two single tree-viewing pit replicates and one set of control replicates and creating a split-plot layout, with repeated measures in most cases. Preplanned contrasts were conducted with Bonferroni protection. All rhizosphere data were collected in the paved systems only.

Results

No significant within-treatment differences in rhizosphere oxygen content profiles were detected ($P = 0.83$), although the low replication of this pilot study could have prevented small differences from being detected. During the first three weeks, there were the expected significant differences between the two treatments at depths where the standard sidewalk subgrade was compared to the test profile. This effect was masked during the last three weeks, from low replication and increased data variability in the standard sidewalk subgrade. Figures 3 and 4 demonstrate this effect from the collection ports at depths of 18.2 and 23.2 in. (46.1 and 58.8 cm). Oxygen levels at 18.2 in. were adequate in both pavement profiles and depressed in the standard sidewalk profiles. Mean rhizosphere oxygen levels at a depth of 23.2 in. fell below 5% in the compacted subgrade of the standard sidewalk treatment in the few weeks where isolated ports were not filled with water.

The weekly temperature data from the 1996 season yielded no differences within or between treatments ($P = 0.52$ and 0.71, respectively). There was a significant difference between measurement depths ($P < .001$). The lower thermocouple layers were very consistent across the entire test area over the entire observation period (Figure 5). The near-surface temperatures had a larger spread, presumably due to changing shade patterns on the wearing surface from the test trees. Based on this information, temperature was tracked hourly the following year. No differences were found within and between treatments in the hourly data sets; Figure 6 displays aggregated measurements at each depth. There were wide temperature fluctuations in excess of $14°C$ ($57°F$) near the surface. The lower two measurement depths show relatively little change in temperature over the testing period shown (Figure 6).

While the neutron and gamma data are not completely converted to density or volumetric moisture levels, pending further calibration, analysis of the raw data yields no within-treatment differences at each testing depth. The expected differences between each pavement layer material and the significant differences between treatments ($P < .001$) were verified. Consistency of moisture content and bulk density within and between the two structural soil profiles was inferred because the analysis yielded no difference between the trenches (P moisture = 0.48, bulk density 0.87) or by depth in trench (P moisture = 0.91, bulk density 0.99).

Roots were first observed in the viewing chamber windows August 5, 1996, during a weekly observation check of the profiles. Root distribution was recorded October 4, 1996, when there were enough roots to make a meaningful data set. Figures 7, 8, and 9 detail the results of the root-grid intersection counts for each species in the two pavement profiles. Most notable is the differential root distribution between the two pavement profiles. The root counts in the standard sidewalk profile were as expected, with no *Acer campestre* or *Tilia cordata* roots penetrating the subgrade, which occurred at the 8-in. (20-cm) depth (Figures 7 and 8). *Malus* 'Adirondack' penetrated 0.4 to 0.8 in. (1 to 2 cm) into the subgrade (Figure 9). The few observations recorded in the standard profile below 8 in. were roots originating higher in the profile, which ran along the viewing window. The test profile surprisingly demonstrated a preferentially deeper root distribution in all three tree species. There were roughly twice as many total root-grid intersections in the test profile for all three species when compared to the standard profile (Figures 7, 8, and 9), but the differences statistically were not well defined ($P = 0.334$), presumably due to the low replication as a pilot study.

The SPAD meter data convincingly demonstrated the differences in plant performance with significant differences ($P < .001$) between the standard sidewalk profile and the other two treatments (Figure 10). The differences in the crabapple may be misleading because all values indicate a healthy condition and were at or above the top range of accuracy for the instrument.

Conclusions

There was an observed benefit to plant establishment by planting trees in the structural soil profile for *Acer campestre* and *Tilia cordata* 'Olympic'. The root distribution of *Malus* 'Adirondack' was preferable in the structural soil profile because it moved the roots away from the wearing surface without negatively impacting on the tree. The proposed structural soil provided a well-aerated rooting zone even after full compaction, as verified by the oxygen data.

Roots moved away from the wearing surface in all trees installed in the structural soil. The density, oxygen content, and relative moisture in the structural soil did not vary with depth, thus eliminating them as causal factors for this phenomena. The even moisture distribution could be an artifact from lateral movement of moisture from beyond the test profile; moisture release studies have been initiated to further clarify the plant-available moisture on hydraulic behavior of these materials. The temperature data roughly agree with prior investigations under pavement structures (7). These large fluctuations and the potential for excessive maximum temperatures suggest that near-surface temperature fluctuations could partially contribute to the preferentially deep root growth in the test profile.

The standard sidewalk profile did not encourage tree establishment and root penetration at depth due to the requisite subgrade and base compaction. The lowered oxygen data and the high soil densities suggest problems for root penetration and establishment in the soil subgrade. The stone base had very little water- or nutrient-holding capacity because silts and clays are carefully avoided when specifying a base material. The trees responded to the problematic situation. Malus fared better than the two other species, with root penetration and leaf color remaining comparable between treatments. Further tests beyond the scope of this discussion indicate a possible reduction in total root volume and above-ground shoot extension in the standard sidewalk profile.

Relative chlorophyll content estimations from the SPAD meter data confirmed a negative impact on plant establishment in the standard sidewalk profile. As noted earlier, *Malus* may or may not have been significantly affected by the differing profiles due to the very high output from all replicates in the study. Two possible causes for the lowered chlorophyll content in the standard sidewalk are high pH and low nutrient availability in the base materials where all roots were observed to exist. Initial testing revealed pH levels of 8.8 to 9.1 during current excavation of the root zones. The base material in the standard sidewalk profile had less than 5% of material passing through the #200 sieve. There is virtually no clay or organic matter in this zone; therefore, moisture retention, cation exchange, and buffer capacities were severely diminished. These possibilities require verification and supplemental testing.

Further work in this area is necessary to verify the root-growth distribution patterns observed in this pilot study, as well as the influencing factors. A repeat of this study might include a carefully devised method for long-term temperature tracking to confirm the data presented. It would also include provisions for tracking the pH creep because the alkaline leachate from the concrete interacts with the near-surface base and sub-base materials. Moisture could be tracked very effectively using a carefully calibrated neutron probe. Time domain reflectrometry should also be considered after calibration to the specific material.

Further testing in this study includes relative chlorophyll content coupled with tissue analysis, shoot growth increment, and total root excavation architecture. All early indications and analysis confirm the improved performance of all species in the structural soil materials. Further establishment of a possible gamma-neutron probe calibration for the structural soil materials is also in progress. These data are not complete but will be presented in a cogent format in the near future.

Literature Cited

1. Abadia, J., and A. Abadia. 1993. Iron and Plant Pigments, pp 327–343. In Iron Chelation in Plants and Soil Microorganisms. Academic Press, San Diego, CA.

2. American Association of State Highway Transportation Officials. 1995. T 99-94: The moisture-density relations of soil using a (2.5 kg) 5.5 lb rammer and a (.305 m) 12 in. drop, pp. 123–128. In Standard Specifications for Transportation Materials and Methods of Sampling and Testing (17th ed.) Part II: Tests. AASHTO, Washington, DC.

3. American Association of State Highway Transportation Officials. 1995. T 193-93: The California Bearing Ratio, pp. 367–373. In Standard Specifications for Transportation Materials and Methods of Sampling and Testing (17th ed.) Part II: Tests. AASHTO, Washington, DC.

4. Dwyer, L.M., M. Tollenaar, and L. Houwing. 1991. *A nondestructive method to monitor leaf greenness in corn.* Can. J Plant Sci. 71:505–510.

5. Grabosky, J. , N. Bassuk, and H. van Es. 1996. Further testing of rigid urban tree soil materials for use under pavement to increase street tree rooting volumes. *J. Arboric.* 22(6):255–263.

6. Grabosky, J., and N. Bassuk. 1995. *A new urban tree soil to safely increase rooting volumes under sidewalks.* J. Arboric. 21(4):187–201.

7. Halverson, H.G., and G.M. Heisler. 1981. Soil Temperatures Under Urban Trees and Asphalt. USDA Forest Service Report NE-481. Washington, DC.

8. Harris, J.R. 1994. Seasonal Effects on Transplantability of Landscape Trees: Periodic Root and Shoot Growth, Seasonal Transplant Response and Effect of Dormancy. Doctoral dissertation. Cornell University.

9. New York State Department of Transportation. 1990. Standard Specifications; Construction and Materials. Office of Engineering, Albany, NY,

10. Yelenosky, G. 1964. *Tolerance of trees to deficiencies of soil aeration.* Proc. ISTC, 127–148.

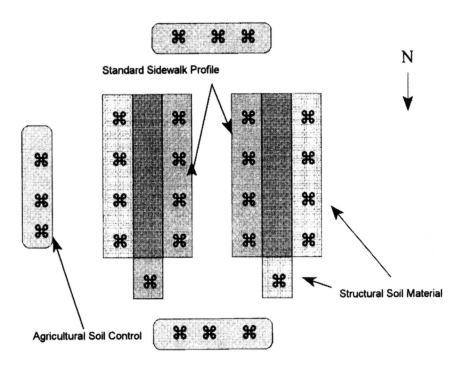

Standard Sidewalk Profile

N

Structural Soil Material

Agricultural Soil Control

Figure 1. Plan view of pavement-tree study.

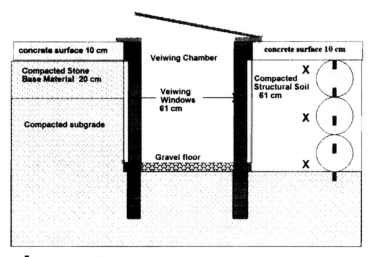

■ Oxygen Sampling Port

◯ Neutron/gamma sampling zone

X Thermocouple site

Figure 2. Elevation plan of the root-viewing chamber.

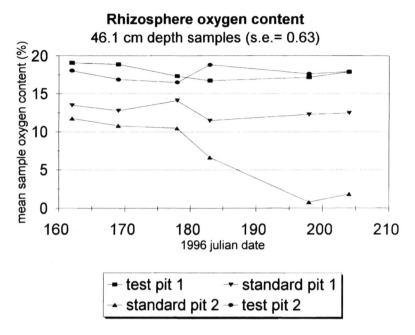

Figure 3. Mean oxygen levels in each trench at 18.2 in. (46.1 cm) show slightly depressed levels in the standard sidewalk profile.

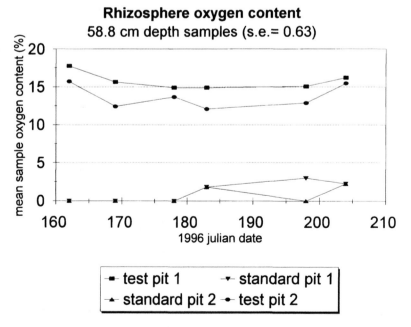

Figure 4. Mean oxygen levels in each trench at 23.2 in. (58.8 cm) show deficient oxygen levels in the standard sidewalk profile.

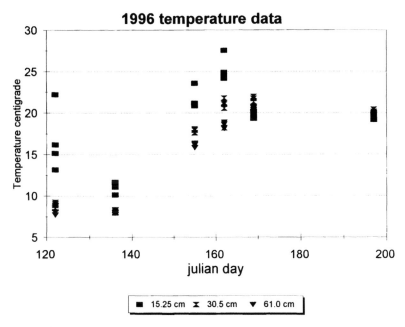

Figure 5. Soil temperatures were similar below each pavement section, with greater variation near the surface.

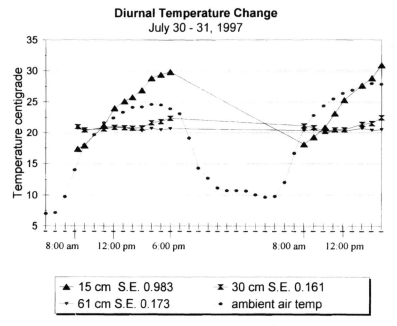

Figure 6. Temperatures below the pavement varied slightly at 12 and 24 in. (30 and 61 cm) but fluctuated widely to excessively high levels at depth of 6 in. (15 cm).

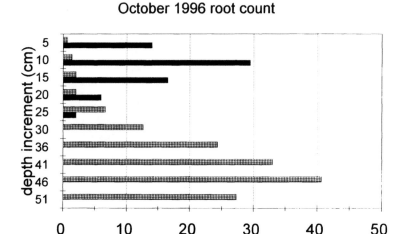

Acer campestre
October 1996 root count

Figure 7. *Acer campestre* root distribution at observation windows. Counts are root-wire grid intersections at each 4-in. (10.1-cm) depth increment.

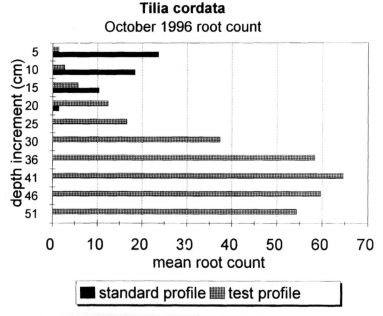

Tilia cordata
October 1996 root count

Figure 8. *Tilia cordata* root distribution at observation windows. Counts are root-wire grid intersections at each 4-in. (10.1-cm) depth increment.

Malus 'Adirondack'
October 1996 root count

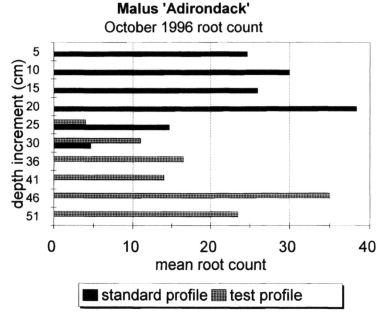

standard profile ▓ **test profile**

Figure 9. *Malus* 'Adirondack' root distribution at observation windows. Counts are root-wire grid intersections at each 4-in. (10.1-cm) depth increment.

Relative chlorophyll content
Mean SPAD Meter readout

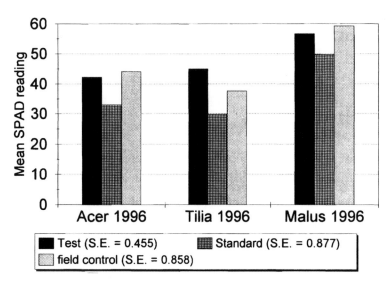

Test (S.E. = 0.455) ▓ Standard (S.E. = 0.877)
▨ field control (S.E. = 0.858)

Figure 10. 1996 SPAD meter data confirming a depression in chlorophyll content in the standard sidewalk treatment.

PART V

WATER UTILIZATION

Irrigation of Newly Planted Street Trees

Roger Harris

It is widely recognized that water stress is the fundamental cause of poor postplanting performance of street trees. Branch dieback is a common sight as transplanted trees begin their second season (Figure 1). Because a transplanted tree has so much of its root system removed (some say as much as 98%) when it is dug, it can quickly become drought stressed. Although the tree in Figure 1 is alive and appears to be establishing, effects of this dieback will be felt for years to come. This tree has essentially been topped by water stress, just as if it had received a haircut from a fly-by-night "arborist." Some extensive corrective pruning will be required if it is to become a desirable street tree. Dieback can be so severe that no amount of pruning will correct the "topping" (Figure 2). This tree probably just dried out soon after it was planted. By the time drought symptoms were noticed and the rootball was irrigated, the damage was already done. This **reactive** style of irrigation may keep a tree alive, but establishment will be slow and dieback will probably occur. It is easy to dismiss this dieback as "transplant shock," an inevitable consequence of transplanting. However, dieback such as this is usually preventable. What is needed is a **proactive**, not a **reactive** irrigation plan.

Watering Strategies

There is evidence that only one drought episode can be detrimental to tree establishment. I tested this on container-grown Turkish hazelnut (*Corylus colurna*) trees (2). Trees that were either dormant or in early active growth were droughted to the same tissue-stress levels. Trees from both growth stages had reduced hydraulic conductivity of their root systems. This means that waterflow through the roots was restricted compared to those trees that were not subjected to the drought. Restricted waterflow through roots can potentially increase dieback, particularly if postplanting irrigation is sporadic. In this experiment, a subsample of trees that were subjected to the drought and well watered thereafter were smaller than those trees that were never allowed to dry out. Wilting trees, waiting beside their planting holes to be planted, may have a much harder time becoming established.

Roger Harris, Assistant Professor, Department of Horticulture, Virginia Polytechnic and State University, Blacksburg, VA 24061.

Figure 1. Branch dieback on a street tree beginning its second season. Similar to a bad pruning job, this tree has been "topped" by drought stress.

Another potential consequence of post-transplanting drought caused by reactive irrigation is the restriction of waterflow through tree stems. Water is conducted from the soil to transpiring leaves through the xylem. Xylem is made up of a series of specialized cells called vessel and tracheid elements (mostly vessels in street trees). There is essentially a continuous column of water within vessels that stretches from the roots to the leaves. Vessels are normally filled with water, except when exposed to freezing winter temperatures or to severe drought. The water column may then "break" in places and individual vessels may fill with air bubbles (called embolism). This is a defense mechanism for many trees native to cold areas, which helps prevent freeze damage to conducting tissues. The vessels are normally filled in the spring when new growth begins (some trees may just grow new vessels). Because water can flow around the air bubbles through holes in the sides of vessels (called pits) (Figure 3), embolism may not pose a serious problem if the tree is always well watered. A problem will probably develop, however, if continued droughts are imposed (reactive irrigation) or if a dormant (highly embolized) tree is planted, as is the normal procedure, and the tree is then improperly irrigated. Recent research at Virginia Tech by Patricia Knight illustrated that root pruning can interfere with natural spring embolism recovery. Turkish hazelnut trees were root pruned to various degrees when dormant and grown in a greenhouse. Trees that were root pruned 50% failed to recover from dormant embo-

Figure 2. Severe branch dieback. Severe structural problems will result if this tree lives and is not removed.

lism levels (Figure 4). Growth, however, was not restricted. The much higher levels of root pruning when harvesting balled and burlapped trees and the common post-transplanting droughts that usually occur would likely result in restricted flow and exacerbated "transplant shock."

Irrigation strategy also affects post-transplant root regeneration. I compared a reactive irrigation strategy to a proactive one on 'East Palatka' holly (*Ilex × attenuata*) in Florida (1). I was interested in the possible interaction between production method (above-ground containers, balled and burlapped, in-ground fabric containers) and irrigation strategy. Although trees from all production methods reacted in a similar way to reactive and proactive post-transplant irrigation (no interaction occurred), proactive irrigation resulted in over three times the weight of new roots growing into the backfill soil compared with those that were irrigated in a reactive manner.

Landscape managers often assume that roots of recently transplanted trees are growing well beyond the original rootball and that normal irrigation spray heads will adequately irrigate the trees. This strategy often results in water-stressed trees, par-

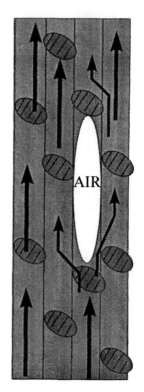

VESSEL ELEMENT

Figure 3. Embolism in xylem.

ticularly for some species, e.g., in a fall-spring transplant comparison of fringe tree (*Chionanthus virginicus*), roots did not begin to emerge from rootballs of fall- or spring-transplanted trees until the first of July (3). Although root regeneration dynamics are undoubtedly species dependent, irrigation should probably be targeted to rootballs for the first season after transplanting.

A Case Study

Developing a sound irrigation strategy for newly planted street trees is obviously very important to the future health of trees. As discussed above, even one severe drought can have lasting consequences. Municipal foresters, increasingly faced with dwindling budgets, simply do not have the workforce to implement a sound proactive irrigation program and must rely on residents to maintain the newly planted trees. David Sivyer, municipal forester for the city of Norfolk, Virginia, recently faced the challenge of developing such a strategy. A simple, easily followed regime was required. Although professional and avid amateur horticulturists and arborists would have little trouble knowing when to water (by feeling the soil, for example) and could be expected to follow instructions that included varying amounts of water and shifting intervals, Sivyer was interested in a recommendation that anyone could and would follow (i.e., how many buckets of water and how often). Borrowing from a model

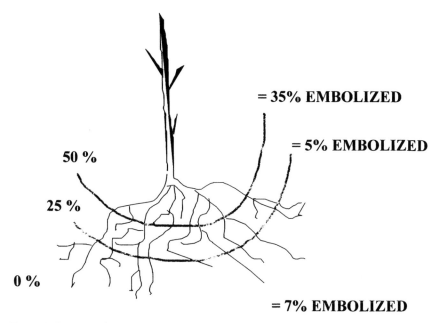

= 35% EMBOLIZED

= 5% EMBOLIZED

50 %

25 %

0 %

= 7% EMBOLIZED

Figure 4. Root-pruning experiment on Turkish hazelnut trees.

published by Lindsey and Bassuk (4), which estimated the amount of soil required to support a tree, a model was developed that estimated the amount and frequency of irrigation required for first-season, 3-in.-caliper shade trees in Norfolk. A brief description follows.

Two question must be asked: "What is the daily water use of the tree?" and "How much water does the rootball hold?" One method of determining plant water use is to refer to how much water evaporates from a standardized pan (Figure 5). These data are kept by state governments at weather stations in various locations. Different crops can indexed to this pan evaporation rate. We assumed an index (crop coefficient) of 20%. To estimate the pan evaporation rate that we would encounter, we averaged the 30-year mean rainfall for the growing season. Like rainfall, pan evaporation data are given in depth. To convert depth (inches) of evaporation to gallons of water, the evaporative surface of the tree must be estimated. This can be done by estimating the crown projection (CP) (shadow cast on ground if the sun were directly overhead) and the leaf area index (LAI) (percentage of CP covered by leaves). Because leaves overlap, the LAI is almost always over 1. We assumed a CP of 50 ft^2 and an LAI of 2 (a total leaf area of 100 ft^2). From the historical pan evaporative data, the crop index, and the estimated total leaf area, we calculated that whole-tree water use would be about 2.7 gal of water a day. To estimate the amount of water available (i.e., in the rootball), the rootball soil was tested and determined to be a clay loam. The percentage of water available to the tree was then determined through a table, and the volume of the rootball was calculated. This resulted in a supply of 9.7 gal of water available to the

Figure 5. An evaporation pan.

tree. It would therefore take approximately 10 gal of water to saturate the rootball, and the tree would use this up in 3.6 days.

The model described above was tested on mulched, 3-in.-caliper callery pear (*Pyrus calleryana* 'Redspire') and river birch (*Betula nigra* 'Heritage') planted in an industrial area of Norfolk (Figure 6). We decided to be conservative by rounding the interval down to 3 days. One group of trees served as a control and were irrigated on an as-needed basis. Moisture sensors were installed in each control tree, and each tree was irrigated when moisture levels dropped to 55 centibars of tension (high numbers reflect drier soil). Trees were therefore irrigated either according to the model or as needed for 2 months. At the end of two months, "as-needed" trees required irrigation an average of every 2.6 to 3.3 days for pears and 2.3 to 3.3 days for birch. The model, therefore, was a fairly accurate prediction of the actual interval required. When we checked actual LAI and CP and adjusted for irrigating at 55 centibars versus the original estimation (available water = irrigate at 150 centibars), we refitted the model and calculated a regime of 5 gal every 3 days. The model therefore resulted in the correct irrigation interval but too much water. However, irrigating with 10 gal versus 5 would ensure that the rootball would be saturated and would wet the area immediately surrounding the rootball where new roots may be emerging. Details of this project have been published in Sivyer et al. (5).

Figure 6. River birch trees used in testing the evaporation pan model.

Conclusion

Proper irrigation of newly planted trees will result in trees that establish faster and have fewer future structural problems. A proactive approach will pay huge dividends. Besides, it should be the birthright of every street tree!

Literature Cited

1. Harris, J.R., and E.F. Gilman. 1993. *Production method affects growth and post-transplant establishment of 'East Palatka' holly*. J. Amer. Soc. Hort. Sci. 118:194–200.

2. Harris, J.R., and N.L. Bassuk. 1995. *The effect of drought and phenological stage of transplanting on root hydraulic conductivity, growth indices, and photosynthesis of Turkish hazelnut*. J. Env. Hort. 13:11–14.

3. Harris, J. R., P. Knight, and J. Fanelli. 1996. *Fall transplanting improves establishment of balled and burlapped fringe tree* (Chionanthus virginicus *L.*). HortScience 31:1143–1145.

4. Lindsey, P., and N. Bassuk. 1991. *Specifying soil volume to meet the water needs of mature urban street trees and trees in containers.* J. Aboric. 17:141–149.

5. Sivyer, D., J.R. Harris, N. Persaud, and B. Appleton. 1997. *Evaluation of a pan evaporation model for estimating post-planting street tree irrigation requirements.* J. Aboric. 23:250–256.

Evaporation and Water Requirements of Amenity Trees with Regard to the Construction of a Planting Site

Jitze Kopinga

Several models have been developed and published for calculating the water requirements of urban trees. To justify the application of these models in practice however, more detailed information is needed on tree transpiration in relation to the development of total leaf area and drought tolerance of amenity trees. This paper highlights some of the gaps in the existing knowledge and presents a short overview of the state of the art in the Netherlands.

For a long time, the water supply of urban trees has been an item of concern for many city foresters and arborists in both temperate and arid regions. After all, it is generally understood that a lack of available water will result in poor tree growth or poor aesthetic value of the tree. Within this framework, models have been developed to estimate or calculate the minimal volumes of rootable soil required for acceptable tree growth under more or less normal climatic conditions (precipitation, evaporation) (2, 11, 12, 14, 15, 16). However, it appears that there are situations in which the dimensions prescribed by the models are not sufficiently met, yet a satisfying tree growth can be observed. Would this imply that the introduced models are much too optimistic, or do additional factors play a substantial role and thus cause considerable flexibility?

The aim of this paper is to explain some of the biological aspects of trees that should be considered, and to point out gaps in existing knowledge, in an effort to understand situations in which satisfactory tree growth occurs, despite a prediction for failure.

The Mechanism of Evaporation

Most of the water a tree needs is used for transpiration (or evaporation, evapotranspiration when total water loss from the individual in its surrounding system is concerned). The rate of transpiration is largely controlled by an energy gradient, also known as an evaporation deficit. The atmosphere "sucks" water from the tree via the leaves. For most tree species, the amount of water that evaporates though the bark is almost negligible. The magnitude of the evaporation deficit is determined by atmospherical conditions such as radiation by the sun and temperature and moisture content of the ambient air. Although water loss can be partly controlled by the tree itself by closing its

Jitze Kopinga, Institute for Forest and Nature Research (IBN-DLO), Wageningen, the Netherlands.

leaf pores (stomata), it is linked to the uptake of carbon dioxide, which is necessary for tree growth. A too-rigid control of water loss thus would imply a lower level of growth. On the other hand, too much water loss may result in desiccation of the tree and possibly its death. The tree in fact has to make a compromise.

In favorable circumstances, water lost by transpiration will be replenished by water extracted from the soil by the tree roots, which requires a sufficient amount of available soil moisture. This in turn is dependent on certain soil properties, the dimensions of the rootable soil volume, and amount and frequency of both the annual precipitation and the precipitation during the growing season.

Required Rootable Soil Volume

A number of papers have been published on the need for sufficient rootable soil in relation to water requirements of trees (2, 8, 9, 14). The models presented in the literature assume a demand of about 0.5 to 0.75 m³ (18 to 26.5 ft³) of rootable soil per m² of crown projection, depending on the richness (organic matter content) of the soil. Initially the Dutch model applies to soils in which the water is supplied by precipitation only (no groundwater influence) and for the average tree, which means a tree with a rounded, oval-to-conical crown shape and an average amount of leaf surface (leaf area index [LAI] of 4 to 5).

Thus far these models seem to be fairly realistic and justifiable because the dimensions of soil volume lie within the same order of magnitude as the models that are developed on the basis of the nitrogen demand of trees (5). However, when comparing the Dutch model with a number of foreign ones, it appears that there are some striking differences in the required dimensions of rootable soil. Some publications (e.g., 11, 15), mention amounts of 0.3 or 0.6 m³ per m² crown projection, which differ by a factor of 2.

Obviously, with regard to these data, the reliability of the Dutch model may be debatable, but the variability is explicable from the differences in assumptions on the water-delivering capacity of the soil and the frequency and quantity of precipitation during the vegetation period together with the expected reference evaporation. This is illustrated already by the two values of 0.5 and 0.75 m³ per m² crown projection of the Dutch model that applies, respectively, to the storage of available water (or water storage capacity [WSC]) of the somewhat poorer soils (organic matter content approximately 4%) and to the richer soils (organic matter content approximately 8%) (Figure 1).

Many trees in the Netherlands grow on sites where soil water supplementation needs can be met partly or even largely by groundwater, depending on the average depth of the soil water table during the growing season and the capillary rise. It is evident that in such situations, this supply can be added to the water storage capacity. In many cases, this supply exceeds the desired storage, so a considerable smaller volume of rootable soil suffices. It must be considered, however, that even when the water demand is sufficiently met by groundwater, an insufficient rootable soil volume may in the long run cause problems with the supply of nutritional elements (especially nitrogen) (5, 8, 9) or even the stability of the tree (windthrow).

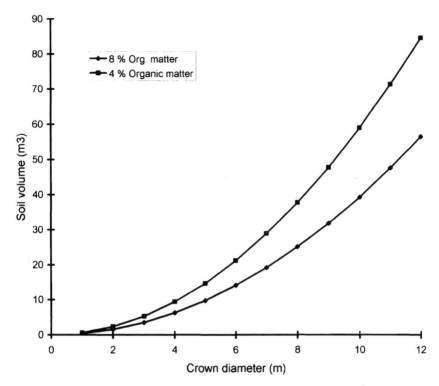

Figure 1. The required amount of rootable soil at two levels of water storage capacity of sand with 8% (upper line) and 4% (lower line) organic matter (after models from Bakker [2] and OBIS [14]).

Calculating the Water Consumption of Trees

In most existing models for determining the minimal required volume of rootable soil, either the open water evaporation (E-O) or the reference evaporation of agricultural crops (E-ref) is taken as basis for the calculation of water loss in trees. The background for this is the positive relationship between the outcomes from meteorological formulas (Penmann, Penmann/Monteith, Makkink) and from the results of experimental research.

The calculation of the annual water consumption of solitary trees, such as street trees, generally is based on data from forestry research combined with a correction factor for the solitary position and the effects of the urban climate. For situations such as those in the Netherlands, this factor has been determined by studies on containerized trees and is established as 1.5 (for park and street trees) with excesses to 2.0 (for trees in a paved sidewalk). This factor is more or less comparable with findings of some other foreign studies (6).

The amount of water (in liters, L) that a street tree would be able to evaporate at optimal water supply (E-pot) is calculated with the following formula:

$$E\text{-pot} = (1.5) \times E\text{-}O \times Cp$$

in which Cp is crown projection of the tree and E-O is open water evaporation. This model can be refined when data are known about the leaf evaporation per unit of leaf surface and the development of total leaf area over the years.

Assuming an equal amount of leaf evaporation throughout a tree crown, the potential daily evaporation of a tree than can be calculated:

$$E\text{-pot} = E\text{-leaf} \times LAI \times E\text{-}O \times Cp$$

An illustration of the application of such a model to a solitary common maple tree is presented in Figure 2.

Designing a Planting Hole

Knowing the local daily E-O and the pattern and intensity of precipitation over the year and assuming that tree root development during the life of a tree is restricted to the planting hole, it is possible to indicate the dimensions of the rootable soil volume that

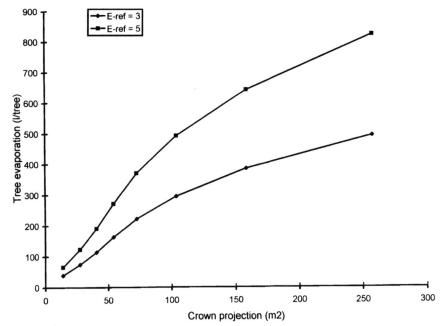

Figure 2. Calculated daily evaporation of common maple at various stages of tree development at reference evaporation levels of 3 (upper curve) and 5 mm per day (lower curve). (Assembled from data of Vrestiak [20] and data presented in this paper [Table 4].)

are required for optimal tree growth. For designing a planting hole, more detailed information is needed about 1) the water requirements of the tree, 2) the water storage capacity and supply of the soil pit mixture, and 3) the amount of infiltrating rain water.

Amount of Required Water and Water Storage Capacity (WSC)

In the Dutch model, the amount of water required for a solitary tree with a leaf area index (LAI) of 4.5 is assessed on 1.5 times the supply of a forest, which is $1.5 \times$ WSC + N-eff, in which WSC is the water storage capacity of the soil and N-eff is the effective precipitation (which is the rainfall, N, minus the interception by the tree).

At a WSC of 75 mm (3 in.) and a precipitation during growing season of 350 mm (13. 8 in.) minus the interception (0.16×350 mm), transpiration can be established as approximately 440 mm (17.3 in.) of rain. The WSC in practice might be more, but preferably not less, because a certain amount of storage is needed to help the tree survive during periods of drought. A water storage capacity of 150 mm (5.9 in.) seems to be a realistic figure, which can be covered by 750 L (198 gal) of sand with 5% organic matter.

It must be emphasized, however, that it is of no use to create a storage capacity that cannot be completely replenished. It must be considered that some drainage of the rooted soil volume is required to prevent accumulation of salts (including deicing salt, if relevant).

For a tree in a pavement with an infiltration rate of 2 mm/hr (0.08 in./hr), the amount of infiltrating precipitation during winter will be $(0.79 \times N) \times 0.90 - 45$ mm, where 0.90 is precipitation minus interception, and 45 mm (1.8 in.) is surface evaporation. For N = 440 mm (17.43 in.), the N-infiltrated amount will be 268 mm (10.6 in.). Because rainfall during wintertime might occasionally be less, a maximum WSC of approximately 220 mm (8.7 in.) seems reasonable.

Based on these calculations, approximately 220 mm must be provided by the infiltration of rain during the growing season. Assuming an interception of 30% (as a worst-case scenario) during growing season, the N-eff will be 0.70×350 mm (13.8 in.) = 245 mm (9.8 in.) minus E-surface, which equals out the model as a difference of approximately 10 mm (0.4 in.) when E-surface = 35 mm (1.4 in.) during summer.

Water Storage

The storage capacity of available water of soils varies according to the composition of the soil. When using medium sand as raw substrate for a planting hole mixture, the capacities are (2, 3):

- medium fine sand (no organic matter): 60 to 70 L/m³
- medium fine sand (2% organic matter): 90 to 120 L/m³
- medium fine sand (5% organic matter):150 to 200 L/m³

Each extra kg of organic matter will increase the storage capacity by about 2 L (0.5 gal) available water.

Amount of Infiltrating Rain Water

Infiltrating rain water is defined as precipitation minus interception, minus runoff from the surface, minus evaporation from the extended root surface. The interception capacity of a solitary tree is more than that of a forest tree and varies widely between 30% in summer and 10% in winter (7). The rate of interception is also related to the leaf area index (1). The amount of runoff depends on the infiltration resistance of the root projection surface and the duration and intensity of rainfall.

Bakker et al. (2, 3) measured the possible infiltration rates through various types of used pavements and determined the minimal infiltration, even when the pavements are old and somewhat dirty (Table 1). Using the data of the so-called "5 minutes rain" in the Netherlands over a period of 12 years, Bakker (2) calculated the percentage of runoff, assuming that the rain falls at a higher intensity than the possible infiltration will run off (Table 2).

The Gaps To Be Filled In

For refinement of the model discussed above with regard to its practical implementation, it is apparent that more and detailed information is needed, especially regarding

- leaf area evaporation of the various tree species
- development of leaf area (the desired amount of foliage)
- the reduction factor r, (the minimal rate of actual transpiration that will provide acceptable growth and performance of the tree)
- drought tolerance (effects of water stress)

Leaf Area Evaporation

Although the water consumption of trees has attracted the attention of researchers for many decades, much of the early research focused on forest trees in forest-like environments and some on focused fruit trees. Studies on amenity trees in a typical urban situation are relatively scarce. Some of the early studies on individual forest and landscape trees, however, clearly demonstrate the differences in leaf transpiration between the species (Table 3) (4).

Table 1. Infiltration rate, by type of soil surface.

Type of soil surface	Infiltration rate (mm/hr)
Loamy soil, wet and compacted	<0.5
Loamy soil, open, not compacted	>200
Sand	>500
Asphalt (tarmac)	0.0
Open asphalt (ZOAB)	>100
Paving stones (30 × 30 × 5 cm)	2–5
Paving stones (60 × 60 × 7 cm)	1–2
Paving bricks (20 × 10 × 10 cm)	10–20

Table 2. Percentage of rain infiltrating through a pavement.

Infiltration rate (mm/hr)	0.5	1	2	5	10	20
Summer (May 1 to Oct 1)	20	37	58	79	89	95
Winter (Oct 1 to May 1)	30	54	79	95	99	100

Table 3. Seasonal transpiration of containerized trees at optimal water supply during the 1972 growing season at Freiburg, Breisgau (4).

Tree species	Water consumption (L/m² leaf area)	Water use economy of stem volume (dm³/100 L)	of leaf area growth (m²/100 L)
Salix alba 'Liempde'	159	0.60	0.63
Populus 'Robusta'	99	0.29	1.00
Populus 'Barn'	97	1.10	1.00
Populus 'Oxford'	90	0.45	1.10
Fraxinus excelsior	96	0.73	0.96
Alnus glutinosa	94	0.90	0.89
Acer pseudoplatanus	87	0.85	0.87
Acer platanoides	56	1.30	1.80

An intriguing question is "To what extent can leaf transpiration of solitary trees be coupled with or predicted from meteorological data?" In this regard, research was carried out by Bakker et al. in the Netherlands at the "Staring Centrum" (the former ICW) and later at the IBN-DLO (the IBG "De Dorschkamp"), both in Wageningen, the Netherlands. Bakker (3) found good correlations (0.86 to 0.90) between potential tree transpiration (Tp) and E-O, and even better correlations (0.91 to 0.96) between Tp and vapor pressure deficit (VPD) and established the relationship:

$$Tp = 0.3 \times E\text{-}O \times LAI$$

which accounted for containerized trees of common maple, Dutch elm ('Vegeta' and 'Dodoens'), and common ash.

Research at the IBN focused on finding relationships between potential tree evaporation (E-pot) per unit of crown projection (Cp) and the crop reference evaporation (E-ref), using:

$$E\text{-}pot = f \times E\text{-}ref$$

in which f stands for the crop factor of the tree, which is determined by multiplying leaf evaporation by LAI.

Data on daily E-ref values were derived from nearby weather stations or were otherwise calculated from the equation:

$$E\text{-}ref = [1/L \times s/(s+pc)] \times 0.65 \times Q$$

in which L = latent heat of vaporization, s = slope of the saturation vapor pressure curve, pc is the psychometric constant at atmospheric pressure (100 kPa), 0.65 is a standard crop factor for turfgrass, and Q is the total global radiation (J/cm²) during the day.

The benefits of this equation are that it is used as a standard method by many Dutch weather stations and that only the temperature (from which the factor between the square brackets can be calculated) and the global radiation has to be measured.

The transpiration appeared to be proportional to the amount of leaf area (Figure 3) and highly correlated to E-ref (Figure 4). The preliminary results justify the assumption of a linear correlation between E-pot and E-ref within the range of E-ref from 0 to 5 mm (0 to 0.2 in.) together with the assumption of an (almost) linear correlation between foliage area and evaporation.

Table 4: Some preliminary data of leaf evaporation of various tree species, assessed by weighing experiments with containerized trees during the period 1994 to 1997 at the IBN at Wageningen, NL.

Tree species	Leaf evaporation correlation to E-ref
Acer platanoides	0.25
Acer pseudoplatanus	0.25
Aesculus hippocastanum	0.22–0.25
Castanea sativa	0.21
Ginkgo biloba	0.23
Pinus sylvestris	0.42
Quercus suber	0.48
Tilia × *vulgaris*	0.23

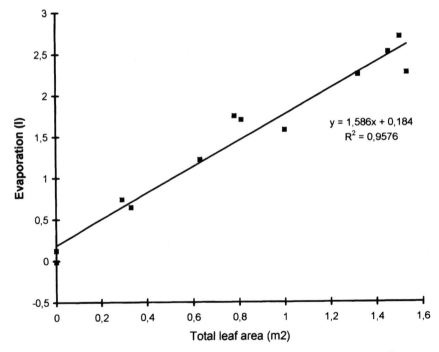

Figure 3. The effect of artificial defoliation on leaf evaporation of containerized European lime trees (*Tilia* × *vulgaris*) at optimal water supply and with more or less equal size and crown projection. Evaporation is expressed as the average values of daily evaporation during four periods of four days during the summer of 1996 (Kopinga, unpublished).

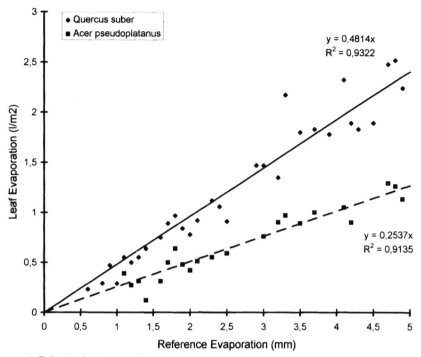

Figure 4. Relation between leaf evaporation and reference evaporation of containerized trees of cork oak (6 years old) and common maple (3 years old) (Kopinga, unpublished).

An overview of some the values of leaf evaporation assessed thus far is presented in Table 4. Within this context, however, it must be noted that the data collected to date apply only to the species studied. Future research will indicate more about the existing differences between the various tree species and the possible differences and variability in leaf evaporation within the crowns of adult trees.

Leaf Area

The amount of leaf area that trees develop as they grow older varies among species. This is illustrated in Figure 1, based on model trees presented by Vrestiak (17, 18, 19, 20, 21) (Figure 5). It is clear that the normal differences in tree size may largely determine the total amount of foliage, but even when the crown volume is taken as reference, the differences in total leaf area are considerable (Figure 6). Apart from the differences between tree species, there also may be substantial differences in total leaf area per unit of crown volume or crown projection between individual trees of the same species.

For honey trees (*Sophora japonica*) 20 years or older, for example, Vrestiak (19) found LAI values ranging from 2.2 to 6.0 at crown densities of 0.2 and 0.6, respectively. For little-leaved lime trees (*Tilia × vulgaris*) 16 years and older, values ranging from 1.2 to 12.9 at crown densities of 0.9 and 2.1 were reported (17).

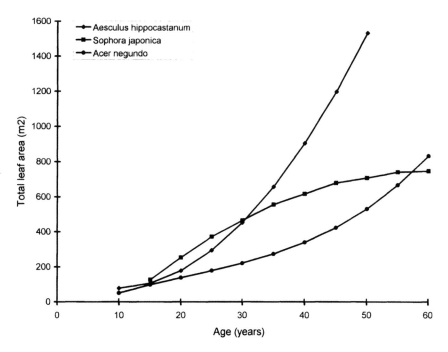

Figure 5. Development of foliage surface on common maple, horsechestnut and honey tree (Vrestiak [18, 19, 20]).

These findings suggest a need further research on the normal foliage development of the various tree species and the impacts of crown density from both a landscape architecture and an urban ecology point of view.

Minimal Required Transpiration

When the water supply is less than optimal, the actual evaporation (E-act) is less than the potential evaporation, according the formula E-act = r × E-pot, in which r is the reduction factor that indicates the quantity of water that will or can be evaporated.

A major question is "At which levels of r will a tree still develop and grow well enough to satisfy the demand?" It is not easy to assess the minimal amount of water needed to keep a tree of a certain size in good condition, nor is it easy to assess the appreciable amenity value of the tree. Formulation of water balance studies *in situ*—studies in which the nature and extent of the rooting system are assessed—are not practicable.

It is also difficult to grow trees in containers at various levels of permanent drought stress. Most of the research therefore has been restricted to the assessment of evaporation (e.g., by sap flow measurements or gravimetric studies on containerized trees) and precipitation in combination with the assessment of the already-mentioned soil and site factors. Until now, arboricultural research results are insufficient to provide satisfying answers. An additional concern are the restrictions in extrapolating the results of such studies to the whole tree system *in situ*.

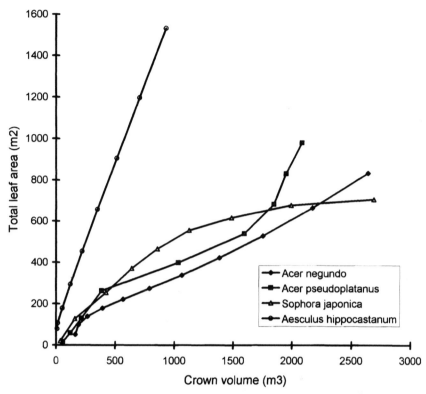

Figure 6. Relationship between development of crown volume and foliage surface for box elder, common maple, honey tree, and horsechestnut (Vrestiak [18, 19, 20, 21]).

For the time being, the magnitude of r that still will give an acceptable growth rate is derived from forestry observations in the Netherlands. These show that in the Dutch climate, all species of trees will grow to 100% capacity when the water storage capacity of the soil is more than 200 mm (7.9 in.). For the survival of the tree at levels of appreciable aesthetic value, a growth rate of more than 40% is required. At that level, acceptable growth can be observed in drought-tolerant species such as pedunculate oak, Dutch elm, white poplar, beech, and birch. Less drought-tolerant species, such as common maple and common ash, require soils with a water storage capacity greater than 125 mm (4.9 in.) in order to maintain their decorative value. On soils with a water storage capacity of 75 mm (3 in.), the actual transpiration will be approximately 75% of the potential transpiration during a year with average E-O and N, and approximately 50% in a dry year (a year with a 10% dry summer) (2, 3).

A shortcoming within the application of the above-mentioned models is the lack of a correction factor per single tree species, that is, a correction for the way the various species manage their water use. The differences between tree species may be quite substantial (Tables 3 and 4), and these differences tend to make the reduction factor r variable, especially towards the lower values, and are part of the explanation of the "stretch" when applying the calculation models in practice.

Drought Tolerance

The ways in which the various trees react on prolonged periods of drought can vary considerably. Some tree species will react by a gradual or sudden, total or partial withering and shedding of leaves. Others will show symptoms of wilting before discoloring and/or withering (which might serve as a signal for the arborist to water a tree). Both the reaction and the recovery of the tree (after watering) may have an impact on growth of the tree during the following growing season (13) and on its aesthetic value.

In nature, drought tolerance of trees sometimes can be ascribed to a favorable root/shoot ratio (the ratio between the amount of functional roots and functional aboveground parts of the tree) (10). It must be considered, however, that the mechanism of "drought avoidance" might be of limited value in urban situations in which the volume of root development is restricted.

It would be of interest to know more about how the duration of drought periods affects the amenity values and recovery capacities of the various tree species.

Conclusions

There are trees that perform well on sites without the amount of rooting space indicated as necessary by some of the existing models for determining the required rootable soil volume on the basis of the water use of trees. It is plausible that the existing differences in leaf area development, single leaf evaporation, and drought resistance will substantially determine the limits of the minimal requirements. For a further refinement of the models, also with regard to their practical implementation and justification, more information about these aspects is needed.

Moreover, in spite of these gaps in knowledge, it is important to note that models based on the nutrient requirements of trees indicate rootable soil volumes that lie within the same order of magnitude as the water-use models. This implies that there is no justification for the supposition that large trees must be able to flourish in just a few cubic meter of rootable soil.

Acknowledgments

The author wishes to express his heartfelt appreciation for the inspiring comments and ideas of the late Jan Willem Bakker during the many discussions in the past on the subject described in this article.

Literature Cited

1. Aston, A.R. 1979. *Rainfall interception by eight small trees.* J. Hydrol. 42: 383–396.
2. Bakker, J.W. 1983. *Groeiplaats en watervoorziening van straatbomen.* Groen 39 (6):205–207.
3. Bakker, J.W. Personal communication.
4. Braun, H.J. 1976. *Rhytmus und Größe von Wachstum, Wasserverbrauch und Produktivität des Wasserverbrauchs bei Holzpflanzen. II.* Acer platanoides *L.,* Acer pseudoplatanus *L. und* Fraxinus excelsior *L. mit einem Vergleich aller*

untersuchter Baumarten einschießlich einiger Populus-Klone. Allg. Forst u. J.-Ztg. 147 (8):163–168.

5. Burg, J. van den. 1988. *Minerale voeding van bomen: bladmonsteranalyse als basis voor een bemestingsadvies.* Groenkontakt 16(1):10–19.

6. Halverson, H.G., and D.F. Potts. 1981. Water Requirements of Honeylocust (*Gleditsia triacanthos* f. *inermis*) in the Urban Forest. USDA Forest Research Paper NE-487, 4 pp.

7. Hiege, W. 1985. Wasserhaushalt von Forsten und Wälder und der Einfluss des Wassers auf Wachstum und Gesundheit von Forsten und Wälder—eine Literaturstudie. Rapport 7a, Studiecommissie Waterbeheer, Natuur, Bos en Landschap (SWNBL), Utrecht. 190 pp.

8. Kopinga, J. 1991. *The effects of restricted volumes of soil on the growth and development of street trees.* J. Arboric. 17(3):57–63.

9. Kopinga, J. 1994. *Bomen in het straatprofiel: enige "teeltkundige" beschouwingen.* Groen 50(1):13–17.

10. Kozlowski, T.T. 1982. *Water supply and tree growth. Part I, Water deficits.* For. Abstr. 43 no. 2:57–95.

11. Lindsey, P., and N. Bassuk. 1991. *Specifying soil volumes to meet the water needs of mature urban street trees and trees in containers.* J. Arboric. 17(6):141–149.

12. Lindsey, P., and N. Bassuk. 1992. *Redesigning the urban forest from the ground below: A new approach to specifying adequate soil volumes for street trees.* Arboric. J. 16:25–39.

13. Neuwirth, G., and H. Polster. 1960. *Wasserverbrauch und Stoffproduktion der Schwarzpappel und Aspe unter Dürrebelastung.* Archiv für Forstwesen, 9. Band, Heft 9:789–810.

14. OBIS. 1988. Bomen in straatprofielen: groeiplaatsberekening, voorbeeldbladen. VNG, 's-Gravenhage, 63 pp.

15. Vrecenak, A.J. 1988. *Shade tree transpiration and water use.* Arboric. J. 12:77–81.

16. Vrecenak, A.J., and L.P. Herrington. 1984. *Estimation of water use of landscape trees.* J. Arboric. 10(12):313–319.

17. Vrestiak, P. 1985. *Auswertung der Winterlinde (*Tilia cordata Mill.) nach der Größe de Blattfläche in den Objekten des Städtischen Grüns von Nitra. Folia dendrologica 12/85:89–109.

18. Vrestiak, P. 1986. *Evaluation of planar and spatial development of leaf biomass in horse chestnut (*Aesculus hippocastanum L.*) in urban greenery.* Ekológia (CSSR) 5(1):33–47.

19. Vrestiak, P. 1986. *Auswertung von* Sophora japonica L. *nach der Größe der Blattfläche und dem Kronenvolumen.* Folia dendrologica 13/86: 143-165.

20. Vrestiak, P. 1987. *Leaf biomass of the sycamore maple (*Acer pseudolatanus L.*) in urban greenery.* Ekológia (CSSR) 6(1):3–14.

21. Vrestiak, P. 1991. *Ash-leaf maple (*Acer negundo L.*) evaluation according to the leaf area size and crown volume in city greenery.* Ekológia (CSFR) 10 (1): 3-18.

Managing Landscapes Using Recycled Water

Nelda Matheny and James R. Clark

Use of secondary- or tertiary-treated recycled water for landscape irrigation is increasing. The quality of recycled water is generally poorer than potable water. In the context of landscape irrigation, water quality refers to the presence and concentration of total salts (TDS, EC_w), specific ions (Cl, Na, B), bicarbonate, pH, trace elements, and nutrients (N, P, K). Guidelines for interpreting water quality are provided. Evaluation of sites for irrigation with recycled water must consider plant salt tolerance, soil texture, chemical characteristics, and drainage, as well as irrigation method and frequency. Lists of tree species' tolerance to salt and boron are provided. Potential problems to plants and soils can be minimized with specific management techniques.

Use of secondary- or tertiary-treated sewage effluent for landscape irrigation is increasing as supplies of potable water become limited. Recycled water can be an abundant source of inexpensive water or in some cases, the only source available for irrigation. Landscape managers, however, often are concerned about the effects recycled water may have on plant appearance and growth. This paper discusses the important factors to consider and management techniques to accommodate use of recycled water.

What Is Recycled Water?

Recycled water, also called effluent or reclaimed water, is water that has been previously used for municipal purposes, industry, or agriculture and has been treated for reuse. Wastewater is the liquid waste collected in sanitary sewers and treated in a municipal wastewater treatment plant (20). The wastewater is subjected to several treatments to make it suitable for irrigation.

- **Preliminary:** coarse screening and grit removal by sedimentation
- **Primary:** removal of settleable organic and inorganic solids by sedimentation and materials that will float by skimming
- **Secondary:** removal of biodegradable dissolved and colloidal organic matter using aerobic biological treatment processes

Nelda Matheny, President, and James R. Clark, Vice President, HortScience, Inc., P.O. Box 754, Pleasanton, CA 94566.

- **Advanced (tertiary):** removal of specific wastewater constituents such as nitrogen, heavy metals, and dissolved solids using chemical coagulation, sedimentation, filtration, or reverse osmosis
- **Disinfection:** killing organisms in water using injection of chlorine (most common), ozone, or ultraviolet light

The California Code of Regulations allows use of primary effluent for surface irrigation of orchards, vineyards, fodder, fiber, and seed crops. Secondary effluent may be used for surface irrigation of food crops, pasture for milking animals, and landscape irrigation of golf courses and cemeteries. Tertiary treatment including coagulation, filtering, and disinfection is required for irrigation of parks and playgrounds, and for spray irrigation of food crops.

Assessing Recycled Water Quality

Water may contain ions or salts that are toxic to certain plants. While good-quality water is suitable for use for irrigation of most any plant, poor-quality water may inhibit plant growth or reduce health. Species selection for the site may be restricted to salt-tolerant species. For recycled water, the quality depends on the components of the water entering the treatment path, as well as the type of use before treatment. For instance, home water softeners exchange calcium in the water with sodium. Recycled water from municipal sources in which water softeners are used therefore has a higher level of sodium than the water entering the system. During sewage treatment, solids and organic materials are removed. However, many of the inorganic compounds, including salts and heavy metals, are retained. Salts can be removed from recycled water through the process of reverse osmosis, although that is an advanced treatment not normally performed for water used in landscape irrigation.

The quality of a given recycled water source may vary throughout the year. In California, the quality of recycled water usually is better during the rainy season (winter) than during the summer and fall drought. Water-quality data may be requested from the treatment facility, or samples may be collected and analyzed by a laboratory. When requesting water-quality data from the treatment facility, ask for the range in measurements in addition to the annual averages normally reported. Water-quality reports usually emphasize constituents of concern for human health. In some cases, additional testing may need to be performed.

In the context of landscape irrigation, water quality refers to the presence and concentration of total salts (TDS, EC_w) as well as several specific ions (Cl, Na, B), bicarbonate, pH, trace elements, and nutrients (N, P, K) (Table 1*). Guidelines for interpreting water-quality data are found in Table 2.

Total Salts

Salinity is the most important measure of water quality for landscape plants. It is expressed as total dissolved solids (TDS) and electrical conductivity (EC_w).

---

*All tables are located at the end of this chapter.

(a)

(b)

(c)

Figure 1. Plant toxicity symptoms from salts and specific ions, especially chloride and boron, usually appear first as necrotic spots or blotches at the leaf edges and extending into the area between veins (a). Chlorosis also may occur (b). In conifers, necrosis begins at the tip of the needle (c). Older foliage shows symptoms first.

When water is applied to soils, some of the salts in the water (notably Na, Cl, and B) remain in the soil. As these salts accumulate in the soil, plant toxicity may occur (Figure 1). Salt toxicity is first expressed as stunting of growth and yellowing of foliage. Burning of the edge of the leaves and defoliation usually follows. In severe cases, plants are killed. The degree of the problem depends on the sensitivity of the plant to salts and the concentration of the accumulated salts in the soil.

Specific Ion Toxicity

While salinity expresses the total salt content, it will not adequately identify potential toxicities from specific ions. Chloride (Cl), sodium (Na), and boron (B) concentrations in recycled water can and often do cause injury to sensitive plants. Boron in particular must be evaluated independently of other salts. It is toxic in such low concentrations (less than 1 ppm) that potential problems cannot be ascertained from the electrical conductivity measurement.

Sodium and chloride concentrations are particularly important if irrigation will be supplied by sprinkler. Plants absorb both ions through their foliage. Toxicity through foliar absorption will occur at much lower concentrations than through soil absorption, particularly under high evapotranspiration conditions.

The toxicity symptoms of the specific ions are often difficult to distinguish from each other. Leaf chlorosis and marginal burning are typical for each. Necrosis associated with boron is often black in color and may appear as small spots near the leaf margin.

As with salinity, plant tolerance to individual ions is highly species-specific. Some plants, such as Indian hawthorn (*Raphiolepis indica*), can tolerate boron in excess of 7 ppm. Others, such as photinia (*Photinia × Fraseri*), are injured at 0.5 ppm. Furthermore, a plant may be relatively tolerant of boron but highly sensitive to chloride.

Little information is available to help develop lists of sensitivity of plants to specific ions. The landscape manager must rely primarily on experience and observation.

Sodium Adsorption Ratio

In addition to affecting plants directly, sodium can have negative effects on soil structure. It may cause dispersion of soil aggregates if present in high concentrations. This decreases both drainage and soil aeration, which may cause plant decline and death. Soils high in clay are particularly susceptible to dispersion of aggregates by sodium.

Sodium hazard to soils is usually assessed from the sodium adsorption ratio (SAR), a value calculated from the sodium, calcium, and magnesium concentrations. However, the permeability problems that can be caused by a high SAR can be partially offset by salts in the water. A more accurate measure of potential problems in irrigation water is the adjusted sodium adsorption ratio (adj R_{Na}) calculated from the salinity, bicarbonate, calcium, sodium, and magnesium concentrations of the water.

Bicarbonate

Bicarbonate affects plants through its influence on pH and interaction with sodium. High bicarbonate concentrations can cause iron chlorosis symptoms in plants. Water high in bicarbonate, carbonate, and calcium and/or magnesium can result in a white precipitate forming on foliage under sprinkler irrigation. Irrigation hardware is also susceptible to damage from bicarbonates—the precipitates can clog drip emitters.

When bicarbonate combines with calcium or magnesium in soils, calcium carbonate and magnesium carbonate precipitate out. Consequently, the SAR of the soil increases, and permeability to water may become a problem. The bicarbonate hazard to soils can be evaluated by calculating the residual sodium carbonate (RSC). The RSC is the sum of the carbonate and bicarbonate ions minus the sum of calcium and magnesium ions (15). Water with an RSC greater than 2.5 meq/L can develop permeability problems.

Heavy Metals

Heavy metals are rarely present in water in sufficient quantities to be directly toxic to plants. However, most metals become tied up in the soil and their concentrations increase over time. Water-quality criteria take the accumulation of the elements with many years of irrigation into account and provide maximum concentrations with long-term use in mind. Effluent derived from domestic sources does not usually have problems with trace elements.

Nutrients

One of the advantages of using recycled water for landscape irrigation is that it contains plant nutrients and reduces the needs for application of fertilizer. Nitrogen (NH_4, NO_3), phosphorus (P_2O_5), and sulfur (SO_4) are the constituents of greatest benefit. Their concentrations are considered when evaluating recycled water to determine fertilization needs. Recycled water usually contains most of the micronutrients needed by plants (25).

A negative aspect of this fertility involves storage of recycled water. Ponded nutrient-laden water develops algae and other aquatic weed problems more rapidly than potable water.

Selection of Sites Suitable for Irrigation with Recycled Water

The ability of a landscape to accommodate irrigation with recycled water depends on the degree to which soil will become degraded and the tolerance of plant materials to salts. The relationship of water quality to soil texture, drainage, and plant sensitivity is summarized in Table 3. Therefore, evaluation of sites for irrigation with recycled water must consider plant and site factors as well as irrigation method. There are five factors to evaluate when considering site suitability for irrigation with recycled water.

1. *Salt-sensitivity of plants in the landscape.* Plants vary widely in their tolerance to salts (Tables 4 through 6). Salt- and boron-sensitive plants have less tolerance to use of recycled water than do more salt-tolerant species. Turf usually is more tolerant of salts than many woody plants because leaf tips where salt accumulates are regularly removed during mowing.

2. *Texture of the soil.* Sandy soils can tolerate a poorer quality of water than clay soils can. As previously noted, as sodium accumulates in the soil it can cause dispersion of aggregated soils and reduce soil permeability. The potential for problems is greater in clayey soils that in sandy soils.

3. *Soil drainage.* Soils that do not drain well accumulate salts and cannot be leached. Therefore, soils with poor drainage for any reason (e.g., hardpan, compaction, high water table) are not suitable for irrigation with poor-quality water, unless highly salt-tolerant plants are used. The poorer the drainage, the more a high-quality water is required.

4. *Irrigation method.* Plants are more sensitive to sodium and chloride toxicity when the water is applied to the foliage as opposed to the soil. Therefore, sensitive plantings irrigated by sprinklers require water lower in sodium and chloride. Drip irrigation emitters can become clogged by calcium carbonate precipitates and suspended solids in the water. Tertiary treatment will eliminate the particulates.

5. *Irrigation frequency.* Drought stress occurs at a higher soil moisture content as water quality declines because the salts increase the osmotic pressure. When using poor-quality water, increase the irrigation frequency to maintain a moist soil. As the soil dries, the salts in the soil solution become more concentrated, and plant damage is more likely to occur.

Sites that are generally suited for irrigation with moderate- to poor-quality recycled water include (Figure 2):
- turf and meadow areas
- established tree and shrub plantings that require only a few irrigations a year
- landscapes composed primarily of plant species that are moderately to highly salt tolerant
- landscapes on sandy to loamy soils with good drainage
- areas of high rainfall where soil salts are leached out of the root zone of landscape plants

Sites to avoid irrigating with moderate- to poor-quality recycled water include (Figure 3):
- any areas with poor drainage
- landscapes with frequent sprinkler irrigation and low to moderately salt-sensitive plants
- soils with high clay content
- landscapes with salt-sensitive plants in areas that are closely viewed
- areas with low to moderately salt-tolerant plants and loamy to clayey soils that cannot be leached

Managing Landscapes Irrigated with Recycled Water

The potential problems to plants and soils can be minimized in a variety of ways, including management and design. All of the management techniques require moni-

Figure 2 (left). Sites generally suited for irrigation with recycled water include turf areas, established tree and shrub areas that require only a few irrigations a year, and sandy to loamy soils with good drainage.

Figure 3 (right). Sites to avoid irrigating with moderate- to poor-quality recycled water include those with salt-sensitive species under sprinkler irrigation. Also avoid soils with high clay content and poor drainage.

toring of soil chemical and moisture characteristics as well as plant responses. The main concerns are salinity and pH. Check the range of recycled water quality before beginning irrigation. In addition, monitor water quality regularly because constituents can vary seasonally. Close cooperation with the treatment facility manager is essential to knowing changes in recycled water composition that might adversely affect plants.

When managing existing sites that will be converted from potable water to recycled water for irrigation, consider the following:

1. *Minimize salt accumulation in the root zone.* Minimizing salt accumulation is important to avoid leaf burn and salt stress, which can predispose plants to other problems. It is accomplished by leaching with heavy irrigations to flush accumulated salts below the roots. Annual rains may be adequate to maintain soil salinity within tolerable levels in some cases (heavy rainfall, well-drained soil). Where soils are heavier, leaching with good-quality water may be needed during the growing season to lower salt levels. Use of recycled water should be avoided in areas with poor drainage because those areas cannot be leached.

2. *Lower sodium concentrations in soils.* If sodium concentrations become too high, drainage is impaired. Incorporating calcium (in the form of gypsum) into the soil and leaching with good-quality water can reclaim soil structure. Routine light applications of gypsum may be advantageous to avoid sodium problems.

3. *Decrease fertilizer applications.* Because recycled water contains significant amounts of nitrogen, phosphorus, and potassium, applications of fertilizer can be reduced and, in some instances, eliminated.

4. *Increase irrigation frequency.* Irrigation with recycled water should occur more frequently to dilute soil solutes, avoid water stress, and minimize toxicity.

5. *Moderate soil pH.* Most plants tolerate a wide range in soil pH. As the pH of the soil begins to rise, however, acid-requiring plants may develop iron deficiency. Should chlorosis symptoms develop, the soil pH could be lowered by applying sulfur, or individual plants can be fertilized with iron to alleviate symptoms.

6. *Install filters on irrigation equipment.* Tertiary-treated water is filtered and will not cause clogging problems. If the water is ponded, however, algae may develop that will interfere with equipment. That water would need to be filtered before entering the irrigation system. Drip systems should have 80-mesh filter screens, or else be designed to be cleared by flushing.

7. *Monitor plant health.* Additional stress factors caused by salts should be considered in the landscape pest-management program. Plant health must be monitored closely to identify stress-related problems that may develop. Some examples are bark beetles (*Ips*) on pines (*Pinus*), borers on alder (*Alnus*), and canker (*Seridium cardinale*) on cypress (*Cupressus macrocarpa*).

8. *Maintain a back-up irrigation system.* It is helpful to maintain a dual irrigation system where possible. This will allow irrigation with good-quality water for leaching sensitive plantings. It also provides back-up in case the supply of recycled water is interrupted. If the recycled water source has acceptable quality throughout the year, and will always be in adequate supply, the expense of a back-up system probably is not justified.

9. *Monitor soil chemical changes.* Soil conditions should be monitored through sampling programs to identify needed leaching or other soil treatments. In most cases, soils should be sampled at the beginning and the end of the irrigation period.

When designing new landscapes that will be irrigated with recycled water, consider the following in the design:

1. *Avoid using salt-sensitive species.* A partial list of species to avoid is provided in Tables 4 through 6. If salt-sensitive plantings cannot be avoided, they should be grouped together and irrigated on separate systems using potable water.

2. *Identify and solve drainage problems before planting.* Good drainage is essential when using recycled water. Adjusting finish grades, eliminating hardpans, and improving soil structure are methods to improve drainage.

3. *Evaluate soil characteristics before planting.* Soils should be tested for chemical and physical characteristics before planting to evaluate their suitability for irrigation with recycled water.

4. *Design irrigation systems with adequate filtration.* Filters should be installed to remove particulates, especially algae.

Conclusion

Recycled water can be an abundant, cost-effective source for irrigation. Landscape designers and managers should consider the quality of the water, soil chemical and physical conditions, and sensitivity of landscape species to water constituents when planning and managing landscapes irrigated with recycled water.

Acknowledgments

The authors wish to thank Larry Costello and Katherine Jones, University of California Cooperative Extension, for their contribution to development of Tables 4 through 7.

Literature Cited

1. Bernstein, L. 1958. Salt tolerance of grasses and forage legumes. USDA Information Bull. 194. 7 pp.
2. Bernstein, L., L.E. Francois, and R.A. Clark. 1972. *Salt tolerance of ornamental shrubs and ground covers.* J. Amer. Soc. Hort. Sci. 97(4):550–56.
3. Branson, R., and W. Davis. 1965. Ornamental Trees and Shrubs Showing Adaptation Characteristics Suitable for San Mateo County. Unpublished manuscript. Agricultural Extension Service, University of Calif. 5 pp.
4. California State Polytechnic University, Pomona. Undated. Soil Materials Syllabus, SS 439. Unpublished manuscript. 233 pp.
5. Dirr, M.A. 1978. *Tolerance of seven woody ornamentals to soil-applied sodium chloride.* J. Arboric. 4(7):162–165.
6. Donaldson, D.R., J.K. Hasey, and W.B. Davis. 1983. *Eucalyptus out-perform other species in salty, flooded soils.* Calif. Agric. 37(9–10):20–21.
7. Driver, C. 1990. Planting in hot arid climates. **In** Clouston, B. (Ed.). Landscape Design with Plants. CRC Press, Boca Raton, FL. 544 pp.
8. Eaton, F.M. 1944. *Deficiency, toxicity and accumulation of boron in plants.* J. Agricul. Res. 69:237–277.
9. Farnham, D.S., R.S. Ayers, and R.F. Hasek. 1977. Water quality affects ornamental plant production. University of Calif. Cooperative Extension Leaflet 2995. 15 pp.
10. Francois, L.E. 1980. Salt injury to ornamental shrubs and ground covers. USDA Home and Garden Bull. #231. 10 pp.
11. Francois, L.E. 1982. *Salt tolerance of eight ornamental tree species.* J. Amer. Soc. Hort. Sci. 107(1)66–68.
12. Francois, L.E., and R.A. Clark. 1978. *Salt tolerance of ornamental shrubs, trees and iceplant.* J. Amer. Soc. Hort. Sci. 103(2):280–283.
13. Francois, L.E., and R.A. Clark. 1979. *Boron tolerance of twenty-five ornamental shrub species.* J. Amer. Soc. Hort. Sci. 104(3):319–322.
14. Glattstein, J. 1989. *Ornamentals for sandy and saline soils.* Grounds Maint. April:52–60.
15. Harivandi, Ali. 1988. *Irrigation water quality and turfgrass management.* Calif. Turfgrass Culture. 38(3,4):1–4.
16. Kvaalen, R. Undated. Roadside ornamental plants and de-icing salts. Assistant Extension Horticulturist, Purdue Univ. Unpublished manuscript. 7 pp.
17. Maas, E.V. 1984. Salt tolerance of plants. **In** Christie, B.R. (Ed.). The Handbook of Plant Science in Agriculture. CRC Press Inc., Boca Raton, FL. 544 pp.
18. Morris, R., and D. Devitt. 1990. *Salinity and landscape plants.* Grounds Maint. April:6, 8.

19. Perry, B. 1989. Trees and Shrubs for Dry California Landscapes. Land Design Publishing, Claremont, CA. 184 pp.

20. Pettygrove, G., and T. Asano. 1985. Irrigation with Reclaimed Municipal Wastewater—A Guidance Manual. Lewis Publishers, Chelsea, MI.

21. Questa Engineering Corp. 1987. Irrigation Water Quality Study, City of Concord. Unpublished manuscript. Point Richmond, CA. 28 pp.

22. San Diego, City of. 1963. Water Reclamation Study for Balboa Park and Mission Bay Park. Unpublished Manuscript. San Diego, CA.

23. Skimina, Conrad A. 1980. *Salt tolerance of ornamentals.* Intern. Plant Prop. Soc. 30:113–118.

24. Van Arsdel, E.P. 1980. *Managing trees to reduce damage from low-level saline irrigation.* Weeds Trees & Turf. June:26–28, 61.

Table 1. Constituents of recycled water that affect landscape plants and soil (20).

Constituent	Measured parameter	Reason for concern
Dissolved inorganics	Total dissolved solids (TDS); electrical conductivity (EC_w); specific elements (Na, Ca, Mg, Cl, B)	Excessive salinity may damaged some plants. Specific ions such as chloride, sodium, boron are toxic to some plants. Sodium may pose soil permeability problems.
Hydrogen ion activity	pH	The pH of water affects metal solubility (e.g., Fe, Mn, Zn, Al) as well as alkalinity of soils.
Heavy metals	Specific elements (e.g., Cd, Zn, Ni, Hg)	Some heavy metals accumulated in the environment and are toxic to plants. Primary concern is for plants with high levels that are ingested by animals.
Nutrients	Nitrogen, phosphorus, potassium	N, P, and K are essential nutrients for plant growth, and their presence normally enhances the value of water for irrigation. When discharged into the aquatic environment, N and P can lead to the growth of undesirable aquatic life. When discharged in excessive amounts on land, N can lead to the pollution of groundwater.
Residual chlorine	Free and combined chlorine	Excessive amounts of free available Cl (> 0.05 mg/L Cl_2) may cause leaf-tip burn and damage sensitive plants. However, most chlorine in recycled water is in a combined form, which does not cause plant damage.
Suspended solids	Suspended solids	Excessive amounts of suspended solids cause plugging in irrigation systems.

Table 2. Interpretive guidelines for water quality for landscape irrigation. Species vary in tolerance to water quality. The poorer the water, the more severe are restrictions on species use (20).

Parameter	Water quality for landscape irrigation		
	Good	Fair	Poor
Salinity			
TDS, mg/L	<450	450–2000	>2000
EC_w, dS/m or mmho/cm	<0.7	0.7–3.0	>3.0
Permeability[y]			
SAR	6	6–9	>9
Specific ion toxicity[z]			
Boron (B) (mg/L)	<0.5	0.5-1.0	>1.0
Chloride (Cl)			
Surface irrigation (mg/L)	<140	140–350	>350
Sprinkler irrigation (mg/L)	<100	>100	
Sodium			
Surface irrigation (SAR)	<3	3-9	>9
Sprinkler irrigation (mg/L)	<70	>70	
Miscellaneous effects			
Nitrogen (Total-N, mg/L)	<5	5–30	>30
Bicarbonate (HCO_3)			
Sprinkler irrigation	<90	90–500	>500
pH		Normal range 6.5–8.4	
Residual chlorine			
Sprinkler irrigation (mg/L)	<1.0	1.0–5.0	>5.0

[y]Permeability affects infiltration rate of water into the soil. Evaluate using EC_w and SAR together. At given SAR, infiltration rate increases as salinity (EC_w) increases.
[z]Plant sensitivity to specific ions varies widely.

Table 3. The quality of recycled water that can be used at a site depends on the degree to which soil will become degraded and the tolerance of the plant materials to salts. The poorer the water quality, the less suitable it is for use at sites with heavy soils and salt-sensitive plants. This table identifies the quality of the water required for sites depending on soil texture, drainage, and plant sensitivity to salts.

Soil texture/drainage	Plant sensitivity to salts[y]		
	Sensitive	Moderate	Tolerant
Sandy/good drainage	Good[z]	Moderate	Poor
Loam/good drainage	Good	Moderate	Moderate
Clay or poor drainage	Very good	Good	Moderate

[y]Refer to salt tolerance ratings of tree species, Tables 4–6.
[z]Refer to water quality interpretive guide, Table 2.

Table 4. Tree tolerance to soil and water salinity and boron.

Scientific name	Common name	Salt tolerance	Boron tolerance	Citation[z]
Acacia farnesiana	Sweet acacia	Moderate		(4)
Acacia greggii	Catclaw acacia	High		(4)
*Acacia melanoxylon	Blackwood acacia	Moderate	Moderate	(3)
*Acacia melanoxylon	Blackwood acacia	High		(22)
Acacia spp.	Acacia	Moderate	High	(4)
Acer macrophyllum	Big-leaf maple	Low		(6)
Acer platanoides	Norway maple	Moderate		(5)
Acer saccarhinum	Silver maple	Low	Low	(24)
Aesculus carnea	Red horsechestnut		Low	(21)
Ailanthus altissima	Tree of Heaven	Moderate		(7)
Albizia julibrissin	Silk tree	Low		(21)
Albizia lophantha (syn. A. distachya)	Plume albizia	High		(4)
Alnus rhombifolia	White alder	Low	Low	(3)
Araucaria araucana	Monkey puzzle	Low		(24)
*Araucaria heterophylla	Norfolk Island pine	High		(9, 23)
*Araucaria heterophylla	Norfolk Island pine	Moderate		(24)
Arbutus unedo	Strawberry tree	High	High	(4)
*Bauhinia purpurea	Orchid tree	Low	Low	(4)
*Bauhinia purpurea	Orchid tree	Moderate		(11)
Betula nigra	River birch	Low		(24)
Betula pendula	European white birch	Low	Low	(4)
Butia capitata	Pindo palm	High		(24)
Callistemon rigidus	Stiff bottlebrush	High		(19)
*Callistemon viminalis	Weeping bottlebush	Moderate		(2)
*Callistemon viminalis	Weeping bottlebush	High	High	(10)
Calocedrus decurrens	Incense cedar	Low		(3)
Calodendrum capense	Cape chestnut		High	(22)
Carya illinoensis	Pecan	Low	Low	(17, 24)
Casuarina	Horsetail tree	Moderate		(9)
Casuarina cunninghamiana	Horsetail tree	High		(4)
Casuarina stricta	Coast beefwood	High		(4)
Catalpa spp.	Catalpa	Low	Low	(4)
Ceanothus thyrsiflorus	Blue blossom	High	High	(4)
Cedrus atlantica	Atlantic cedar	Low	High	(23)
*Cedrus deodara	Deodar cedar	High	High	(4)
*Cedrus deodara	Deodar cedar	Low		(23)
Celtis australis	European hackberry	Low	Moderate	(3)
Ceratonia siliqua	Carob	Moderate	Moderate	(3, 21)
Cercidium floridum	Blue palo verde	High		(4)
Cercidium spp.	Palo verde	High		(4)
Cercis occidentalis	Western redbud	High		(4)
Cercis spp.	Redbud	Low	Low	(7)
Chrysobalanus icaco	Coco plum	Moderate		(4)
*Cinnamomum camphora	Camphor	High		(22)
*Cinnamomum camphora	Camphor	Low		(23)
Citrus spp.	Lemon, Orange	Low	Low	(7, 8, 23)
Coccoloba floridana	Pigeon plum	High		(4)
Cragaegus phaenopyrum	Washington thorn	Low	High	(3)
Crataegus × lavallei	Carriere hawthorn	Low		(3)
Crinodendron patagua	Lily-of-the-valley tree		High	(22)
Cupressus forbesii	Forbes cypress	Low		(3)
Cupressus macrocarpa	Monterey cypress	Low		(3)
Cupressus sempervirens	Italian cypress	High	High	(4)
Cupressus sempervirens 'Glauca'	Arizona cypress	Moderate		(23)
Cupressus spp.	Cypress	Low		(7)
Diospyros virginiana	Persimmon	Low		(17)
Eriobotrya deflexa	Bronze loquat	Low		(3)
Eriobotrya japonica	Loquat	Low	Moderate	(17)

(Table 4 continued, next page)

Table 4 (cont.). Tree tolerance to soil and water salinity and boron.

Scientific name	Common name	Salt tolerance	Boron tolerance	Citation[2]
Erythea armata	Brahea blue fan plam	High		(4)
Erythrina caffra	Kaffirboom coral tree		Low	(22)
Eucalyptus camaldulensis	Red river gum	High	High	(6, 19)
Eucalyptus citriodora	Lemon gum	High	High	(4)
Eucalyptus cladocalyx	Sugar gum	High	High	(4)
*Eucalyptus ficifolia	Red flowering gum	Low	Moderate	(3)
*Eucalyptus ficifolia	Red flowering gum	High		(4)
Eucalyptus globulus compacta	Dwarf blue gum	High	High	(4)
Eucalyptus gunnii	Silver dollar gum	High		(6)
Eucalyptus microtheca	Flooded box	High		(6)
*Eucalyptus polyanthemos	Silver dollar gum	High	Moderate	(4)
*Eucalyptus polyanthemos	Silver dollar gum		High	(21)
Eucalyptus pulverulenta	Silver mountain gum	Moderate		(4)
Eucalyptus rudis	Swamp gum	High	High	(6, 19)
Eucalyptus sargentii	Salt river mallet	High		(6)
*Eucalyptus sideroxylon var. rosea	Pink ironbark	Moderate	Moderate	(3)
*Eucalyptus sideroxylon var. rosea	Red ironbark	High	High	(4)
Eucalyptus spp.	Eucalyptus	High		(7)
Eucalyptus tereticornis	Forest red gum	Moderate		(4)
Eucalyptus torquata	Coral gum	High		(19)
Euphorbia tirucalis	Milkbush	High		(4)
Ficus benjamina	Weeping chinese banyan	Low		(23)
Ficus carica	Fig	Moderate	Low	(8, 17)
Ficus microcarpa	Indian laurel fig	High		(23)
Ficus microcarpa nitida		Low		(3)
Ficus rubiginosa	Rusty leaf fig	Low		(3)
Ficus spp.		Moderate		(7)
Fraxinus americana	White ash	Low		(24)
Fraxinus oxycarpa 'Raywood'	Raywood ash		High	(21)
Fraxinus pennsylvanica	Green ash	High		(24)
Fraxinus pennsylvanica var. lanceolata	Green ash	Moderate		(4)
Fraxinus velutina	Arizona ash	High	High	(24)
*Fraxinus velutina 'Modesto'	Modesto ash	High	High	(4)
*Fraxinus velutina 'Modesto'	Modesto ash		Low	(21)
Ginkgo biloba	Maidenhair tree	Low		(6, 24)
Gleditsia triacanthos 'Moraine'	Moraine locust	Low		(3)
Grevillea banksii	Banksii forsteri	High		(4)
Grevillea 'Canberra'	Canberra silk oak	High		(6)
Grevillea robusta	Silk oak	High		(4)
Hymenosporum flavum	Sweetshade		High	(22)
Jacaranda acutifolia	Jacaranda	High	High	(4)
Juglans nigra	Black walnut	Low	Low	(9)
*Juglans regia	English walnut	Low	Low	(17)
*Juglans regia	English walnut		Moderate	(21)
Koelreutaria paniculata	Goldenrain tree	High		(22)
Kopsia arborea	Blume	Moderate		(4)
Lagerstroemia indica	Crape myrtle	Low	Moderate	(11)
Lagunaria patersonii	Orchid tree	High	High	(4)
Laurus nobilis	Grecian laurel		High	(21)
*Liquidambar styraciflua	Sweetgum	Moderate	Moderate	(11)
*Liquidambar styraciflua	Sweetgum	Low		(24)
Liquidambar styraciflua 'Festival'	Festival sweetgum		Low	(21)
Liriodendron tulipifera	Tulip tree	Low	Moderate	(11)
Maclura pomifera	Osage orange	Moderate		(24)

(Table 4 continued, next page)

Table 4 (cont.). Tree tolerance to soil and water salinity and boron.

Scientific name	Common name	Salt tolerance	Boron tolerance	Citation[z]
*Magnolia grandiflora	Southern magnolia	Moderate		(11)
*Magnolia grandiflora	Southern magnolia	Low	Low	(23)
Magnolia spp. (deciduous)	Magnolia	Low	Low	(22)
Malus spp.	Crabapple		High	(21)
Malus sylvestris	Apple	Low		(17)
Maytenus boaria	Mayten		High	(21)
Melaleuca armillaris	Drooping melaleuca	High		(4)
Melaleuca nesophila	Pink melaleuca	High		(19)
Melaleuca quinquenervia	Cajeput tree	Moderate		(9)
Metrosideros excelsus	New Zealand Christmas tree	High		(19)
Morus alba	Mulberry	Low	Low	(21)
Morus alba 'Fruitless'	Fruitless mulberry	Moderate	Low	(4)
Morus nigra	Black mulberry	Low		(7)
Myoporum laetum	Myoporum	Moderate		(3)
Nerium oleander	Oleander	High		(19)
*Olea europaea	Olive	High	High	(4)
*Olea europaea	Olive	Moderate	Moderate	(9, 17)
Parkinsonia aculeata	Palo verde	High	High	(4)
*Persea americana	Avocado	Low	Low	(17)
*Persea americana	Avocado	High		(24)
Phoenix loureiri	Pigmy date palm	Low		(4)
Picea pungens	Blue spruce	Low		(4)
Pinus brutia	Brutia pine	High		(6)
Pinus canariensis	Canary Island pine		High	(21)
Pinus eldarica	Mondale pine	Moderate		(6)
Pinus elliottii	Slash pine	Moderate		(24)
Pinus halepensis	Aleppo pine	High	Moderate	(7, 12)
Pinus nigra	Austrian pine	High		(24)
Pinus pinaster	Cluster pine	High		(7)
Pinus pinea	Italian stone pine	High	Moderate	(11)
Pinus radiata	Monterey pine	High		(7)
Pinus sylvestris	Scots pine	Moderate		(24)
Pinus taeda	Loblolly pine	Moderate		(24)
Pinus thunbergiana	Japanese black pine	Moderate	Moderate	(12)
Pistacia chinensis	Chinese pistache	Moderate	Low	(3)
*Pittosporum phillyraeoides	Desert willow	Moderate		(9)
*Pittosporum phillyraeoides	Desert willow	High		(19)
Platanus occidentalis	American sycamore	Low		(24)
Platanus racemosa	California sycamore	High	High	(4)
Platanus × acerifolia	London plane		Moderate	(21)
*Platycladus orientalis	Oriental arborvitae	Moderate	Moderate	(2)
*Platycladus orientalis	Oriental arborvitae	Low		(13, 17)
Plumeria rubra	Frangipani plumeria	Moderate		(4)
Podocarpus gracillior	Yew pine		High	(21)
*Podocarpus macrophyllus	Southern yew	Low	Moderate	(10)
*Podocarpus macrophyllus	Japanese yew	High		(24)
*Populus fremontii	Cottonwood	High		(4)
*Populus fremontii	Cottonwood	Moderate		(24)
Populus spp.	Cottonwood		High	(21)
Populus × canadensis	Carolina poplar	High		(4)
Prosopis grandulosa var. torreyana	Honey mesquite	High		(4)
Prunus armeniaca	Apricot	Low		(17)
Prunus avium	Cherry	Low	Low	(8, 17)
Prunus besseyi	Sand cherry	Low		(5)
Prunus cerasifera	Cherry plum	Moderate		(11)
Prunus cerasifera 'Atropurpurea'	Purple leaf plum		High	(21)
Prunus domestica	Plum, prune	Low	Low	(17)

(Table 4 continued, next page)

Table 4 (cont.). Tree tolerance to soil and water salinity and boron.

Scientific name	Common name	Salt tolerance	Boron tolerance	Citation[z]
Prunus dulcis	Almond	Low		(17)
Prunus ilicifolia	Hollyleaf cherry	High	High	(4)
Prunus lyonii	Catalina cherry	High	High	(4)
Prunus persica	Peach	Low	Low	(8, 17)
Prunus serrulata	Flowering cherry		Moderate	(21)
Prunus tomentosa	Nanking cherry	Low		(5)
Prunus × *blireiana*	Flowering plum	Moderate		(3)
Punica granatum	Pomegranate	Moderate		(17)
Pyrus communis	Pear	Low		(17)
Pyrus kawakamii	Evergreen pear	High	High	(11)
Quercus agrifolia	Coast live oak		High	(21)
Quercus ilex	Holly oak		Moderate	(21)
Quercus lobata	Valley oak		High	(21)
Quercus marilandica	Black jack oak	Moderate		(24)
Quercus palustris	Pin oak	Moderate		(24)
Quercus suber	Cork oak		High	(21)
Quercus virginiana	Southern live oak	High		(24)
Salix babylonica	Weeping willow	High	High	(4)
Salix matsudana 'Tortosa'	Corkscrew willow		High	(21)
Sapium sebiferum	Chinese tallow tree	High	High	(24)
Schinus molle	California pepper	High	High	(4)
Schinus terebinthifolius	Brazilian pepper	High	High	(19)
Sequoia sempervirens	Coast redwood		Low	(21)
Sophora japonica	Japanese pagoda tree		Moderate	(21)
Taxodium distichum	Bald cypress	High		(3)
Tilia spp.	Linden	Low		(24)
Ulmus alata	Winged elm	Low		(24)
Ulmus americana	American elm	Low	Low	(8, 17, 24)
Ulmus crassifolia	Cedar elm	Low		(24)
*Ulmus parvifolia	Evergreen elm		Moderate	(21)
*Ulmus parvifolia	Evergreen elm		Low	(22)
*Ulmus pumila	Siberian elm		Low	(21)
*Ulmus pumila	Siberian elm	High	Moderate	(24)
Vitex luscens	New Zealand chaste tree		High	(22)
× *Cupressocyparis leylandii*	Leyland cypress	High		(23)
Zelkova serrata	Sawleaf zelkova		Moderate	(21)
Zizyphus jujuba	Chinese jujuba	High		(19)

*Species that were rated in more than one category.
[z]Refer to Table 7 for methods and criteria used in evaluating salinity and boron tolerance.

Table 5. High, moderate, and low salt tolerance of tree species (see Table 4 for common names and citations).

High tolerance	Moderate tolerance	Low tolerance
Acacia greggii	Acacia farnesiana	Acer macrophyllum
Acacia melanoxylon	**Acacia melanoxylon**	Acer saccarhinum
Albizia lophantha (syn. A. distachya)	Acacia spp.	Albizia julibrissin
Araucaria heterophylla	Acer platanoides	Alnus rhombifolia
Arbutus unedo	Ailanthus altissima	Araucaria araucana
Butia capitata	**Araucaria heterophylla**	**Bauhinia purpurea**
Callistemon rigidus	**Bauhinia purpurea**	Betula nigra
Callistemon viminalis	**Callistemon viminalis**	Betula pendula
Casuarina cunninghamiana	Casuarina	Calocedrus decurrens
Casuarina stricta	Ceratonia siliqua	Carya illinoensis
Ceanothus thyrsiflorus	Chrysobalanus icaco	Catalpa spp.
Cedrus deodara	Cupressus sempervirens 'Glauca'	Cedrus atlantica
Cercidium floridum	Eucalyptus pulverulenta	**Cedrus deodara**
Cercidium spp.	**Eucalyptus sideroxylon var. rosea**	Celtis australis
Cercis occidentalis	Eucalyptus tereticornis	Cercis spp.
Cinnamomum camphora	Ficus carica	**Cinnamomum camphora**
Coccoloba floridana	Ficus spp.	Citrus spp.
Cupressus sempervirens	Fraxinus pennsylvanica var. lanceolata	Cragaegus phaenopyrum
× Cupressocyparis leylandii	Kopsia arborea	Crataegus × lavallei
Erythea armata	**Liquidambar styraciflua**	Cupressus forbesii
Eucalyptus camaldulensis	Maclura pomifera	Cupressus macrocarpa
Eucalyptus citriodora	**Magnolia grandiflora**	Cupressus spp.
Eucalyptus cladocalyx	Melaleuca quinquenervia	Diospyros virginiana
Eucalyptus ficifolia	Morus alba 'Fruitless'	Eriobotrya deflexa
Eucalyptus globulus compacta	Myoporum laetum	Eriobotrya japonica
Eucalyptus gunnii	**Olea europaea**	**Eucalyptus ficifolia**
Eucalyptus microtheca	Pinus eldarica	Ficus benjamina
Eucalyptus polyanthemos	Pinus elliottii	Ficus microcarpa nitida
Eucalyptus rudis	Pinus sylvestris	Ficus rubiginosa
Eucalyptus sargentii	Pinus taeda	Fraxinus americana
Eucalyptus sideroxylon var. rosea	Pinus thunbergiana	Ginkgo biloba
Eucalyptus spp.	Pistacia chinensis	Gleditsia triacanthos
Eucalyptus torquata	**Pittosporum phillyraeoides**	'Moraine'
Euphorbia tirucalis	**Platycladus orientalis**	Juglans nigra
Ficus microcarpa	Plumeria rubra	Juglans regia
Fraxinus pennsylvanica	**Populus fremontii**	Lagerstroemia indica
Fraxinus velutina	Prunus cerasifera	**Liquidambar styraciflua**
Fraxinus velutina 'Modesto'	Prunus × blireiana	Liriodendron tulipifera
Grevillea banksii	Punica granatum	**Magnolia grandiflora**
Grevillea 'Canberra'	Quercus marilandica	Magnolia spp. (deciduous)
Grevillea robusta	Quercus palustris	Malus sylvestris
Jacaranda acutifolia		Morus alba
Koelreutaria paniculata		Morus nigra
Lagunaria patersonii		**Persea americana**
Melaleuca armillaris		Phoenix loureiri
Melaleuca nesophila		Picea pungens
Metrosideros excelsus		**Platanus occidentalis**
Nerium oleander		Platycladus orientalis
Olea europaea		**Podocarpus**
Parkinsonia aculeata		**macrophyllus**
Persea americana		Prunus armeniaca
Pinus brutia		Prunus avium
Pinus halepensis		Prunus besseyi
Pinus nigra		Prunus domestica
Pinus pinaster		Prunus dulcis
Pinus pinea		Prunus persica

(Table 5 continued, next page)

Table 5 (cont.). High, moderate, and low salt tolerance of tree species (see Table 4 for common names and citations).

High tolerance	Moderate tolerance	Low tolerance
Pinus radiata		*Prunus tomentosa*
Pittosporum phillyraeoides		*Pyrus communis*
Platanus racemosa		*Tilia* spp.
Podocarpus macrophyllus		*Ulmus alata*
Populus fremontii		*Ulmus americana*
Populus × canadensis		*Ulmus crassifolia*
Prosopis grandulosa var. *torreyana*		
Prunus ilicifolia		
Prunus lyonii		
Pyrus kawakamii		
Quercus virginiana		
Salix babylonica		
Sapium sebiferum		
Schinus molle		
Schinus terebinthifolius		
Taxodium distichum		
Ulmus pumila		
Zizyphus jujuba		

Species in bold text appear in more than one column (see also Table 4).

Table 6. Boron tolerance of selected tree species (refer to Table 4 for common names and citations).

High tolerance	Moderate tolerance	Low tolerance
Acacia spp.	*Acacia melanoxylon*	*Acer saccarhinum*
Arbutus unedo	*Celtis australis*	*Aesculus carnea*
Callistemon viminalis	*Ceratonia siliqua*	*Alnus rhombifolia*
Calodendrum capense	*Eriobotrya japonica*	*Bauhinia purpurea*
Ceanothus thyrsiflorus	*Eucalyptus ficifolia*	*Betula pendula*
Cedrus atlantica	**Eucalyptus polyanthemos**	*Carya illinoensis*
Cedrus deodara	**Eucalyptus sideroxylon** var. *rosea*	*Catalpa* spp.
Cragaegus phaenopyrum	**Juglans regia**	*Cercis* spp.
Crinodendron patagua	*Lagerstroemia indica*	*Citrus* spp.
Cupressus sempervirens	*Liquidambar styraciflua*	*Erythrina caffra*
Eucalyptus camaldulensis	*Liriodendron tulipifera*	*Ficus carica*
Eucalyptus citriodora	**Olea europaea**	**Fraxinus velutina**
Eucalyptus cladocalyx	*Pinus halepensis*	**'Modesto'**
Eucalyptus globulus compacta	*Pinus pinea*	*Juglans nigra*
Eucalyptus polyanthemos	*Pinus thunbergiana*	**Juglans regia**
Eucalyptus rudis	*Platanus* × *acerifolia*	*Liquidambar styraciflua*
		'Festival'
Eucalyptus sideroxylon var. *rosea*	*Platycladus orientalis*	*Magnolia grandiflora*
Fraxinus oxycarpa 'Raywood'	*Podocarpus macrophyllus*	*Magnolia* spp. (deciduous)
Fraxinus velutina	*Prunus serrulata*	*Morus alba*
Fraxinus velutina 'Modesto'	*Quercus ilex*	*Morus alba* 'Fruitless'
Hymenosporum flavum	*Sophora japonica*	*Persea americana*
Jacaranda acutifolia	*Ulmus parvifolia*	*Pistacia chinensis*
Lagunaria patersonii	**Ulmus pumila**	*Prunus avium*
Laurus nobilis	*Zelkova serrata*	*Prunus domestica*
Malus spp.		*Prunus persica*
Maytenus boaria		*Sequoia sempervirens*
Olea europaea		*Ulmus americana*
Parkinsonia aculeata		*Ulmus parvifolia*
Pinus canariensis		**Ulmus pumila**
Platanus racemosa		
Podocarpus gracillior		
Populus spp.		
Prunus cerasifera 'Atropurpurea'		
Prunus ilicifolia		
Prunus lyonii		
Pyrus kawakamii		
Quercus agrifolia		
Quercus lobata		
Quercus suber		
Salix babylonica		
Salix matsudana 'Tortosa'		
Sapium sebiferum		
Schinus molle		
Schinus terebinthifolius		
Vitex luscens		

Species in bold text appear in more than one column (see also Table 4).

Table 7. Methods and criteria used in evaluating salinity and boron tolerance for literature cited in Table 4.

Reference	Relative tolerance			Methods and/or criteria
	Low	Moderate	High	
Salinity of Irrigation Water—EC$_w$				
Bernstein et al. (2)	0.75–1.5	1.5–3.0	>3.0	Plots salinized with NaCl and CaCl$_2$ to provide 0.7, 4.4, and 7.8 mmhos/cm in irrigation water. Tolerance evaluated by growth reduction and appearance.
Cal Poly (4)		1.0–2.5		Observations at landscapes in San Bernadino County, CA. Plants irrigated with water with conductivity 1.0–2.5 mmhos/cm.
Farnham et al. (9)	0.75–1.5	1.5–3.0	>3.0	Results of work done by Branson et al., Univ. of California Cooperative Extension.
Maas (17)				No ratings given.
Morris and Devitt (18)				
Skimina (23)	180–300 mhos × 10^{-5}	400–800	1000–12000	Source of salts: 50% fertilizer and 50% NaCl. Plants grown in containers. Soil salinity usually 2–3 times higher than irrigation water. Classification based on not more than 50% relative growth reduction, no leaf burn, negligible mortality.
Van Arsdel (24)				Ratings based upon personal experience with waters containing 48–140 ppm Cl and 188–445 ppm Na.
Salinity of Soil—EC$_e$				
Bernstein (1)	2.0–3.0 mmhos/cm	4.0–6.0	6.0–12.0	No methods stated.
Cal Poly (4)				No methods stated.
Dirr (5)				Container plants irrigated with 0.25N NaCl daily. Plants ranked on an appearance index.
Francois (10)	2.0–4.0 dS/m	4.0–6.0	6.0–8.0	Methods not given. Plants in EC$_e$ 8.0–10.0 rated with good tolerance.
Francois (11)	<4.0	4.0–6.0	7.0–9.0	Maximum root zone salinity without foliar injury. Methods similar to Francois and Clark.

Reference	Relative tolerance			Methods and/or criteria
	Low	Moderate	High	
Francois and Clark (12)	<3.0	3.0–6.0	6.0–9.0	Rating criteria: <50% growth reduction; no leaf injury; plants aesthetically appealing. Experiment run for 3 years in sandy loam soil. Plants irrigated with NaCl and $CaCl_2$ added to yield EC_w of 0.7 (control), 4.4, and 7.8 mmhos/cm. Averge EC_e was 1.0, 4.3, and 7.0 mmhos/cm. Soil salinity was uniform with depth throughout the root zone during summer.
Glattstein (14)				No methods stated; authors assumed plants included in list were in "moderate" category.
Harivandi (15)	<4.0 dS/m	4.0–8.0	8.0– >16.0	Field soil.
Morris and Devitt (18)				Plants grown for 8 years in silty clay loam soil with saline groundwater. EC_w 26.0–40.0 at 3-ft. depth. EC_e in root zone 8.0–13.0 mmhos/cm. Authors ranked trees by appearance.
Perry (19)				No methods stated.
Boron—EC_w Cal Poly (4)				Rating criteria not given.
Eaton (8)	<1.0	5	10.0–25.0	Plants grown from seed, out-of-doors, in large sand culture. Irrigated with 0.03, 1, 5, 10, 15, and 25 ppm B.
Farnham et al. (9)	0.5–1.0 mg/L	1.0–2.0	2.0–10.0	Adapted from USDA Technical Bulletin #448.
Francois and Clark (12)	0.5	2.5	7.5	Plants grown out-of-doors in sand culture. Classification based on growth reduction and overall plant appearance.
Questa (21)				Inventoried plants growing in Concord, CA, parks that were irrigated with high-boron water. Evaluated species for injury and ranked according to sensitivity, based on boron concentration in soil and water, and severity of toxicity symptoms.
San Diego (22)		0.75–3.0		Observations at landscapes in San Bernardino County, CA, irrigated with boron water; ratings based on growth and leaf injury.